ASSASSINATION

ASSASSINATION

Miles Hudson

SUTTON PUBLISHING

First published in 2000 by
Sutton Publishing Limited · Phoenix Mill
Thrupp · Stroud · Gloucestershire · GL5 2BU

Paperback edition first published in 2002

British Library Cataloguing in Publication Data
A catalogue record for this book is available from the British Library

ISBN 0 7509 2795 X

Typeset in 12/15 pt Garamond.
Typesetting and origination by
Sutton Publishing Limited.
Printed in Great Britain by
J.H. Haynes & Co. Ltd, Sparkford.

CONTENTS

ACKNOWLEDGEMENTS

Of the many people who have helped with this book, I would like to single out my friends Sir John Stanier and Philip Merridale, who have read and commented on the whole manuscript, as indeed have my sons Mark and Richard and my long-suffering wife, Mercedes. She has also had to put up with the loss of the use of the nursery table which has groaned under a load of books for eighteen months. Others who have greatly helped have been Sir John Graham, Lord Holderness, John Snodgrass, Stanley Uys, Frank Taylor, Gary Rudas, Oren Root, Marie Hudson and Anthony Wigram. The Duke of Devonshire kindly let me peruse the archives of Chatsworth House. The staff of the London Library have consistently been polite and understanding as they attempted to cope with a computer-illiterate idiot.

Vikki Tate has again typed and retyped the whole manuscript several times with great skill and aplomb.

Everything in the book is, of course, wholly the author's responsibility.

INTRODUCTION

This book is about the practice of assassination, what it achieves (if anything) and why. A personality is removed from the scene for a purpose – that is what assassination is about. What is the result? Is the assassin successful in that the objective is achieved? Or does something else happen – perhaps the exact opposite of what is intended? Or perhaps nothing happens at all apart from the disappearance of the victim.

Of course, every situation is different – not only different but complex, and most modern historians would probably agree that even when we think we know what happened we can very rarely, if ever, be certain, and even less so about why it happened. Memories are highly fallible and often constrained by wishful thinking. Both the written word and the camera can lie. There are nuances and pressures which defy analysis even if known, and often knowledge is gained purely by chance.

In spite of all this, it is the intention of this book to establish some kind of pattern for assassinations and their repercussions, and this in turn might throw light on questions of current interest. There have been many situations in the recent, and not so recent, past where an individual leader has seemed to hold the world to ransom and to personify an evil against which others feel they must fight, for one reason or another. The idea has often been floated that if this person were to be removed from the scene – and assassination is one way of doing this – the threat which he poses would vanish and, hey presto, normal life would be resumed.

For instance, in July 1998 it became known that the Special Operations Executive of the British Secret Service had planned to kill Hitler before the war ended. If they had been allowed to proceed and if they had succeeded, would the war have finished and the Allied war aims have been achieved earlier? Or would it have continued for longer than it in fact did, since Hitler might have acquired martyr status and perhaps been succeeded by somebody who did not make the vast strategic blunders which Hitler, in his megalomania, undoubtedly did?

Britain and the USA made it clear in 1999 that their Middle Eastern policy was shaped round the aim of removing Saddam Hussein of Iraq. The sanctions against that country and the subsequent bombing of it were designed to foster such strong opposition to him that he would be ousted and the evil he represented would subside, if not vanish. Would that be achieved if he were to be assassinated? Would his successor be more reasonable and less of a danger to peace in the region? Or would he perhaps be even worse?

In the 1990s Slobodan Milosevic, with his racist policies of securing a greater Serbia from the ruins of the old Yugoslavia, posed appalling problems for the world community. This led to considerable military activity by the United Nations and later by NATO, which was costly in money and lives. If, instead of all that, he had been assassinated, would the situation have been greatly eased, if not completely changed?

There can be no definitive answers to these questions, but there may be some relevant guidelines. In *The Rhetoric of Reaction*, Alfred Hirschman, the well-known American social scientist, has sought to explain the rationale behind reaction as a political policy. He has some interesting things to say about what reactionaries see as attempts to steer society in a changed direction, which can be applied to this, albeit very different, context.[1] He puts forward three theories – Perversity, Futility and Jeopardy:

The Perversity theory holds that society may well move as a result of pressures of various kinds, but often in the opposite direction to what is intended. The French Revolution is cited as an example. Hirschman calls in aid Edmund Burke's *Reflections on the Revolution in France*, which shows how Liberté, Egalité, Fraternité turned into the dictatorship of the Comité de Salut Public (and later into that of

Bonaparte). He goes on to quote Schiller, who in 1793 wrote: 'The attempt of the French people to install the Holy Rights of Man and to conquer political liberty has only brought to light its impotence and unworthiness in this regard. The result has been that not just France but alongside it a considerable part of Europe and a whole century has been thrown into barbarism and servitude.' We will touch on these matters when we examine the assassination of Marat.

The Futility theory argues that actions intended to promote change in fact have little, if any, effect. To illustrate this theory Hirschman quotes De Tocqueville, who claimed that the French Revolution produced what he called only 'the illusion of change'. De Tocqueville made the point that even the famous Rights of Man which were 'solemnly declared' in April 1789 had already been instituted by the anciens régimes long before that date. A number of the so-called achievements of the Revolution from administrative centralization to widespread owner-operated small-scale farming were already in place well before the Revolution. De Tocqueville went on: 'Each time since the Revolution that we wanted to destroy absolute power we have succeeded only in placing the head of liberty on the body of a slave.'

The argument of the Jeopardy theory is that the proposed change, though perhaps desirable in itself, can produce costs or unforeseen consequences of one sort or another which are wholly unacceptable. A classic example of this, which will be examined in more detail, is the assassination of Archduke Franz Ferdinand in 1914, when an attempt to free Bosnia from the Austro-Hungarian Empire led to a world war, with the deaths of many millions from all continents of the world except South America and Antarctica – a result certainly never desired or envisaged by those involved in the assassination plot.

Although not studied by Hirschman in his book, obviously there could also be occasions when a push for change achieves precisely what is intended, no more and no less. This book will try to establish if that ever happens and, if so, in what circumstances.

A further, perhaps more basic, aspect of this study, which inevitably arises, concerns the role of the individual in history. Can the removal of one person actually change the course of history in the long or short term? Or are individual leaders merely the froth thrown up by the wave, seeming to wield great and even decisive power but in fact merely the result, not the cause, of vast, collective movements of opinion and political and social change? Do they determine these movements by the force of their personalities? Do leaders lead or are they led by the circumstances in which they find themselves? Tolstoy in his massive novel *War and Peace* argues that 'in historic events the so-called great men are labels giving names to events and, like labels, they have but the smallest connection with the event itself'. He goes on to explain the problem in deterministic terms: 'Every act of theirs, which appears to them an act of their own will, is in an historical sense involuntary, and is related to the whole course of history and predestined from eternity.'[2]

It is not the intention of this book to make any examination of the question of free will or determinism. However, in studying eighteen major assassinations, the question is asked whether the death of these leaders did or did not change the course of history, either on a long- or a short-term basis. This leads on, naturally, to the perennial question: 'To what extent, if at all, does any individual matter in historical terms?'

The *Oxford English Dictionary* defines the word 'assassin' as:

1) a hashish eater. Certain Moslem fanatics in the time of the Crusades, who were sent forth by their sheikh, the Old Man of the Mountains, to murder the Christian leaders and, hence, 2) one who undertakes to put another to death by treacherous violence. The term retains so much of its original application as to be used chiefly of the murderer of a public personage, who is generally hired or devoted to the deed and aims purely at the death of his victim.

In fact the origin and use of the word is a subject of considerable debate and is not at all as clear as the *OED* suggests. (For more information see the appendix.) For the purposes of this book it will be assumed that in its present received meaning, the word 'assassin' denotes the murderer of a public personage by treacherous violence; furthermore the deed would have a political purpose of some kind.

Even using the narrowest definition of the word, there must have been thousands of assassinations since the beginning of recorded history. However, rather than merely describing many of these events, this book will confine itself to a comparatively small number of well-known assassinations, together with a detailed examination of their causes and repercussions.

Clearly an explanation is required as to why certain victims have been chosen for closer scrutiny. However, first let us look at why some well-known figures have not been chosen. President J.F. Kennedy has not been included because it is not known for certain why he was assassinated, and if one is to examine whether the deed attained its objective, it is clearly necessary to know the reason for it. The same applies to a whole range of assassinations by madmen, the only exception to this being the case of Hendrik Verwoerd, whose assassin, albeit insane, did have a political purpose. A further group of assassinations which have not been included are those committed by anarchists. The political philosophy of anarchism became highly important in the last decade of the nineteenth, and the beginning of the twentieth, century. The bearded anarchist with his bomb became a dreaded symbol of militant evil to successive generations in the Western world. In the 1930s the children's cartoon in the *Daily Mail*, 'Pip, Squeak and Wilfred', with its stereotyped anarchist villain (Popski) lurking about with his cloak and smoking round black bomb, sank deep into the author's consciousness, as no doubt it did into many others', confirming his assumptions about the anarchists. That this feeling was to a great extent unfair is almost beside the point. A book dealing with assassination which does not even mention anarchism could justifiably be criticized for ignoring a major aspect of its subject.

Like most philosophic doctrines the idea of anarchism (although not given that name until the second half of the nineteenth century) originated with the Greeks, continuing through Sir Thomas More and his *Utopia,* the English writer William Godwin in the late eighteenth century, the Frenchman Pierre Joseph Proudhon with his famous aphorism 'property is theft', the Russians Bakunin and the gentle Prince Kropotkin and then to Tolstoy and William Morris with his idyllic rural vision put forward in *News from Nowhere.*

The basic idea of anarchism is that humankind is essentially good; evil comes through government. Do away with government and the result would be general happiness as people would, without inhibition, follow those finer instincts that exist in all of us. The authoritarian state would be replaced by some form of non-governmental cooperation between free individuals or collections of individuals such as trades unions. Even political parties are barred by the true anarchist since, as Proudhon said – 'All parties without exception, in so far as they seek for power, are varieties of absolutism.'

The majority of anarchists have always been opposed to violence. They believed that their idea of a perfect society would be achieved through peaceful persuasion and education. Furthermore, there would be no transitional period. Unlike the Marxists with whom they had fundamental, often very bitter, disagreements and who foresaw a period of the 'dictatorship of the proletariat' before the state would 'wither away', the true anarchists saw an almost immediate transition from authoritarian rule to liberty. In their view, the state must not be taken over, but abolished. In fact, contrary to popular belief, anarchism was a deeply moralistic philosophy.

However, there were indeed some anarchists towards the end of the nineteenth century, notably Bakunin, who believed that violence was necessary to get rid of authoritarian rule. Unlike the Russian nihilists who thought that violence was an end in itself, these anarchists, always a minority of the movement, believed that violence was indeed evil, but a necessary evil for a greater good. In order to bring down the state apparatus it was necessary to create a situation of chaos by killing its major representatives.

It was in the 1890s that these people put their ideas into practice, assassinating Carnot (the President of France), Elizabeth Empress of Austria, Humbert I, King of Italy, and William McKinley, President of the United States, together with numerous other lesser figures, particularly in France and Spain. It was these acts of terrorism which gave anarchism the name it still has in the minds of generations of newspaper readers. As far as Britain was concerned, anarchism fell on deaf ears with the British Labour movement almost totally ignoring it. The only casualty of anarchist violence in England was a Frenchman, Marcel Bourdin, who, in 1884, accidentally blew himself up in Greenwich Park with a home-made bomb intended for use abroad – thus giving Joseph Conrad the plot for his brilliant book *The Secret Agent*.

Anarchism as a political doctrine hardly exists now except in some rarefied intellectual circles. It faded out after the early 1930s, with only a short period of some fifty years in which it was a factor to be considered seriously in international and national affairs. This is not surprising: whatever the rights and wrongs, it must now be clear that the vision of society existing happily and serenely without any form of government or law constraining its citizens is an absurdity. It must be true that government is not the only evil; human beings are not wholly good and, even if they were, some form of government would be necessary to regulate their activities. That being so, there is little point in examining anarchists' assassinations in this book since they could not, in any circumstances, achieve their political aim. Anarchists' assassinations are by definition certain to fail to achieve their objectives. Even if the actual deed is successful, subsequent disillusionment is inevitable.

One inclusion in this book which might occasion some surprise is the crucifixion of Jesus Christ, an event which is clearly not assassination in the common usage of that term - perhaps judicial murder would be a better description. His death was hardly caused by 'treacherous violence' – although it might just be possible to use both those words if pushed to it. The reason for his inclusion, however, is that Jesus Christ was removed from the scene by his

enemies in order to silence him for ever and, in the context of the
eventual results of murder with a political purpose, the
repercussions of his death seem to be highly relevant here.

It is of course possible to criticize the selection of assassinations
contained in this book. There are other notable exclusions apart
from John Kennedy, but this is inevitable given such a vast field of
possibilities. The aim has been to cast the net wide both in terms of
geography and time, and those chosen have been grouped because of
similarities in context. The result is as follows:

> Julius Caesar / Thomas à Becket
> Mahatma Gandhi / Jesus Christ
> Jean Paul Marat / Leon Trotsky
> Lord Frederick Cavendish / Archduke Franz Ferdinand
> Tsar Alexander II / Abraham Lincoln
> Field Marshal Sir Henry Wilson / Michael Collins
> King Abdullah of Jordan / President Anwar Sadat of Egypt /
>   Prime Minister Yitzhak Rabin of Israel
> President Hendrik Verwoerd / Martin Luther King / Malcolm X

This list comprises – one Roman, two Jews, one Indian, one
Frenchman, two Russians, one Austrian, one Jordanian, one
Irishman, one Anglo-Irishman, two Englishmen, one South African,
three Americans and one Egyptian. Therefore both the nationalities
and the eras are spread, though with perhaps a bias towards the
nineteenth and twentieth centuries.

It is argued that this list is wide enough to draw some firm
general conclusions about the practice and repercussions of
assassination. Furthermore, a pattern emerges which can be used to
answer questions about the role of the individual in history. These
matters will be dealt with in the Conclusion.

NOTES

1. A.O. Hirschman, *The Rhetoric of Reaction*, Harvard University Press, 1991.
2. L.N. Tolstoy, *War & Peace*, Macmillan, London, 1942, p. 667.

CHAPTER 1

JULIUS CAESAR /
THOMAS À BECKET

It is extremely difficult, if not impossible, to visualize the context of Becket's life 850 years ago, let alone that of Julius Caesar after two millennia. There is much contemporary or near contemporary evidence in both cases but beliefs, assumptions and codes of behaviour have changed vastly since then, quite apart from the massive advances in scientific knowledge. It is too easy, and can be very misleading, to project oneself into their times and expect to understand why, and how, they did what they did. But human nature does not change all that much and there are some certainties about both men. They were both assassinated because some of their contemporaries thought that they were becoming, or indeed had become, too big for their boots. The scale of their achievements and their importance to world history are, of course, very different – Caesar, near master of the known world of his day; Becket, thorn in the flesh of Henry II, King of England. But those who assassinated them, in both cases, hoped to achieve significant changes – in Caesar's case to halt the slide towards dictatorship and return power to the Senate; in Becket's case to help the monarch in his attempt to redraw the boundaries between Church and State. As we shall see in both cases the assassinations failed in their purpose and, in both cases, the assassins were repudiated by many, if not all, of their contemporaries.

Both men certainly were arrogant, ruthless, opinionated, ambitious and in their own different ways very powerful characters. Whether they were ambitious solely for themselves or whether, and to what extent, they had philanthropic motives, is a matter for debate, and this can be argued both ways. As already mentioned, there are vast differences between the two: Caesar was a soldier, politician and statesman; Thomas à Becket a trusted and very powerful civil servant and Archbishop. However, their deaths, were broadly similar. Both were struck down by their own nationals in the centre of their respective worlds – the Roman Senate (with daggers) and Canterbury Cathedral (with swords). These were dramatic events indeed, so much so that both have been marked by major dramas by great English playwrights.

Gaius Julius Caesar was probably born on 12 July 102 BC, although the precise year is not known. He came from an aristocratic or patrician family that claimed legendary descent from Iulus, the grandson of Venus. His great grandfather on his father's side claimed descent from the fourth king of Rome. On his mother's side was Lucius Aurelius Cotta and his son of the same name, both of whom were consuls (in 144 and 119 BC respectively). The most famous of Caesar's relations was, however, not a blood relation. Caius Marius, the son of a poor farmer, married Caesar's Aunt Julia – the sister of his father. Marius was a highly successful soldier in North Africa and was elected consul on no fewer than seven occasions.

Rome had become a republic in 509 BC, having expelled its seventh king, Tarquinius Superbus, whose reign had been an unmitigated disaster. This had led to an endemic hatred of monarchy, which was to play its part in Julius Caesar's assassination. The basic system of a Citizens' Assembly modelled on the Greek city-state was clearly not suitable to rule over what was becoming an empire. The result was the bloody turmoil of the final two hundred years of the Roman Republic. Cynical manipulation, bribery, debauching of the electorate, patronage and factional rivalries inexorably moved events on to a series of skirmishes, producing dictator figures who still ruled under the fig leaf of the old democratic forms and titles. There was a continuous struggle for power between the patricians who mostly claimed descent from the original people whom Romulus, the first king, had brought to Rome, and the plebeians who were freed slaves or strangers who had come to the city. However, as is so often the case, class distinctions were becoming less rigid. By the time of Caesar's birth the aristocracy was composed largely of plebeian families with an ancestor who had served Rome well either in the city or elsewhere in the army. The focus of the struggle for power shifted to the rivalry between the Optimates and the Populares. The former believed that the Senate, composed of members of the old and new aristocracy, should have all the power. It represented the wisdom and experience of the past and should rule Rome and its empire. The Populares, on the other hand, believed that the people should have the major influence on all decisions. They derided what they saw as the selfish and corrupt rule of a collection of self-interested, so-called aristocrats. (The basis of this conflict seems to be endemic to mankind – snobbery, direct and inverse, abounded then as it does now.)

Marius, himself of plebeian stock, supported the Populares. A struggle developed between Sulla, an aristocratic consul representing the Optimates, and Marius. Sulla marched on Rome and broke the power of the Populares. He then went to the East where revolts had broken out against the Romans in Asia Minor and Greece. A complicated and bloody period of alternating power ensued in Rome, culminating in the final return of Sulla in 82 BC. He ordered the execution of 1,700 of his opponents including forty senators. Three thousand unfortunate Samnite prisoners who had opposed his return to Rome were also butchered in the Circus Maximus as an entertainment. If this kind of behaviour qualifies as 'barbarism', then barbarism existed in full measure in Rome at the time. (The antics of Madame Guillotine and her tricoteuses probably furnished the nearest equivalent in modern times – the gas ovens were hardly 'entertainment' – but the scale, horrifying as it was, was very different.)

Julius Caesar appeared to have had the normal education of a young Roman of his class and status. This would have included the study of Latin grammar, arithmetic, Greek language, history and philosophy and, later, oratory. He was steeped in Hellenic culture, although his way of thinking was always more Roman than Greek. As a young man he wrote a tragedy and some boyish love songs, which were banned long after his death by Augustus, believing that they would add to Caesar's fame.

When he was sixteen Caesar married Cornelia, the daughter of Cinna, an arch-enemy of Sulla who, on his return to Rome, ordered Caesar to divorce her. Showing an extraordinary courage, Caesar refused. Surprisingly, Sulla was persuaded to spare his life. But Caesar wisely left Rome to join the staff of the new governor of Asia, Thermus. Like Becket, as we shall see, Caesar was clearly an impressive youth whose bearing, intelligence and energy led to almost immediate preferment.

Caesar's career now took off. He showed great courage in battle, being decorated with the Civic Crown, the highest award for bravery which Rome could award, and distinguished himself in a diplomatic mission to Nicodemes, the King of Bithynia. On the death of Sulla, Caesar returned to Rome where he flourished as an advocate. However, on a journey to Rhodes he was captured by some pirates and held to ransom for six weeks. He seems to have had a jolly time in captivity, eating and drinking with his captors and promising them with jocularity that when he was freed he would return and crucify them. The ransom was paid and he did indeed return and crucify them, being praised later for his mercy in ordering them to be stabbed to death before being nailed to their respective crosses.

Sulla's death in 78 BC had led to further turmoil in Rome. Three powerful figures emerged, all of whom were to have a great influence on Caesar's life – Pompey, Crassus and Cicero, the latter a brilliant orator and boyhood friend who ultimately turned against him. A continuing struggle for power ensued. However, all internal squabbles were swept into the background by a slave revolt led by Spartacus, an escaped gladiator. For two years Spartacus defeated every Roman army sent against him, until Pompey and Crassus between them eliminated the slave insurrection, crucifying Spartacus.

However, Pompey and Crassus were rivals. In their quest for popularity they vied with each other in their extravagant entertainments and banquets for the people. Meanwhile Caesar managed to get himself elected to a quaestorship (the lowest grade of the magistracy), becoming heavily in debt in the process. A very successful tour in Spain was followed by election as aedile (the third grade of magistracy), for which he staged the biggest gladiatorial show ever, with three hundred pairs of combatants dressed in silver armour. Like Becket, in his youth he flaunted wealth. Not surprisingly, his indebtedness increased as a result. He was then elected pontifex maximus (chief priest), defeating the Optimates candidate. This was followed by his election as praetor (the magistrate next to consul in seniority) and his return to Spain as governor in 61 BC. He became consul in 60 BC and formed a triumvirate with Pompey and Crassus, under which he brought in a number of much-needed agrarian and administrative reforms. He then left for his remarkable period in Gaul, during which he won victory after victory – immortalized in his books, to the delight of scholars and the dismay of generations of schoolboys. He established Roman rule over the whole of France and Belgium and parts of Switzerland, Holland and Germany, invading Britain twice in the process. It has been estimated that during Caesar's campaigns 1,192,000 of his enemies were killed.[1]

Crassus was immensely rich, even by Roman standards. However, he suffered, from vanity. He wished to become a great military figure like Pompey and Caesar – the comparatively simple matter of defeating Spartacus had not satisfied him. He determined to attack Parthia, the only power that could confront Rome and hope to win. He took an army with him, paid for out of his own pocket, and marched to his death and that of many of his soldiers in a futile invasion of Parthia in 53 BC. Pompey became the sole consul in Rome, with the Optimates in firm control.

It was clear to Caesar that he and Pompey would not be able to co-exist. He decided that he would have to fight for his position and, with his army, he crossed the River Rubicon in northern Italy on his way back to Rome, thus breaking the inviolable rule that generals should leave their armies behind them when approaching Rome. This was a massive affront to the Senate and a decisive step towards civil war, with Caesar championing the Populares against Pompey's Optimates. He defeated Pompey, who escaped to Egypt but was subsequently murdered. Caesar entered Rome and held a series of triumphs. Four hundred lions were hunted to death in the Circus (it must have been a massive task getting them there) and gladiators fought each other not only individually but in groups. A naval battle was staged and as a grand finale in the Circus Maximus two armies composed of war captives and condemned criminals – a thousand foot, two hundred horse and twenty elephants on either side – fought each other to the death.[2] When the last triumph had been celebrated, the populace was entertained at a feast for which 22,000 tables were laid and after it Caesar was escorted to his house by much of the populace and twenty elephants carrying torchbearers.

Not content with this bonanza Caesar then went to Egypt, where he won yet more victories and confirmed Cleopatra as queen of Egypt. He went on to Judaea (Palestine), where he enjoyed a further military triumph. Rather belatedly – having been delayed perhaps by Cleopatra's charms – he then returned to Rome. The Optimates were still holding out in North Africa, however, and Caesar now set off for the North African coast with 3,000 foot soldiers and 150 cavalry, winning yet another massive victory at Thapsus.

Caesar did not return to Italy until July 46 BC. On his triumphal reappearance he was made dictator for ten years and a mass of honours was heaped upon him. He was decreed a thanksgiving of fifty days and a temple of liberty was ordered to be built at public cost. Although ostensibly resisting it, he was virtually deified and swamped the Senate with his supporters, increasing its membership from six hundred to nine hundred. He then set about a whole mass of reforms, proclaiming a general amnesty, pardoning nearly all of his enemies and promoting many. He ordered the rebuilding of Carthage and Corinth, abolished the existing tax system and appointed commissioners to carry out the allotment of land for his discharged veterans. He also projected the establishment of colonies in what had in effect become an empire for those Romans who wished to settle there. For the year 44 BC he selected Mark Antony as his partner in the Consulate, in spite of his dissatisfaction with Mark Antony's performance as his deputy during his absence abroad. He clearly valued loyalty above efficiency as, disastrously, have many other leaders throughout history.

In addition, he ordered the digging of a canal through the Isthmus of Corinth and in Italy a canal was to be dug from the Tiber near Rome to Tarracina in order to drain the Pontine Marshes. A new trunk road was planned from the Adriatic over the Apennines to the Tiber valley. Meanwhile the whole of Greek and Roman literature was to be collected in one vast library and the whole body of civil law was to be unified in one work. As with Napoleon, his influence seemed to reach into every corner of national life.

As a result of all this he was granted the title of father of his country; his birthday was declared a public holiday; statues of him were to be set up in all the temples of Rome; the month of his birth was to be renamed Julius (July); his dictatorship was extended for life; his son, or adopted son, was to be designated pontifex maximus, a veiled recognition of hereditary monarchy, and all senators swore an oath that they were ready to protect his life. His future governmental actions were declared valid in advance; every four years games were to be held in his honour; during all gladiatorial games in Rome and Italy one day was to be dedicated to Caesar; he was given a golden chair and a golden wreath adorned with jewels for the games; what was considered to be his divine image was to receive a holy resting place like other deities. The one honour which he refused, with what some considered to be mock modesty, was the title of rex (king). Supreme power undoubtedly rested in Caesar's hands and he was fully aware of this. The power of the Optimates and indeed of the Senate itself appeared to be broken for ever.

Caesar was a remarkable man by any standards. He had great restless energy and inspired total devotion in his various armies.

He was intelligent, decisive, brave, unpredictable and imaginative in his military campaigns. He could be ruthless and thought nothing of ordering thousands of his enemies to be slaughtered but he could be very forgiving when he deemed it to be in his interests. He was a master of intrigue and had a magnetic personality with boundless egoism. He was prepared to flatter, even to grovel, when it suited him. He was also a generous patron of the arts and wrote surprisingly well himself. A leader to his fingertips, he was contemptuous of the old guard of the Senate and determined to reform a system that had failed to give stability. He was arrogant, versatile, determined and brilliantly successful, establishing Rome as the centre of Europe. There can be few, if any, other men in world history with such a record of achievements. However, many of his contemporaries were vastly jealous of him and he was assassinated at the zenith of his power.

Thomas Becket (known as Thomas à Becket) was born in AD 1118. His background was what would, in France until perhaps recently, be called the haute-bourgeoisie. His mother was a native of Caen. His father came from Rouen, but emigrated to London before Thomas was born; he became a prosperous merchant and at one time was sheriff of London. Thomas was educated in London and then in Paris. He returned to England aged twenty-two and served as clerk and accountant to a rich businessman. He was, clearly, an outstanding young man and Theobald, the Archbishop of Canterbury, took him into his household. He obtained the confidence of the primate and accompanied him on a visit to Rome and to the Council of Rheims in AD 1148. He gained a number of valuable livings as a clerk in holy orders and after being ordained deacon became archdeacon of Canterbury, a position of some power and authority. On Theobald's recommendation, Henry II appointed him as Chancellor of England. At this stage he still had not been ordained as a priest.

Henry II was only twenty-one years old when he became King of England. He was the grandson of Henry I by his daughter Matilda.

On Henry I's death, the Norman barons who exerted power in England bypassed Matilda and crowned his nephew, Stephen, as King. Stephen attempted to crown his son Eustace as the future king but Theobald refused to sanction it, a refusal which would later have a fateful echo.

Civil war broke out between Matilda and Stephen, which was only really resolved on Stephen's death and his succession by Henry II. Henry himself was more French than English. He was born in Normandy, reared in France and spoke Norman French rather than English. Most of his life was spent on the continent and England comprised only a part of his empire, which included Normandy, Anjou, Maine, Poitou and Aquitaine, with sovereign claims over Toulouse, Wales and Scotland.[3] On Thomas's appointment as Chancellor, he and Henry became firm friends, jointly indulging in their passion for hunting. They began to deal with the abuses that had grown up during the years of civil war. A large number of mercenaries had found their way into England and their presence was the cause of much disorder. Henry decreed that they should leave, and they did. Furthermore the barons and bishops had built a number of unlicensed castles and these were all pulled down. Within six months law and order, which had largely broken down, was restored; 'the fields were cultivated and the valleys were thick with corn, the pastures full of oxen and the folds of sheep'.[4] It was a remarkable achievement for two young men inexperienced in government. Henry II's energy was prodigious. Among many other reforms during his reign he established a system of circuit courts and juries, which, although much amended, is still in place today.

As Chancellor, Becket was chief officer of the royal chapel. He was in charge of the Great Seal and all important documents passed through his hands. He had a finger in every pie and being very close to the king was showered with gifts by those hoping to obtain favours. He was in a position to obtain money from church preferments and a number of other sources, and did so. In short, apart from the King, he was probably the most powerful man in England.

Becket had a love of luxury and ostentatious wealth similar to that of Julius Caesar. Like Caesar, he was both a brave and successful leader in war, fighting on Henry's behalf in the south of France, and a successful diplomat. Henry sent him to France to negotiate with the French king, Louis VII, about a marriage between Henry's son, still an infant, and Louis's daughter, who was only a few months old! Becket took with him two hundred men on horseback as well as soldiers, clerks, butlers, serving men, knights and several youths of noble family. All were dazzlingly dressed in new and brilliant clothes. Becket himself took twenty-four changes of clothing. There were eight carriages in his train, each drawn by five enormous horses. Two of the carriages were filled with beer in iron-bound casks intended as gifts to the French. One carriage was used for the chancellor's chapel, another for his sleeping compartment and another for his kitchen. Others carried different sorts of meat and drink, others again cushions, bags of bedding, night attire and so on. Eight coffers that formed part of the luggage were filled to the brim with Becket's gold and silver cups, his pitchers and his basins, his spoons and his knives. To add a few finishing touches each carriage had a large dog tied to it which looked savage and strong enough to have tackled a lion, and on the back of every packhorse rode a long-tailed monkey. The cavalcade passed through the villages in an apparently endless stream, the footmen going first, 250-strong and singing lustily. Next came the dogs with their keepers, the packhorses, the grooms, the squires, the falconers, the butlers, the attendants, the knights and the clerks and so on, until at last the climax of the whole display – the Chancellor, and with him some particular friends. The French villagers could hardly believe their eyes. 'What a remarkable man the king of England must be,' they exclaimed, 'if he has such a great man as this for his Chancellor!'[5] Partly because of all this, the arrangements for a marriage were successful and it was agreed that it should take place as soon as the infants were old enough.

Henry had been having trouble with the Church under Theobald, as the Archbishop would not defer to his wishes in many areas.

When the latter died he thought that, by installing his friend Thomas as Archbishop, he would avoid similar problems in the future. He was to be very wrong.

Thomas accepted the post of Archbishop of Canterbury with great reluctance, telling Henry that he expected that their relations would totally change and that they might well find themselves at odds in the future. However, Henry, was determined to make his friend Archbishop. Thomas was therefore ordained priest one day (2 June 1161) and consecrated archbishop the next. He was forty-four. All the evidence is that Becket transformed himself overnight. As Nesta Pain put it:

He put aside his rich clothing and wore the sober habit of a monk. Next to his skin he put on a hair shirt of the roughest kind which fell to his knees, and swarmed, so a devoted admirer tells us, with lice. His charities, his persistence in prayer, his mortifications became as famous as his banquets had been in days gone by. He changed his manner as well as everything else and he now spoke in a solemn tone. He himself ate little; scarcely enough to sustain life and his favourite drink was said to be 'water in which hay had been boiled'. Each meal was taken to the accompaniment of reading from a holy book and it was shared by troops of poor men who were ostentatiously ushered into the hall before everybody else. Every day he went down on his knees and washed the feet of thirteen paupers and he wept. His weeping reached 'almost miraculous proportions' according to John of Salisbury and when he celebrated Mass his tears fell like rain. His nights were passed in prayer, rather than sleep, and now more frequently than ever his back was bared to the lash.[6]

It is difficult to know the real reason for the abrupt transformation which was eventually to lead to Becket's assassination. It is certain that, at a stroke, ostentatious wealth, devotion to his monarch and a love of display were transformed into an ostentatious hair shirt, to prayer and to devotion to what he held to be the interests of his Church, regardless of the consequences. It is possible that this stemmed from a genuine spiritual conversion, as with St Paul on the road to Damascus. It is also possible that this came from what many would hold to be a defect in his character: a determination to carry whatever role he was playing to the extreme, come what may. As Chancellor he would show off his wealth and power to the greatest possible extent; as Archbishop he would make his mark by an opposite ostentation of poverty and by flaunting his temporal and spiritual power at the expense of his monarch. The very fact that he had been Henry II's great friend added to the drama.

Whatever the truth of this, he began, almost immediately to oppose the King. The problems started when Becket presented the living of Eynesford to one of his household clerks. With Henry's support the current lord of the manor opposed this, but, without hesitation Becket excommunicated him. Henry was furious and, in this case, Becket relented. The second serious dispute was about a voluntary tax paid by some householders to the sheriffs, in return for which they undertook certain defensive duties. Henry demanded that the money should go to his treasury. However, Becket refused to pay for his lands and churches. The third, and by far the most important, quarrel was about what was called 'criminous clerks'. It was this issue, in essence, which eventually led to Becket's assassination.

The problem was that there were two legal systems existing side by side in England – Church and State. The precise boundaries of their jurisdiction had been a matter of argument for some time. William the Conqueror had brought England into line with Norman practice by separating the two: the 'Courts Christian' had power to deal with cases which concerned the Church or which lay within the moral sphere, while secular courts dealt with the rest. Henry I, Henry II's grandfather, had tightened up the system. Any letter from the Pope or even a legate from him was not allowed into England without royal licence, and appeals from Church courts could only go to Rome if Henry I agreed. A further, and to modern minds extraordinary, canon ordained that the wife of a man who had become a priest, if she refused to separate herself from her husband, should be sold into slavery.

However, the situation under Stephen, had been very different. He was a weak personality and could not stand up to the pressures exerted by the Church. Furthermore, he was distracted by the civil war he was fighting against his cousin Matilda and during this time the secular courts became almost entirely ineffective while Church courts succeeded in greatly widening their power.

When Henry II came to the throne, he was determined to re-establish the position of royal, as opposed to Church, revenue, and State, as opposed to Church, jurisdiction, as it had been at the time of his grandfather. He claimed that the archdeacons, of whom Becket was one, extracted more money from the people of England every year than the whole of his own revenue, and took action to redress the balance. Above all, control of the respective areas of jurisdiction had become absurd. Almost every crime could be said to be within the jurisdiction of the Church, as could almost all civil cases. Marriage, divorce, legitimacy, property, wills – all came under Church jurisdiction. Furthermore, crimes committed by clerks in holy orders were dealt with by Church courts. These could not impose sentences that included the shedding of blood and, in practice, Church court sentences were almost always restricted to fines. Over a hundred murders were said to have been committed by clerks in holy orders during the first nine years of Henry II's reign. It was very easy to be consecrated as a clerk in minor orders: there were no tests of character or education. A clerk could not marry, but he could have as many mistresses as he pleased, and many did. Henry II may have been exaggerating when he said that half of those in holy orders were adulterers, robbers, fire raisers and murderers, but clearly there was more than a grain of truth in that remark.

This situation, as Henry II saw it, could not be allowed to continue. He proposed that, as was the custom in his grandfather's day, 'criminous clerks' would be degraded from their orders and handed over to secular courts for punishment. Becket refused to accept this. This refusal of what seemed to Henry and many others to be a reasonable request was the equivalent of Julius Caesar crossing the Rubicon. The die of inevitable and escalating confrontation was cast.

The quarrel continued. Henry drew up a document known as the Constitution of Clarendon, named after his hunting lodge near Salisbury. This document, with sixteen clauses, contained all the rights which had been reserved for Henry I, including one dealing with the treatment of 'criminous clerks'. Becket managed to get all the bishops to agree not to accept any of it. But to everyone's surprise, he suddenly gave in. He then repented of his weakness and wrote to the Pope to apologize. However, he continued to oppose Henry on other matters, for instance refusing to allow Henry's brother to marry the widowed countess of Varenne because of consanguinity, and opposing him on the rights of a man, John Marshal, to appeal to the king against a decision made by an ecclesiastical court. Becket compounded his defiance by refusing to attend the king's court to argue his case. Henry then summoned a Great Council at Northampton on 6 October 1164 attended by all the leading men in England. Becket was charged with contempt of the king's majesty and found guilty. He was heavily fined and ordered to repay all the money he had received as Chancellor from the Archbishopric of Canterbury when the see had been vacant. The quarrel escalated and eventually Becket escaped to France, travelling in disguise by night. The King of France, Louis VII, supported Becket and helped him with money. The whole issue was greatly complicated because the papacy was in dispute. Pope Alexander had been expelled from Rome and his papal court was at Sens in France. A rival Pope, Pascal III, was in Rome. The attitude of Louis and, even more so, Henry was of great importance in establishing papal legitimacy. Alexander wished to support Becket but not at the risk of Henry transferring his support to Pascal. However, he did condemn the Constitution of Clarendon and told Becket to live the life of a simple monk at the monastery at Pontigny, thereby hoping to dampen down the whole affair. However, Henry was furious at Alexander's action over the Clarendon Constitution. His attitude towards Becket was becoming increasingly intransigent and vindictive. He confiscated all the property of the see of Canterbury and sent all Becket's relatives — four hundred people including women and children — into exile. Many were in great distress, but Louis came to the rescue and gave them financial and other support.

Becket refused to take Alexander's advice and to lie low. He sent furious letters in all directions and threatened Henry with excommunication. However, Becket was losing support in England: the English bishops backed Henry and sent a letter to Becket to that effect. Hostilities between the two of them escalated even further. Henry managed to bring pressure to bear on the Cistercians, the order of the monastery in which Becket was living, and forced him to move. Becket went to a Benedictine abbey at Sainte Colombe, not far from Sens. Both Henry and Becket sent embassies to Rome — the rival Pope had died in the meantime — in an attempt to gain support from Alexander, who had returned there. In April 1169 Becket excommunicated a large number of leading lay and ecclesiastical figures in England. The sentence of excommunication was not valid unless it was personally served. Henry had the English ports blockaded against any emissary from Becket carrying documents, but Becket managed to persuade a young man, not in holy orders, to risk his life by smuggling the letters into England. The Archbishop of York and the Bishop of London were both served with their sentences of excommunication.

Becket then decided to take the ultimate step open to him. He lay England under interdict. This meant that there could be no church services or marriages and no confessions could be heard except from the dying. Henry tried to prevent the sentences being delivered and published a decree to the effect that anyone found carrying letters from the Pope or from Becket containing sentence of interdict was to be arrested and punished as a traitor. No one was to leave England or to return without the king's permission. There would be no appeal to the Pope. Everyone in the kingdom over the age of fifteen was to swear to observe these decrees. Henry then determined to add insult to injury. He had his son crowned as heir to the throne not by Becket who as Archbishop of Canterbury had the sole right to perform the ceremony, but by his long-time rival and enemy, the Archbishop of York, whom Becket had already excommunicated. The situation between Henry and Becket had become impossible. Efforts had been made on all sides to effect a reconciliation and to resolve the various problems between them, all of which could have been solved given sufficient will. Two meetings between Henry and Becket took place in France. At one stage it seemed that they had made up their differences but it all fell through when the King refused to give Becket 'the kiss of peace'.

Becket now returned to England. He narrowly evaded arrest on landing and went to Canterbury. On Christmas Day he preached a sermon in Canterbury Cathedral, weeping as he foretold his own death. He excommunicated several new leading figures and reaffirmed his sentences of excommunication on many of the Bishops in England: 'Accursed of Jesus Christ let them be for sowing hatred and strife between me and my lord! Blotted out be their memory from the company of Saints!' And with these words Becket dashed the candles to the ground – a token of their utter extinction.[7] In those days there was an almost universal fear of God, and excommunication was a terrible fate.

News of Becket's Christmas sermon and fresh sentences of excommunication reached Henry II in France, probably on Boxing Day 1170.

Caesar was assassinated on 15 March 44 BC in the Forum in Rome while attending a meeting of the Senate. He had gone there in order to receive an endorsement for his forthcoming expedition against the Parthians, intended to bring them to heel after their defeat and killing of Crassus. His wife, Calpurnia, had had a premonition of something terrible happening to him, but he had brushed this aside:

whatever he may or may not have been, he certainly was no coward. Furthermore he thought himself safe because of the chaos that would certainly ensue if he was killed and he imagined that this would stay the hand of any enemies he might have. He was very mistaken: he had many powerful enemies in the Senate and elsewhere who sought his death. As is the case with almost all assassinations, the assassin's motives were mixed. There was, for some, an all-consuming jealousy. Power was held by one man – Caesar – but it should be shared, and many of his enemies believed that they would receive a major, and profitable, piece of it. There was greed for the spoils which would accrue to those who killed him. There was also a genuine belief that Caesar, having overturned centuries of traditional democratic rule, had become a tyrant, all-powerful and immune from criticism and not open to influence of any kind. By his assassination, some believed they would bring freedom to a long-suffering people. Perhaps the most notable of these was Marcus Junius Brutus, an old friend of Caesar of high moral character, who may even have been his natural son. He had fought against Caesar in the civil war, but had been pardoned. In all there were about sixty conspirators in the Senate.

When Caesar entered the hall where the Senate was sitting that day and sat on his special chair, he was approached by a senator, Tullius Cimber, whose brother had been banished and who besought Caesar to end his exile. Caesar refused. As a sign to the other conspirators Cimber grabbed his purple toga and pulled it off his shoulder. Caesar was stabbed again and again by many of the conspirators and he died, sinking to the ground in front of Pompey's statue.

The assassins thought that their action would be acclaimed by the people of Rome, that Caesar's death would lead to a resumption of power by the Senate without further bloodshed and that they themselves would be seen as heroes who had dared to make a stand against tyranny. (As John Wilkes Booth, Abraham Lincoln's assassin, was to shout, in an imagined imitation of Brutus, 'Sic semper tyrannis'.)

They were wrong on all counts. They were not supported by the people of Rome as a whole. Caesar's death was followed by a bitter and long drawn out civil war between Octavian, Caesar's great nephew, adopted son and designated successor, and Mark Antony. Thirteen years later Octavian, given the title of Augustus, emerged as an omnipotent Emperor, becoming as autocratic as Caesar ever was. This status he achieved with great subtlety, avoiding confrontation with the Senate by a mixture of flattery, dissimulation and sheer natural cunning. Thus the Republic became the Empire, giving Rome two hundred years of comparative peace and prosperity.

Henry II, in France, had become ever more infuriated by Becket's total intransigence, and uttered the words (which have been variously quoted, but the meaning of which was undoubtedly clear): 'Who will rid me of this turbulent priest?' – probably not meaning the injunction to be taken seriously. However, four knights of Henry's household took him at his word, went to England and entered Canterbury Cathedral. In circumstances of high drama they killed Becket, who is said to have behaved with great dignity during his ordeal. He refused to escape and faced his assassins' swords with quiet composure, reportedly uttering the final words: 'For the name of Jesus and the safety of the church I am ready to die.'[8]

Becket's assassination was a great shock to the whole of Western Christendom. A cult of the martyr was started, many miracles were ascribed to him and he was canonized in 1173. His shrine became a popular resort for pilgrims, not least for Chaucer's famous company.

If the assassins hoped to ingratiate themselves with Henry, they failed. Henry was appalled. He seemed to be stupefied with grief and remained in his room for three days. He sent an envoy to the Pope protesting that he knew nothing of the knights' plans. Nevertheless, Pope Alexander confirmed Becket's excommunication of the Archbishop of York and the Bishops of London and Salisbury and threatened to excommunicate Henry, who then ordered that all the ports of Normandy were to be closed to any representative of the Pope and set sail for England. Partly to avoid contact with the Pope he led an expedition to Ireland in 1171 where he was to play a major part in that country's tangled and tragic history. On his return in 1172 he purchased the Pope's absolution by renouncing all customs harmful for the Church that had been introduced during his reign. All Church lands and goods were restored exactly as they had been a year before Becket had left England. Above all, clerks found guilty of crimes by ecclesiastical courts were not to be retried or sentenced by secular courts. The four knights, however, managed to evade any terrible retribution, ironically by calling in aid the custom whereby even those who killed a prelate could only be tried by ecclesiastical courts.

The assassins had hoped to please the monarch by killing the man who was trying to hold on to and even to expand Church jurisdiction and power in a number of areas which the king thought should belong to him or to his agents. However, they did not please him and the Church did retain its position. Their failure was absolute. Indeed Becket was probably more powerful in death than he would have been alive – martyrdom is a potent advocate.

The question remains as to whether Becket was predominantly a saint or a sinner, and there are knowledgeable and wise protagonists of each position. His supporters claim that his austere way of life after becoming archbishop was not just for show. Following his assassination his hair shirt was found to be crawling with maggots, not a penance easily accepted even in those unhygienic days. He really did lead a frugal and unostentatious life, a complete contrast to his previous opulent existence. His translation from Chancellor to Archbishop did transform him in almost every way. But was there not a strong element of personal and vainglorious pride in his subsequent dealings with Henry? Could and should he not have been prepared to make some kind of compromise with his erstwhile friend in the interests not only of good relations between Church and State but of his Church itself? It is difficult to absolve him from the sins of vanity and self-importance, even though they were expressed in remarkably different ways when his role changed, or was changed for him against his will.

Henry underwent a very public penance in Canterbury Cathedral in 1174. Every one of the cathedral monks, and several Bishops and Abbots, lashed his naked back. He put on sackcloth and prayed before the tomb. The rest of his life was a disaster, as one after the other of his sons rebelled against him including his favourite son, John.

The conclusion, therefore, is that both Julius Caesar and Thomas à Becket were assassinated because their contemporaries thought that they were a menace to peace and stability, that they were too autocratic and that sensible administration and rule would be restored if they were out of the way. In both cases, the exact opposite happened. Caesar's death was followed by a period of chaos and then by an autocratic rule which surpassed even his own, while Becket's assassination failed to create a more sensible division of the responsibilities of Church and State in England. The Church was able to maintain much of its domination of affairs – in particular its jurisdiction over criminous clerks – until the Reformation, centuries later, swept away much of the old ecclesiastical order.

NOTES

1. M. Gelzer, *Caesar*, Blackwell, Oxford, 1968, p. 284.
2. J.F.C. Fuller, *Julius Caesar*, Eyre & Spottiswoode, London, 1965, p. 285.
3. T.W. Moody, *The Course of Irish History*, Mercier Press, Cork, 1967, p. 125.
4. Nesta Pain, *The King and Becket*, Eyre & Spottiswoode, London, 1964, p. 47.
5. Ibid., p. 50.
6. Ibid., pp. 84, 85.
7. Ibid., p. 234.
8. Ibid., p. 241.

CHAPTER 2

MAHATMA GANDHI /
JESUS CHRIST

Some would consider it almost sacrilegious to compare Mahatma (or 'Great Soul' as his supporters called him) Gandhi and Jesus Christ and in particular to examine the similarity of the circumstances and repercussions of their deaths. But this must be wrong: on the contrary it is surely sacrilegious for a Christian to imagine that Jesus Christ cannot stand up to comparison with anyone. There are, of course, many great differences between the two men but there are also some startling similarities which will become apparent.

There are many problems in making a comparison of this sort. One lies in comparing situations in one age with another. It is difficult, some would say impossible, to make the imaginative leap necessary if one is to grasp the very different contexts involved. This is exacerbated when the material available varies so greatly. Then there is the problem of selectivity – what evidence does one use? In Gandhi's case eyewitness accounts of his life, times and beliefs abound. He wrote what amounts to an autobiography of the first half of his life and there is a myriad of contemporary accounts of his life and death. In Jesus Christ's case there is the New Testament, and in particular the Gospels. And even with these remarkable documents there are scholarly disputes about just how much they are, indeed, based on contemporary or near-contemporary accounts. It is not the intention of this book even to touch on the fringes of the vast theological treasure chest of writing about every possible facet of the life and times of Jesus Christ.

Neither will the post-facto judgements of the Church, whether divinely inspired or not, be taken into account. The New Testament alone will be used.

Gandhi was born on 2 October 1869, the fourth and last son of his father's fourth marriage. His mother was a deeply religious Hindu. His father was chief minister in the very small state of Porbandar in the west of India. The family belonged to the Vaisya, the merchant or shopkeeper, caste. This stood third in the Hindu pecking order, below the Brahman, the priestly, which was top, and the Kshatriyas – the rulers and soldiers. The Sudras, the working and farming class, were the lowest except, of course, for the untouchables who were hardly even to be mentioned in polite society. The untouchables were descendants of the inhabitants of India at the time of the Aryan invasion from the north in about 2000 or 3000 BC. They had originally retreated into the hills and forests, but had gradually returned and were allowed to perform menial tasks for the conquerors, who established their own caste system, largely reflecting the occupations of their members. Each caste had a large number of sub-castes. The original inhabitants were not allowed to participate in this caste system and were relegated to the most menial of tasks. In some areas a Brahman was not supposed even to pass under the shadow of an untouchable and had to be purified if he did. Indeed, in these areas untouchables were supposed to ring a bell as they moved about to warn Brahmans of their approach.

In order to escape this humiliation, after the Mogul invasion many of these outcasts became Moslems and, subsequently, others became Christians, both religions believed that all human beings are equal in the sight of God. This gave added force to the hatred of many Hindus for the Moslems, many of whom had previously been untouchables.

Gandhi was married at thirteen to a girl of the same age, Kasturbai, who was illiterate. The marriage lasted sixty-two years until her death. Without his knowledge, Gandhi had been betrothed twice before. In the Hindu tradition, marriage was a matter to be dealt with by the respective families: the participants had no say in the matter. In later life Gandhi strongly opposed child marriage, this custom being one of the features of Hindu society which he believed to be totally wrong, as indeed was the whole concept of untouchability. Gandhi's view of the caste system changed: in 1921 he defended it but by 1946 he went so far as to accept and encourage intercaste marriages. Furthermore, Gandhi did not drink alcohol and was steeped in the whole concept of vegetarianism, which was an article of faith of the Vaishnavis, a Hindu sect to which Gandhi's parents belonged. Indeed the whole question of diet was to play a major part in his lifestyle to an increasing degree in his later years.

At that time the law was a major avenue of advancement for a bright young Indian and when not quite eighteen years of age, Gandhi went to study law at the Inner Temple in London, leaving his wife and child behind. This move, largely financed by a devoted brother, was bitterly opposed by his sub-caste. Not for the last time Gandhi ignored what he saw as illogical and stultifying opposition by conservative and stuffy elements from his own background. When in England the young Gandhi tried to ape the clothes and manners of the English, an absurdity which he chronicled with amused self-tolerance in his autobiography. He bought a chimney-pot hat for the very expensive price of nineteen shillings and an evening dress suit from Bond Street for ten pounds. His brother sent him a gold watch chain. He learnt how to tie his tie and spent ten minutes every day examining his appearance in front of a mirror. He took lessons in dancing, French and elocution. He also joined the Vegetarian Society in England and made his first speech, a total failure, in that environment. He was shy and a very bad speaker. It was his personality, his beliefs and his lifestyle which had such a charismatic appeal to millions, not his oratory, which remained second rate throughout his life.

It was in England that he began to think seriously about religion. He met, and admired, some deeply religious Christians. He was persuaded to read the Bible. He did not think much of the Old Testament and quickly became bored with it – 'but the New Testament produced a different impression, especially the Sermon on the Mount which went straight to my heart. The verses "But I say unto ye that ye resist not evil: but whosoever shall smite thee on thy right cheek, turn to him the other also. And if any man take away thy coat, let him have thy cloak too," delighted me beyond measure.'[1] Indeed he took the Sermon on the Mount with him throughout the rest of his life, but could not accept either the divinity of Jesus Christ or the exclusive nature of his teaching. For the first time too, he really began to study his own religion in some depth, reading the Bhavagard Gita, the Song of Heaven. This had a very powerful effect on him and probably led to his belief in the end not justifying the means, but the means shaping the end – a very different matter. He also read Thomas Carlyle's essay on Mohammed. He found time, somehow, to take the University of London matriculation, his subjects being Latin, French, English language, history, geography and science. He found mathematics tiresome. It was in England that he first read Tolstoy's *The Kingdom of God is Within You*. This had a very great effect on him, both in its exposure of the outrage of the Tsarist autocracy's treatment of the peasantry – to him reminiscent of the Raj in India – and, above all, in its espousal of non-violence as a creed. Tolstoy's insistence on the simple rural life as against the so-called 'civilized' urban rat race also must have affected Gandhi and perhaps led later to his love affair with the spinning wheel and all that entailed. Indeed, Gandhi was to have a fascinating correspondence with Tolstoy. They exchanged three letters each in 1909/10, finding themselves in complete agreement about the need for a peaceful, painful refusal to serve or obey evil governments including 'no police duty, no military duty, no payment of taxes'. Tolstoy was a very old man, soon to die, whereas Gandhi was a young forty year old.[2] Ruskin, too, later had a great influence on him (in 1904), particularly with his insistence on the redemptive quality of labour.

Gandhi passed all his examinations and was called to the Bar. He sailed for India on 12 June 1891 and began to try to make his way as a lawyer.

We have a detailed knowledge then of Gandhi's early life, his actions and even his inner thoughts, which he chronicled with total honesty even when these were far from being favourable to himself, including an admission of stealing from his brother. In contrast we know little about Jesus's life except for the circumstances of his birth, an appearance in the temple as a youth and a period of three years before his death. A great deal has been inferred, some would say with scant evidence. We do know from the Gospels, however, that Jesus was greatly opposed to the Scribes and Pharisees who dominated the practice of the Jewish religion. He inveighed at length against their hypocrisy. Indeed the importance of the reality of religious practice against the almost total irrelevance of form and ritual is one of his major themes: Gandhi had similar views. The parable of the Good Samaritan suggests that Jesus Christ would not have accepted the caste system, repudiating the current received dogma of social hierarchy and prejudice. That Jesus Christ thought for himself is clear. Indeed much of what he said had revolutionary connotations in terms of the existing morality. Unlike Gandhi, as far as we know Jesus Christ had no dietary hang-ups, other than the contemporary Jewish customs, which he seems to have accepted. Indeed he remained very much a Jew with the central Jewish religion and beliefs until his death. He therefore avoided Gandhi's expenditure of time and energy on what, to much of the Western mind, is a peripheral matter. Jesus Christ did not marry, whether by design or circumstance we do not know: the Gospels do not contain much about Christ's attitude to sex (perhaps obsessive interest in this subject is a modern phenomenon). He does say that 'whosoever looketh on a woman to lust after her hath committed adultery with her already in his heart'.[3] And we do know that

Jesus Christ was deeply opposed to divorce – though one gospel,[4] tantalizingly gives 'fornication' as a legitimate reason for 'putting away a wife'.

As for Gandhi, his wife became pregnant when they were both fifteen. Indeed when his father was dying, instead of remaining at his bedside Gandhi sought sexual gratification with his young wife and, as a result, he was affected by a continuing deep guilt. That may well have been partly why, except for the purpose of procreation, he ever after associated the sexual act with the concept of guilt. In 1906, when he was thirty-seven, Gandhi eventually took a vow of celibacy while remaining married to his unfortunate, but devoted, Kasturbai. Gandhi said that celibacy 'means search after God. It signifies control of all the senses at all times and places in thought, word and deed. . . . It rules out hate, anger, violence and untruth. It creates equability. It is desireless.'[5] Such was Gandhi's determination to overcome carnal desire that for much of his later life, his cousin's granddaughter, Manu, a devoted disciple, shared his bed with him so that he could demonstrate to himself his defeat of lust.

Gandhi did not seem to be making much progress in his profession of the law in India and after less than two years there a business firm of Porbandur Moslems offered to send him to South Africa for a year as their lawyer. He gladly seized the opportunity, leaving his wife, now with two children, behind him. He arrived in South Africa at the age of twenty-two and remained there for twenty-one years. These were the formative years of his life. He underwent some very unpleasant and demeaning experiences of colour prejudice, on one occasion being ejected from a first-class compartment in a train in spite of having a valid ticket. This was, in fact, against the law at the time, as the rigours of apartheid were not officially adopted until 1948. Most of the Indians in South Africa were Hindu labourers who had been indentured for five years to work on the sugar plantations of Natal (152,184 Indians arrived there between 1860 and 1911) or on the coal fields or elsewhere. Other Indians, mostly Moslem merchants, paid their own way to South Africa and established successful businesses there. These Indian communities were, therefore, a sizeable minority by the time Gandhi appeared – in 1896 Natal's population comprised 400,000 blacks, 50,000 whites and 51,000 Indians.[6] There was considerable discrimination against them by the whites, who even began to talk of an 'Asian peril', an ironic term in view of the fact that it was the whites themselves who had introduced the Indians into South Africa and, in the case of indentured labour, had paid for their passage. This discrimination gradually became adopted in law and it was as a result of this that Gandhi became heavily involved as an Inner Temple trained lawyer, emerging quite soon as the leader of the Indian community. On one occasion he was nearly lynched by a frenzied crowd of whites who resented his intrusion into what they thought to be their domain to rule as they thought fit. In this incident he was rescued by the white wife of a white police superintendent, an act which he never forgot. When warned of this assault on his person, Gandhi replied, 'I hope God will give me the courage and sense to forgive them and to refrain from bringing them to law. I have no anger against them. I am only sorry for their ignorance and their narrowness. I know that they sincerely believe that what they are doing is right and proper. I have no reason therefore to be angry with them.'[7] He, therefore, refused to allow a case to be taken against those who had physically assaulted him and enjoined his supporters to do likewise in similar situations.

It was in South Africa that he adopted two of the foremost themes of his life – political activity against discrimination and non-violence, combining the two in the new and dynamic idea of peaceful resistance or non-cooperation. He believed profoundly that violent action was not only evil in itself but would prove ineffective by giving an excuse to use violence in return. He refused to obey what he saw as unjust discriminatory laws and successfully courted arrest, as did thousands of his followers. On one occasion Smuts, the South African Minister of the Interior, had to give way, withdrawing the requirement for Indians to register and carry passes and abolishing the system of indenture. However, Gandhi failed to move Smuts on other issues. The match between the two would have to be scored as a draw. Smuts, also a very religious man, recognized the stature of his opponent and came to admire him. Gandhi became a figure to be reckoned with and when Joseph Chamberlain, the British Colonial Secretary, visited the country, Gandhi, who was in India at the time, was hurriedly sent for to represent his countrymen in talks with the great man. He continued to have many Christian friends and to accept many of their beliefs and teachings without changing his views about the exclusively divine nature of Jesus Christ.

When he arrived in South Africa Gandhi strongly believed in the essential fairness of the British Empire and its promise (in a proclamation of Queen Victoria on 1 November 1858) of equality before the law for all citizens of the British Empire. He continued in that belief while in the country. This explains the perhaps surprising support he gave to the British during the Boer War and in the subsequent Zulu revolt. During both these conflicts he raised an ambulance corps. The former consisted of 300 'free' and 800 'indentured' Indians. Gandhi led it on one occasion, at Spion Kop, evacuating the wounded while under fire, and receiving British thanks and admiration as a result. The Zulu revolt was a very small affair in comparison and did not last long, but Gandhi received the official rank of sergeant major!

During the First World War, too, Gandhi supported the British, trying to help in raising Indian volunteers. With his record of opposition to the government of South Africa and later to that of India, these were difficult decisions to take. He justified them on two grounds: first, the British Government in London was not responsible for the conduct of the colonial government in South Africa, whose colour prejudice was, he thought, quite contrary to the British tradition;[8] secondly, 'I accept the benefits and protection of the British Empire; I have not tried to destroy it; why should I allow it to be destroyed?'[9]

Jesus Christ, clearly, had no experiences similar to those of Gandhi in South Africa, though he would have been fully aware of the status of Jews as second-class citizens in a Roman province, with all that entailed. But he consciously and consistently refused to have anything whatever to do with political life. He expressed his feelings on these matters in that memorable sound bite – 'Render therefore unto Caesar the things which are Caesar's: and unto God the things which are God's.'[10] He was exclusively concerned with spiritual matters and did not seem to share Gandhi's belief in the connection between the two and hence the necessity to act on both fronts. He appears to have been almost totally disinterested in temporal matters or how people earned their living: 'Take no thought for your life, what ye shall eat: neither for the body, what ye shall put on.'[11] He told the rich young man seeking perfection to sell all his goods and give the resulting money to the poor. Gandhi initially attempted to follow a similar path seeing his mission as spiritual, not political. But he was very quickly drawn into political struggles, both in South Africa and then in India where, soon after his return there, he found himself leading a strike of textile workers in Ahmedabad.

However, on the theme of non-violence Gandhi was in total agreement with Jesus Christ, whose admonitions are quite clear: 'Resist not evil', 'Turn the other cheek', 'Put up thy sword', 'Love your enemies' and so on. Jesus Christ was a militant pacifist, if this is not a contradiction in terms, in precisely the same way as was Gandhi nearly two millennia later. In this context, the difference between the two was that Jesus Christ did not combine non-violence with political activity against injustice, as Gandhi did in his campaigns of civil disobedience. Jesus Christ eschewed political activity, unlike some modern prelates, concentrating entirely on individual not corporate social virtue. It could be argued that in practice the political ramifications of Jesus's teaching have been profound. The concepts of equality in the sight of God and 'love your neighbour as yourself' are often cited as a main source of inspiration for liberalism and socialism. There may or may not be truth in these assumptions: the point, however, is that, Jesus's activity was centred on spreading his message in isolation from the particular circumstances of his life; whereas Gandhi's was almost exactly the reverse.

On the other hand the Sermon on the Mount, with its emphasis on personal humility and forgiveness, chimed exactly with Gandhi's beliefs and activities in South Africa. It was in South Africa that Gandhi adopted the Tolstoyan determination to live out his beliefs in practice and to return to the simple life without the encumbrances of so-called civilization. Jesus Christ clearly had similar views: 'Lay not up for yourselves treasures on earth.'[12] Indeed, his whole life emphasized a spiritual not a material ethic.

After a visit to England Gandhi returned to India, landing on 19 January 1915. He was to live for another thirty-three years before his assassination, and during this time he became a world-renowned figure and the leader of the Indian struggle for freedom. There are a number of different aspects to his philosophy of life, all of which, as he saw it, stemmed from the same ethical base. There was the political fight for independence itself and the belief in non-violence. There was the struggle against the concept of untouchability and the drive to bring the Moslems and Hindus together, above all avoiding intercommunal violence. On a more mundane level he campaigned against uncleanliness and spitting. Lastly there was his opposition to industrialization and his espousal of the concept of the spinning wheel. Gandhi believed that the Western-financed cloth factories were destroying the pattern of village life in India with its simplicities and self-help virtues. Indians should spin their own cloth and make their own clothes. He abandoned Western garb and wore a loincloth made out of cotton (the dhoti) which he or his close associates had personally spun. He urged the Indians, all four hundred million or so of them, to do the same. Indeed this loincloth became his trademark in Western eyes, Winston Churchill arrogantly dubbing him a half-naked fakir. When he visited England for the second Round Table Conference in 1931 he went to see King George V. He was told afterwards that he had been rather rude only to wear a loincloth. He replied that he could not imagine why this was so as the king had worn enough clothes for both of them.

On top of all this he fashioned for himself a distinctive lifestyle, dwelling in his own hermitage, or ashram, where he, some of his family and friends (shortly to be his disciples) lived a simple existence, sharing all the chores including, controversially, the removal of the night soil. He maintained this regime for the rest of his life. He kept and even increased his very strict regime of vegetarianism, refusing to eat eggs or any product of the cow, and he was very sceptical about medical science, preferring his own remedies of mud baths, enemas and meditation. He nearly killed himself on one occasion by refusing to take any cows' milk when this was essential, and only survived because, to his own disgust, he accepted goats' milk as a substitute. He probably was responsible for his wife's death, because he refused to allow a doctor to give her penicillin injections. She died when she was with him in prison in 1943.

The political methods he used in his efforts to achieve all these ends were varied. He undertook fasts – his first major one was in September 1924 when he started a twenty-one day fast for Hindu / Moslem friendship. He edited and wrote in various journals, and addressed meetings. He organized demonstrations and strikes and vast movements of non-cooperation. He met, pestered and cajoled the leading political figures of the time, both British and Indian, thus dominating much of the political agenda. He also played a leading part in the activities of the Indian National Congress, and courted arrest, spending 2,089 days in Indian and 249 days in South African prisons. Whatever he did or said, he was hot news. His famous march to the sea in protest against the salt tax and his symbolic picking up of salty mud off the seashore (in fact there was little salt there) became world news.[13]

Whatever means he used, he succeeded in becoming the most famous man on the whole Indian sub-continent, admired, feared and waited upon by viceroys, listened to with great attention by intellectuals and virtually worshipped by hundreds of millions of Indian peasants. There was no television, little radio and, certainly, there were no spin doctors in those days. Indeed, a great deal of the time he was out of touch with the media in any form as he walked through the villages of India, sometimes attended by only one interpreter. There was a magic in his presence. He was able to speak straight to the hearts of all Indians and arouse their most passionate feelings. He refused, in so far as he was able, to accept that he was divine any more than was any other human being. On one occasion when he was on a train an Indian lawyer fell out of it on to his head. The train stopped and the man was picked up, apparently unhurt. He came to see Gandhi and thanked him for his divine help, saying that he must have worked a miracle on his behalf. Gandhi indignantly refuted this and went on – 'If I was divine you would not have fallen out of the train at all.'

The great difference between Jesus Christ and Gandhi was, of course, that, unlike Gandhi, Jesus Christ claimed to be divine, the Son of God, and indeed, according to the Gospels, performed a large number of miracles whereby the normal rules of nature were overturned. As we have already noted, also, Jesus Christ had no political objectives. We cannot imagine him fomenting a strike or organizing demonstrations. But he did have an overwhelming magic about him. He, too, spoke straight to the heart of those who heard him. Thousands flocked to be near him and to hear what he said. Like Gandhi he had disciples who were prepared to give up everything to follow him and propagated his message before and after his death. Like Gandhi he revolted against the status quo: Gandhi inveighed against the British Raj, while Jesus Christ strongly attacked the hypocrisy of the scribes, pharisees and chief priests who controlled the existing Jewish religious establishment together with the money changers and other merchants who invaded the temple in Jerusalem. Jesus Christ's lifestyle would certainly have been based on simplicity. He eschewed all sins of the flesh, constantly reiterating his renunciation of the temptations of this world.

Gandhi was aware of the criticism he occasioned because of the way he treated his family. He did not send his children to school to have a 'literary education', preferring to keep them with him and to teach them himself as best he could in the sparse intervals of his very busy life. His eldest son, Harilal, went right off the rails, submerged in a welter of drink and dishonesty for which Gandhi held himself largely to blame. At one time he became a Moslem, probably to spite his father. Gandhi's other two sons, however, largely satisfied their very demanding father who was proud of the 'simplicity and spirit of service they show in their lives'.[14] When asked 'Who is your family?', Gandhi is reported to have said, 'All of India is my family.'[15] These words are very similar to those used by Jesus Christ, except that Jesus did not limit it to his nation. As he was preaching to a multitude he was told that his brothers and his mother were waiting and wished to see him. He replied, 'Who is my mother or my brethren?' And he looked about him and said, 'Behold my mother and my brethren. For whoever shall do the will of God, the same is my brother, and my sister, and my mother.'[16] Indeed, he seems not to have been at all impressed by what many now hold to be the importance of family life.[17]

This is not the place to sift through the many twists and turns of Gandhi's life between his arrival in India and the achievement of independence on 15 August 1948. However, there are two aspects of his life during this period which would repay a little examination. The first is his relationship with Congress and the second is his trial, which took place on 18 March 1922; the latter is particularly significant because of the similarities to the trial of Jesus Christ.

The Indian National Congress was founded in 1885 by a dignified English civil servant, Octavian Hume, in order to channel the protests of the rising numbers of educated Indians into a moderate body which would conduct a gentlemanly dialogue with the English who ruled the sub-continent. Far from restricting itself to this purpose, however, Congress became the focus of revolt and on his return to India, Gandhi devoted a great deal of effort in attempting to use it as a means of implementing his policy of peaceful resistance to British rule. At times he was officially part of the leadership, at others he was not and had major disputes with it, but throughout his life he had an enormous influence on it. Indeed many see him as its conscience.

In the early stages there were two main issues within Congress – violence or non-violence and cooperation or non-cooperation with the British. At its meeting in Surat in 1907 Congress had split into the so-called moderates and the extremists, characterized by Gandhi as 'the slow party' and 'the impatient party'.[18] Gandhi used all his persuasive powers, and these were very considerable, in favour of non-violence and non-cooperation. His first intervention came in March 1919 when he called for a hartal, a strike, against the findings of a committee set up under Sir Sidney Rowlat. The committee recommended the continuation of the wartime system of justice, which most Indians saw as very unjust. Gandhi called for a day to be spent in fasting and prayer, followed by a campaign of civil disobedience. Much to his distress, this led to many incidents of violence and a number of deaths. This was followed by the massacre at Amritsar on 13 April 1919 when General Dyer ordered his troops to open fire on what undoubtedly was a peaceful meeting, killing no fewer than 379 people and wounding 1,200. Gandhi blamed himself for launching his campaign prematurely. He confessed to 'a blunder of Himalayan magnitude' and called it off.

Towards the end of 1921 Gandhi resumed the campaign of non-cooperation. During December 1921 and January 1922 ten thousand Indians were thrown into prison for political offences. Many Indians in government offices left their jobs. Gandhi continued to preach his doctrine of non-violence – 'If India takes up the doctrine of the sword, she may gain momentary victory, but then India will cease to be the pride of my heart.'[19] But eventually, and in retrospect probably inevitably, passions boiled over and violence occurred. At Chouri Chaura in the United Provinces twenty-two police constables were burnt to death by a mob. Again, Gandhi, appalled by the evil he seemed to have unleashed, called off his campaign of civil disobedience. However, he was arrested and tried for sedition on 18 March 1922 before Mr Justice Broomfield, an event which will be examined shortly.

During the rest of the period between his trial and the achievement of independence, Gandhi's relations with Congress and its leaders varied between titular leadership of it and sometimes bitter dispute. However, his views and personality were always a prime factor in shaping Congress's policy towards the British Raj. There were, of course, ups and downs. In fact Gandhi did at one stage come to an agreement with the current Viceroy, Lord Irwin – later Lord Halifax. Irwin was a deeply religious Anglican. Gandhi said, 'I submitted not to Lord Irwin but to the honesty in him.' For his part, Irwin came to admire the spiritual nature of his antagonist but never really trusted him, calling him 'a most baffling enemy, generous, irrational and illusive and as hard to pin down on a point of logic as a butterfly on the plains of his native Gujerat'.[20] As he put it in a letter to the King:

> I must confess to your Majesty that I was, too, greatly interested in having the opportunity of discussion with this strange little man. I had met him of course before two or three other times, but never in circumstances that permitted conversation to be entirely free. I think that most people meeting him would be conscious, as I was conscious, of a very powerful personality, and this, independent of physical endowment, which indeed is unfavourable. Small, wizened, rather emaciated, no front teeth, it is a personality very poorly adorned with this world's trimmings. And yet you cannot help feeling the force of

character behind the sharp little eyes and immensely active and acutely working mind.[21]

Clearly, from the Nationalists' point of view the great bonus of this meeting was that here was their leader talking on equal terms with the Viceroy – a new and, to them, massively important development. This was not lost on Churchill, who was revolted by 'the nauseating and humiliating spectacle of this one time Inner Temple lawyer, now seditious fakir, striding half-naked up the steps of the Viceroy's palace there to negotiate and parley on equal terms with the representative of the King Emperor'. However, the truce thus achieved, came to an end after a totally unsuccessful second Round Table Conference in London which Gandhi attended. He turned down flat the concessions which were offered as being unacceptable.

Gandhi continued his campaigns on all fronts – independence, anti-untouchability, a return to the simplicities of village life and the spinning wheel, non-violence and, gradually, reconciliation between the Hindus and Moslems, an issue which finally was to become the focus of his activities and lead to his assassination. Jinnah, the ascetic, cold, rigid and brilliant lawyer who came to dominate the Moslem community in India, both east and west, in spite of personally adhering to virtually none of the tenets of the Moslem religion, had originally been a member of Congress. Despairing of Moslem politics, however, he returned in 1929 to Britain where, like Gandhi, he had been trained as a lawyer. He did not return to India until 1935. He gradually became convinced that the only solution to the problems of the Indian sub-continent was partition and the creation of a separate state of Pakistan. He was prepared to go to almost any lengths to achieve this. Gandhi was totally opposed to partition, believing that Moslem and Hindu should live and thrive together in a unified India. Jinnah was to succeed in his aim, but at the cost of perhaps hundreds of thousands of lives.

In fact, Gandhi was to fail in nearly all his political objectives except for the achievement of independence. He made some progress on untouchability but this stigma on Indian and Hindu life still exists. As far as the spinning wheel is concerned, India is becoming an industrial country with all that entails, and although it retains a vast rural hinterland there are few spinning wheels about now. Moslem/Hindu hatred thrives, although it is now sanctified by government policy on both sides rather than a matter for personal violence. In fact, between 1954 and 1964 only 344 people were killed in Hindu / Moslem riots.[22] This is minuscule compared to the immediate post-independence figure. Jail sentences, fasts, meetings, marches (notably the phenomenally successful salt march of March 1930), non-violent campaigns of one sort and another: Gandhi's activities continued with unabated vigour. Although during the whole period there was in fact a slow movement towards independence of one sort of another – at times a dyarchy, at times dominion status – it was the Second World War which really brought matters to a head. This was followed by the election in Britain in 1945 of a Labour Government, resulting in the appointment of Lord Mountbatten and the almost immediate granting of independence, albeit to a divided sub-continent and within the British Commonwealth.

Gandhi's trial in 1922 took place twenty-six years before his death; Jesus Christ's, before Pontius Pilate, a few hours before his crucifixion. Gandhi's resulted in a sentence of six year's imprisonment, of which he served only two, being released as a result of illness (appendicitis). Jesus Christ's culminated in a cruel death by slow torture followed, according to the New Testament, by his resurrection about two days later. Both men were guilty of disturbing the status quo and neither attempted to deny this guilt. Both courted their arrest and their sentence: indeed, according to his followers, Jesus Christ's death was an essential element in the universal forgiveness of sins, a belief which ever since has been a vital part in the religion he established.

Gandhi's trial must have been one of the most remarkable ever held. He was accused of running a campaign to spread disaffection openly and systematically, to render government impossible and to overthrow it. Gandhi having pleaded guilty, the advocate general,

Sir Thomas Strangman, opened the proceedings by asking for a severe punishment. Gandhi replied:

Before I read this statement, I would like to state that I entirely endorse the learned Advocate General's remarks in connection with my humble self. I think that he was entirely fair to me in all the statements that he made because it is very true that I have no desire whatever to conceal from this Court the fact that to preach disaffection towards the existing system of government has become almost a passion with me. . . . I wish to endorse all the blame that the learned Advocate General has thrown on my shoulders in connection with the Bombay, Madras and Chouri Chaura occurrences. Thinking over these things deeply, and sleeping over them night after night and examining my heart, I have come to the conclusion that it is impossible for me to dissociate myself from the diabolical crimes of Chouri Chaura or the mad outrages of Bombay. He is quite right when he says that as a man of responsibility, a man having received a fair share of education, having had a fair share of experience of this world, I should have known the consequences of every one of my acts. I knew that I was playing with fire. I ran the risk, and if I were set free I would still do the same. I would be failing in my duty if I did not do so. I have felt this morning that I would have failed in my duty if I did not say what I have said here just now. I wanted to avoid violence. Non-violence is the first article of my faith. It is also the last article of my creed. But I had to make my choice. . . . I do not ask for mercy. I do not plead any extenuating act. I am here, therefore, to invite and cheerfully submit to the highest penalty that can be inflicted upon me for what in law is a deliberate crime and what appears to me to be the highest duty of a citizen. The only course open to you, Mr Judge, is, as I am going to say in my statement, either to resign your post or inflict on me the severest penalty if you believe that the system and law you are assisting to administer are good for the people.

Gandhi then turned to the reasons for his campaigns:

> I came reluctantly to the conclusion that the British connection
> had made India more helpless than she ever was before
> politically and economically. . . . The law itself in this country
> has been used to serve the foreign exploiter. My unbiased
> examination of the Punjab Martial Law cases has led me to
> believe that at least ninety-five per cent of convictions were
> wholly bad. My experience of political cases in India leads me to
> the conclusion that in nine out of every ten the condemned men
> were totally innocent. Their crime consisted in the love of their
> country. . . . The greatest misfortune is that Englishmen and
> their associates in the administration of the country do not
> know that they are engaged in the crime I have attempted to
> describe. I am satisfied that many Englishmen and Indian
> officials honestly believe that they are administering one of the
> best systems devised in the world, and that India is making
> steady, though slow, progress. . . . I have no personal ill-will
> against any single administrator, much less can I have any
> disaffection towards the king's person. But I hold it to be a
> virtue to be disaffected to a government which in its totality
> has done more harm to India than any previous system. . . .
> I am endeavouring to show to my countrymen that violent non-
> co-operation only multiplies evil and that as evil can only be
> sustained by violence, withdrawal of support of evil requires
> complete abstention from violence.

Mr Justice Broomfield then delivered his judgement:

> Mr Gandhi, you have made my task easy in one way by
> pleading guilty to the charge. Nevertheless, what remains,
> namely the determination of a just sentence, is perhaps as
> difficult a proposition as a judge in this country could have to
> face. The law is no respecter of persons. Nevertheless, it would
> be impossible to ignore the fact that you are in a different

category from any person I have ever tried or am likely to try. It would be impossible to ignore the fact that, in the eyes of millions of your countrymen, you are a great patriot and a leader. Even those who differ from you in politics look upon you as a man of high ideals and of noble and even saintly life. . . . I do not presume to judge or criticize you in any other character. It is my duty to judge you as a man subject to the law who by his own admission has broken the law and committed what to an ordinary man must appear to be a grave offence against the state. I do not forget that you have consistently preached against violence and that you have on many occasions, as I am willing to believe, done much to prevent violence but having regard to the nature of your political teaching and the nature of many of those to whom it was addressed, how you could have continued to believe that violence would not be the inevitable consequence, it passes my capacity to understand.

It might be thought unfair to compare Mr Justice Broomfield to Pontius Pilate, but there are some similarities in the position both found themselves in. Pilate, as procurator of Judea, was answerable to the Roman governor of Syria and through him to Emperor Tiberius to whom he was related by marriage. His job was to keep order, maintain the authority of Rome, collect taxes and arbitrate in cases involving Roman jurisdiction – a far wider brief than that of Broomfield, who only had to administer the British law. But both men bore allegiance to a 'foreign' state and both had clear responsibilities for keeping order. Pilate would be in great trouble if he failed to deal with a potential security threat. (Tiberius's method of reprimand for failure was to have the offending official thrown off the cliff at Capri, where he lived in brooding suspicion and debauchery.) Clearly, as Pilate saw it – and we shall deal with this situation shortly – Jesus did represent a serious threat. Like Broomfield he found himself in a dilemma, having to take punitive action while personally admiring the culprit.

After the sentence of six years' imprisonment had been imposed, Gandhi declared – 'So far as the sentence itself is concerned, I certainly consider that it is as light as any judge could inflict on me, and so far as the whole proceedings are concerned I must say that I could not have expected greater courtesy.'

To add to the extraordinary nature of the proceedings there was general acclaim for the way that Gandhi had conducted his case, for the prosecutor and for the judge himself. Mrs Naidu, a poetess and a prominent nationalist, wrote in the *Bombay Chronicle* that Broomfield was 'an admirable judge deserving of our praise alike for his brave and resolute sense of duty, his flawless courtesy, his just perception of a unique occasion and his fine tribute to a unique personality'. The advocate general warmly shook hands with Gandhi before departing.[23]

In some ways the contrast of these proceedings with the tragic absurdities of the trial of Jesus Christ could not be more marked. But there are some very close similarities. Not surprisingly, the Gospels vary slightly in their accounts. Matthew and Mark are almost the same: Jesus is accused by the chief priests and elders of calling himself 'King of the Jews'. He is then taken before Pilate who asks if this is true, to which he replies, 'Thou sayest' – a polite method, in the Greek, of saying 'Yes'. Pilate can find no fault with him and attempts to avoid the issue by asking the Jews if, in accordance with the custom of releasing one prisoner on that particular day, he can release Jesus. The crowd, which may well have been a rent-a-crowd furnished by the chief priests, although there is no evidence to that effect, vehemently calls for another prisoner, Barrabas, to be released and for Jesus Christ to be crucified. Jesus resolutely refuses to make any plea – in fact, according to these two Gospels, apart from the words quoted above he says nothing at all when before Pilate.

This story is a little expanded by Luke, who says that the statements made include the accusation that, by calling himself the

King of the Jews, Jesus Christ was in effect forbidding the Jews to pay their tribute to Caesar. This, clearly, would directly affect Pontius Pilate, the Roman procurator. Then a short examination by Pilate reveals that Jesus Christ is a Gallilean and therefore subject to Herod, who happens to be in Jerusalem at the time.[24] Jesus is therefore taken to him, but Herod gets no further with the matter in his examination, and Jesus is returned to receive judgement from Pilate. Again, he refuses to answer his accusers. In all four Gospels there are, in effect, two trials – one by the Jewish authorities and one by the Roman procurator who, alone, can order a death sentence.

John expands even further and in his Gospel Jesus is taken first before Annas and thence to his father-in-law, Caiaphas, the high priest at the time. Caiaphas asks Jesus Christ about his doctrine, to which Jesus replies that he has nothing to hide. He has spoken quite openly and those who have heard him can tell what he said. He is then taken to Pilate, who again asks him if he is the King of the Jews. Jesus replies that he is indeed a king but not of this world. The rest of the story is much the same, with slightly more emphasis on Pilate's reluctance to have Jesus crucified.

The remarkable similarity between the two cases, therefore, is that both men lived under the control of an occupying power and both refused even to attempt to avoid judgement and sentence. In both cases, paradoxically the accused's triumph lay in his conviction: it was the jurisdiction which was shown to be at fault. In Gandhi's case, of course, the proceedings were merely one step on the road to eventual success in achieving independence. In the case of Jesus Christ, as he and his followers saw and still see it, his death saved the world by expiating the sins of mankind. Indeed Jesus's actions at his trial can only be explained in the context of that message.

The priests' motives in having Jesus crucified are not explicitly covered in the Gospels. However, as well as fearing what they undoubtedly saw as a possible rival centre of attention and source of doctrine, they were probably incensed by Jesus's cleansing of the temple; the latter would have denuded them of one of their major sources of income, as acceptable offerings were bought by pilgrims at monopoly prices and the profits accrued to the chief priests.

Jesus is reported to have asked God to forgive his torturers – 'Forgive them for they know not what they do.'[25] Likewise Gandhi told his disciples in advance that if he was murdered they were to forgive his assassins. After a failed attempt to assassinate him in Delhi, just before the successful act (which will be dealt with later), Gandhi said, 'No-one should look down on the misguided youth who had thrown the bomb. He probably looks upon me as an enemy of Hinduism. . . . The young man should realise that those who differ from him are not necessarily evil.' Sikhs visited him and assured him that the would-be assailant was not a Sikh. 'What does it matter,' Gandhi asked, 'whether he was a Sikh, a Hindu or a Moslem? I wish all perpetrators well.'[26]

One contrast between the two men was that Gandhi questioned his own beliefs and actions. He certainly did not claim to be perfect. Jesus Christ, on the other hand, as the Son of God, did not appear to have doubts. This difference between the two could perhaps be summed up by saying that Gandhi operated from profound moral conviction, Jesus Christ with moral authority.

The outbreak of the Second World War put Gandhi, as it did much of the Indian Nationalist movement, in some difficulty. On the one hand, clearly the British were in a weaker position to resist internal upset in India: they had very many, to them more important, problems elsewhere. On the other hand, though, the Indians did not wish to see one imperialism succeeded by another as the Japanese arrived at their gates in May 1942. After much deliberation, at Gandhi's instigation, Congress launched a 'Quit India' campaign in August 1942. As Gandhi saw it, the issue was to put their own house in order by getting rid of British rule before repelling the Japanese invasion. Quite how they hoped to do this was never clear. There was certainly no intention of encouraging people to join Subha Bose's Indian national army, which was set up in order to support the Japanese in July 1943. In fact this movement was to fail and fade out after the Japanese defeat at Imphal and subsequent retreat from Burma.

The Indian Government reacted strongly and immediately against the Quit India campaign with its rebellious overtones. Its leaders were immediately arrested and Gandhi was sent to jail on 9 August 1942. After some initial chaos, order was imposed – though no fewer than fifty-seven British regular battalions were tied up in India during this period.[27] Gandhi was released on 6 May 1944 after another serious illness. His wife, sharing his imprisonment with him, died during this time.

With the end of the conflict, the question of Indian independence became ever more urgent. In the aftermath of a highly debilitating war, Britain simply could not afford to continue to rule India even if she had wished to – and, apart from a few die-hard Conservatives, she did not. There were two major questions – should India remain united or should she split into two on religious lines? And, almost equally important, was the problem of timing – when should independence come? The advent of a Labour Government with its declared policy of Indian independence brought the whole issue into even sharper focus.

The current Viceroy was Wavell, a cultivated Field Marshal, incisive, percipient, honest almost to a fault, but lacking in small talk and obvious charm. He believed that a quick handover of power was vital, but had failed to extract from the Labour Government a clear plan to that effect, in spite of a cabinet delegation sent to India for that purpose. Very understandably, he had, become dispirited and exasperated with his government and many of the Indian politicians with whom he had to deal, including Gandhi. Indeed Gandhi undoubtedly was a very tiresome person in many ways. For instance, on one day of the week, generally Monday, he would never speak, however important it might be for him to do so. Elusive, opinionated, apparently unyielding, even bloody-minded, sometimes interested only in what appeared to be totally peripheral matters, he tried the patience of most, but not all, of those British people who perforce had to deal with him. In any event, rightly or wrongly Wavell obviously had to be replaced. Prime Minister Attlee appointed Lord Mountbatten as Viceroy: in the circumstances it was a brilliant choice. Mountbatten and his wife were very different to their predecessors. He had demanded and won plenipotentiary powers from Attlee before accepting the job. (Wavell had had to obtain permission from his secretary of state before meeting any prominent Indian politician.) He was vain, conceited, glamorous, very ambitious, quick-thinking, decisive and possessed legendary aristocratic charm. Mountbatten and Gandhi hit it off immediately (as did Mountbatten and Nehru, who greatly admired and even revered Gandhi while holding very different views on industrialization. As we have seen, Jinnah was very different: there was never any warmth in Jinnah's relations with anyone.)

By 1946 Gandhi's relations with Congress had changed. There was talk of Congress 'dropping the pilot' and Gandhi himself said that he had become 'a back number'. However much truth there was in that, Gandhi remained, until his death, a pivotal figure around whom others revolved during the appallingly difficult transition period.

Jinnah and the Moslem League had called for a Direct Action Day on 16 August 1946 and this led to very widespread communal violence. There were savage riots in Calcutta with, by official estimate, five thousand killed and fifteen thousand wounded. In Bihar, Hindus killed, by Gandhi's estimate, more than ten thousand Moslems. There were appalling scenes in the rural area of Noahkali in Bengal where Moslems killed Hindus, forcibly converting Hindus to Islam, raping Hindu women and burning Hindu houses and temples. Gandhi went to the area and travelled around by himself with only one interpreter for months, staying in a total of forty-nine villages, living with the Moslems, talking to and praying with them. He lived on local fruits, vegetables and goats' milk. He was seventy-seven years of age. His message to Hindu and Moslem alike was in effect taken word for word straight out of the New Testament – 'But I say unto you, love your enemies, bless them that curse you, do good to them that hate you and pray for them which despitefully use you and persecute you . . . for if ye love them which love you, what reward have ye?'[28] Gandhi sent many of his disciples into other villages carrying the same message. The mission was largely successful and the killings subsided.

In the event Mountbatten really had no alternative to accepting partition. Jinnah would settle for nothing else and he had the power to throw the whole sub-continent into bitter civil war. Gandhi was bitterly disappointed. He had fervently hoped and worked for a united India with Moslem and Hindu living peacefully together. This was impossible and Gandhi reluctantly accepted partition, though he spent Independence Day itself in fasting and prayer.

As for what date independence should start, the question was solved by Mountbatten, who announced that it would happen much earlier than anyone expected – 15 August. However, in response to the superstitions of many contemporary Indians this had to be changed to midnight on 14 August, because of a universal cry by astrologers that 15 August was a most unpropitious day. Unlike the bulk of Indian Hindus, Gandhi had always derided the practice of astrology as ridiculous rubbish.

When independence became imminent, Calcutta was like a tinder-box, with massive riots clearly about to break out. Mountbatten asked Gandhi if he would go there and attempt to divert the disaster which was threatening. Gandhi asked the Moslem former Prime Minister of Bengal, H.S. Suhrawardi, to go with him and they walked together through the streets arm in arm. The violence subsided. However, before long, the violence began to erupt again. On 1 September 1947 Gandhi decided to fast until it stopped. He was prepared to continue the fast until death if necessary. Hindus and Moslems alike in Calcutta were appalled and delegations from both communities implored him to end his fast. He refused to do so until he had a written pledge signed by all sides to the effect that there would be no more trouble in Calcutta. They duly signed and at 9.15 p.m. on 4 September Gandhi ended his fast. From that moment on both parts of Bengal remained riot free. Gandhi had worked a near miracle. Mountbatten, by now Governor General of the new Indian Republic, at Nehru's request, wrote a letter:

My dear Gandhi,

In the Punjab we have fifty-five thousand soldiers and large scale rioting on our hands. In Bengal our forces consist of one man, and there is no rioting. As a serving officer as well as administrator, may I be allowed to pay my tribute to the one man boundary force.[29]

Elsewhere the situation was very different. It had been impossible to draw a boundary without placing very large numbers of Moslems and Hindus alike on the wrong side of the line. As far as Pakistan was concerned, nearly half of the Moslems on the sub-continent were placed on the wrong side of the boundary. Hindus and Sikhs were fleeing from the new Pakistan in their millions, while millions of Moslems moved in the opposite direction. Soon the killing began in Delhi itself. Gandhi immediately went there and his very presence quietened the situation. However, he was not satisfied and decided to commence what turned out to be his last fast. It was a fast unto death directed, as he said, 'to the conscience of all': to the Hindus and Moslems and the Indian Union and to the Moslems of Pakistan. He could not accept the hatred that existed between the two communities and hoped, by his action, to bring love instead of hatred into their hearts. A further issue was that the government of India had not paid the government of Pakistan the forty million pounds it owed as Pakistan's share of the assets of prepartition India. Gandhi's fast had enormous publicity. The whole of the Indian sub-continent held its breath while doctors issued daily bulletins. He could not drink water: it caused nausea. His kidneys were functioning poorly. He lost much strength and his weight dropped by two pounds each day.

The first result of his fast came when the Indian government paid up the £40,000,000 pounds. An endless queue filed past the bed on which he lay. Many meetings took place between representatives of the two communities in an attempt to find a solution to this appalling and acute problem of preventing Gandhi's death. Nehru by this time was Prime Minister, having become President of Congress through Gandhi's nomination in spite of greater support by Congress activists for his rival Patel. Not surprisingly he was in constant touch with all sides. Eventually, on the morning of 18 September, five days after the fast had begun, a pledge was drafted and signed by representatives from all the communities involved. The Hindus undertook to protect the life, property and faith of the Moslems and promised that the incidents which had taken place in Delhi would not happen again. Moslems would be able to move about just as they could in the past. 'The mosques which had been left by Moslems which are now in the possession of Hindus and Sikhs will be returned. The areas which have been set apart from Moslems will not be forcibly occupied.' Moslems who had fled could return and conduct their business as before. A Hindu representative then reported to Gandhi on the touching scenes of fraternization which had taken place that morning, when a procession of 150 Moslem residents was given an ovation and then fêted by the Hindus of the locality. Gandhi then asked about the Moslem attitude. Moslem scholars spoke and assured Gandhi that Moslems did not wish to attack or even to exterminate Hindus. The Pakistan ambassador addressed a few friendly words to the Mahatma. A Sikh representative added his pledge. Finally Gandhi announced that he would break his fast. The girls of Gandhi's entourage sang a Hindu song and 'When I survey the wondrous cross', Gandhi's favourite Christian hymn. Gandhi's last fast did indeed perform what many, though not Gandhi, believed to be a miracle. Delhi was pacified and there was an end to religious riots and violence throughout both India and Pakistan. Gandhi then decided to go ahead with his intention of visiting Pakistan to carry his message of love to that country too. In the meantime he remained in Delhi.

All religions seem to spawn some fanatical extremists, and Hinduism is no exception. This particular breed was known as the Rashtriya Sevak Sangua (the National Volunteer Force or RSS). They were violent, bigoted and zealous. As partition approached, together with a group of Sikh extremists they attempted to assassinate Jinnah. Their aim was to plunge the whole sub-continent into civil war and anarchy, after which the numerically superior Hindus would emerge with total power. Their plan was to assassinate Jinnah and Lord Louis Mountbatten during their triumphal drive through Karachi on 14 August, the eve of independence. The plot failed, probably because the man who was to throw the grenade at the car in which the two were sitting lost his nerve. Mountbatten and Jinnah both knew that there was a plot to assassinate them during the drive. As thousands crowded around them it was a supreme test of nerve for the two of them, triumphantly overcome.

The RSS had seen Gandhi as an enemy, if not *the* enemy, for many years. Their dream was to recreate a great Hindu Empire with sway over the whole of the Indian sub-continent. Gandhi's continued and powerful message of Hindu / Moslem reconciliation was anathema to them. They saw the Moslems as usurpers whose presence stemmed from the Moghul invasion of the sixteenth century. In fact, as we have seen, many Moslems in India were the descendants of Hindu untouchables, who had become Moslem because that religion did not accept the caste system in any shape or form but saw all human beings as equal in the sight of Allah, the one and only God. The fact that many, if not most, Moslems in India, were, as the RSS saw it, the descendants of renegades from the true religion only served to exacerbate the extremists' hatred. Although Gandhi had strongly resisted partition, with mind-boggling irony they held him responsible for it because of his fervent support of Moslem rights and the dignity of the Moslem religion: he regularly read from the Koran at his prayer meetings and his concept of non-violence was totally opposed to what they saw as the proud unyielding strength of the Hindu people.

The RSS had been responsible for many of the massacres of Moslems before, at and after independence. In particular one such outrage had led to Gandhi's fast unto death in Calcutta. They had initiated the violence in Delhi which had led to Gandhi's return there. A particularly fanatical group of RSS were based on Gwalior, some two hundred miles south-east of Delhi. Their leader was the homeopath Dr Dattatrya Parchure. One of his followers was Madanlal Pahwa, who boasted that he slaughtered Moslems on trains – a common method of mass murder. 'We stopped the train. We got on board. We murdered them.'[30] The outstanding leader of the Hindu fanatical fraternity was Vinayak Savarkar, like Gandhi a graduate of London's Inns of Court. He had been instrumental in two successful assassinations – a British bureaucrat and the governor of the Punjab. He had also been implicated in an unsuccessful attempt on the life of the Governor of Bombay. He had twice been president of the Hindu Mahasabha, the right-wing Hindu political party whose military arm was the RSS (it had been affiliated to the Mahasabha since 1932). Furthermore, he was the inspiration behind the extremist newspaper in Poona, *Hindu Rashtru*, which was edited and run by two men, Nathuram Godse and Narayan Apte. It was these two who on 13 January 1948 decided to kill Gandhi.[31] They were joined by Madanlal Pahwa and Vishnu Karkare, the owner of a guesthouse.

On 19 January 1948 Nathuram Godse, his brother Gopal Godse, Narayan Apte and Vishnu Karkare gathered in Delhi in order to kill Gandhi. They were joined by Digamber Badge, who supplied the arms, and Madanlal Pahwa. Their original plan was to carry out the assassination on 20 January during Gandhi's regular prayer meeting. Two bombs were to be detonated and Gopal Godse would open fire from a previously reconnoitred cell just behind Gandhi, at point-blank range. However, coordination was poor and only one bomb was actually detonated, with no great effect. Madanlal was arrested and the others escaped.

There was no doubt that if the police had acted with determination and speed the rest of the conspirators would have been arrested before the second, successful, attempt at assassination. But they were dilatory and totally lacking in urgency. In fact Indian revolutionaries had been hopelessly incompetent in their attempts at assassination for a long time. Attempts had been made to murder Viceroy Hardinge and many other British officials. Few had succeeded and a cynic might argue that violence having failed, Gandhi's non-violence was given a chance to succeed – hence Congress's support of it!

At first Gandhi had thought the bomb on 20 January to be an army unit practising. When he was told the truth he said to Lady Mountbatten who, with her husband, had rushed to see him, that there was no need to congratulate him as he had shown no bravery. 'If someone fired at me point blank and I faced his bullet with a smile, repeating the name of Rama [God], then I should indeed be deserving of congratulations.' Fatally, he refused to allow suspicious characters coming to his prayer meetings to be searched. 'Rama is my protector,' he said. 'If he wants to end my life no-one can save me.'

Overcome with shame at the failure of the first attempt, the remaining conspirators decided to try again. With Madanlal in police hands they knew the authorities would probably be on to them soon – 'We must get Gandhi before the police get us.' Godse and Apte had escaped to Bombay. They flew back to Delhi and thence to Gwalior, where they procured a pistol from Badge. They returned to Delhi and were joined by Karkare. They decided that they would assassinate Gandhi at his daily prayer meeting at 5.00 p.m. on 30 January.

At 4.30 p.m. Nathuram Godse went to the gardens at Birla House where Gandhi was staying. He was joined by Karkare and Apte. For the first time since his fast Gandhi was able to walk by himself to his prayer meeting in the garden. As he walked towards the little platform from which he would conduct the meeting, Nathuram Godse with Apte and Karkare at his side stepped forward and shot him three times in the chest. Gandhi gasped, 'Hé Rama' ('Oh, God') and died.

Mountbatten heard the news as he trotted back to Government House after a ride. He immediately grasped the vital point that if the assassin were a Moslem, the whole country would erupt. Previous massacres would pale into insignificance compared to the anarchic mass murders which would follow. Before he knew who the murderer was, he announced that the assassin was a Hindu. His relief when he knew that this was indeed the case must have been very great.

Grief at the Mahatma's death was all-encompassing. Bombay and Calcutta were silent; Pakistan was engulfed with sorrow. Hundreds of thousands of people flocked to Delhi to attend the funeral. Pope Pius, the Dalai Lama, the Archbishop of Canterbury, the Chief Rabbi in London, the King and Prime Minister of Great Britain, President Truman, Chiang Kai-shek, the President of France and many other world leaders all expressed their grief. George Bernard Shaw made the memorable remark, 'His murder shows how dangerous it is to be good.' The Security Council of the United Nations paused to pay tribute, and the United Nations flag flew at half-mast. Lord Mountbatten (himself to be assassinated by evil fanatics) expressed the hope that Gandhi's life might inspire our troubled world to save itself by following his noble example. Sir Hartley Shawcross, the British Attorney-General, said that Gandhi was the most remarkable man of the century, while Albert Einstein declared that 'in our time of utter moral decadence [Gandhi] was the only statesman to stand for a higher human relationship in the political sphere'.[32] In the *Hindustan Standard* the editorial was ringed in black and read: 'Gandhi has been killed by his own people for whose redemption he lived. This second crucifixion in the history of the world has been enacted on a Friday – the same day Jesus was done to death one thousand nine hundred and fifteen years ago. Father forgive us.'

In the presence of well over a million people, Gandhi was cremated. In the presence of some Roman soldiers, a few women (including his mother) and two thieves, Jesus Christ was crucified on Good Friday AD 33. There was no great outpouring of universal grief: indeed, he was probably completely unknown outside Palestine.

Gandhi was assassinated: Jesus Christ was judicially executed. The perpetrators of both acts were from the victims' own backgrounds. Nathuram Godse and Narayan Apte were hanged (ignoring Gandhi's wishes). Karkare, Gopal Godse and Madanlal were imprisoned for life. Badge, the arms pedlar, turned state witness and was released. Savarkar was acquitted.

There were three main parties to Jesus Christ's crucifixion – Judas Iscariot who betrayed him, the chief priests who accused him and Pontius Pilate who handed him over to be crucified. Judas Iscariot hanged himself, but we do no know what happened to the chief priests. Pontius Pilate was recalled to Rome shortly after the crucifixion, in AD 36. The early Church tended to exonerate him. His life and death thereafter are the subject of controversy and there is no certainty about what happened to him. It is true, however, that he was canonized by the Abyssinian Church and that his wife Procla was canonized by the Greek Church.

Were those who brought about Jesus Christ's and Gandhi's deaths successful in their aims? We can be in no doubt that the chief priests were not. Quite apart from any theological arguments, the attempt to humiliate and then to remove Jesus from the scene had the precise opposite effect. His influence spread throughout the area very quickly, engulfed Rome, and eventually Christianity became a dominating, almost world-wide, religion. The chief priests are long forgotten, whereas their victim's life and death remain a massive inspiration for millions.

Matters are not so clear cut as regards Gandhi. The objective of the assassination was to eliminate the major influence for Hindu / Moslem reconciliation, thereby setting the whole sub-continent aflame, from which, it was hoped, a unified Hindu India would emerge, phoenix-like, from the flames. Some of the conspirators were also motivated by personal revenge and blind irrational hatred.

But insofar as there was rationality to the act, it was to kill the peacemaker, thereby igniting civil war. This failed: the immediate effect of Gandhi's assassination was to calm intercommunal passion. Both parties took a deep breath and the enormity of what had happened led to a near cessation of personal violence.

However, in the long term Hindu / Moslem hatred has not been curbed to any great extent, let alone abolished. At the time of writing there are worries about a nuclear arms race and even a nuclear war between India and Pakistan. Had he been alive, Gandhi would have been appalled: he would undoubtedly have initiated a fast unto death in an attempt to halt the development of nuclear weapons either by India or Pakistan. In some ways his life has turned out to be a failure. It could well be argued that his campaigns against the concept of untouchability, against industrialization and against partition and intercommunal hatred have all failed and that only the campaign for independence succeeded and that would have happened anyway sooner or later. But these are all political matters. It is impossible to measure what effect Gandhi's life and death has had and will continue to have on the minds of men and women. Perhaps he will be forgotten in two hundred years, or perhaps he will be seen as a major spiritual influence foretelling the dangerous repercussions of industrial-ization, materialism and intercommunal hatred. His assassination and the identity of his assassins probably added to his fame by dramatizing the circumstances of his death. After all, he was an old man and would probably not have been long for this world.

The circumstances of Jesus Christ's crucifixion undoubtedly dramatized his death and, to Christian believers, redoubled the impact of his resurrection. It is difficult now to visualize an old Jesus Christ dying naturally in his bed. Jesus certainly courted arrest. According to the Gospels, he knew that his last journey to Jerusalem would end in his trial and death – and told his disciples so. Whether as the Son of Man he deliberately engineered the whole proceedings in order that the Son of God could redeem the sins of the world is a question perhaps best left to theologians.

Gandhi surely did not engineer his own death, although this has been suggested. He was certainly not naïve and realized that his assassination by Hindu fanatics was quite likely. But he had made plans to go to Pakistan in an attempt to calm Moslem fears and ameliorate their hatreds: he did not think that his work on earth was finished. He was deeply upset by partition and in many ways he died a disappointed man. But, as he saw it, he had tried his best and accepted what God had decided for him.

NOTES

1. *M.K. Gandhi, An Autobiography*, Penguin, Middlesex, 1982, p. 77
2. L. Fischer, *The Life of Mahatma Gandhi*, HarperCollins, London, 1997, pp. 125–30.
3. St Matthew 5 v28.
4. St Matthew 5 v32.
5. Fischer, *Gandhi*, p. 96.
6. A. Copley, *Gandhi – Against the Tide*, OUP, Oxford, 1987, p. 19.
7. *M.K. Gandhi*, p. 181.
8. Ibid., p. 166.
9. Fischer, *Gandhi*, p. 158.
10. St Matthew 22 v21 and St Mark 12 v17. See also St John 6 v15.
11. St Luke 12 v22. See also St John 6 v27.
12. St Matthew 6 v19.
13. P. French, *Liberty or Death*, Flamingo, London, 1998, p. 79.
14. *M.K. Gandhi*, p. 190.
15. Fischer, *Gandhi*, p. 164.
16. St Mark 3 v31, 35.
17. St Matthew 4 v21, 22; St Matthew 8 v21, 22; St Matthew 10 v35; St Matthew 19 v29; St Luke 8 v19–21; St Luke 9 v59, 60; St Luke 13 v53; St Luke 15 v26; St John 2 v4.
18. Copley, *Against the Tide*, p. 37.
19. Fischer, *Gandhi*, p. 248.
20. Copley, *Against the Tide*, p. 47.
21. The Earl of Birkenhead, *Halifax*, Hamish Hamilton, London, 1966, p 299.
22. French, *Liberty*, p. 382.
23. F. Watson, *The Trial of Mr Gandhi*, Macmillan, London, 1969, pp. 154–63.
24. This is Herod Antipas, the Jewish tetrarch of Galilee and Peraea. He is not to be confused with Herod the Great (his father) who ordered the massacre of the innocents.
25. St Luke 23 v34.
26. L. Collins and D. Lapierre, *Freedom at Midnight*, HarperCollins, London, 1997, pp. 623, 624.
27. French, *Liberty*, p. 160.
28. St Matthew 5 v44, 46.

29. P. Ziegler, *Mountbatten*, Collins, London, 1985, p. 436.
30. Collins, *Freedom*, p. 421.
31. Ibid., p. 474.
32. Fischer, *Gandhi*, pp. 20, 21.

CHAPTER 3

JEAN PAUL MARAT /
LEON TROTSKY

Were anyone asked to name the most important events in
world history in the past two and a half centuries, they
could not fail to include, near the top of the list, the French and
Russian revolutions. The two world wars of the twentieth century
would perhaps be rivals, but the revolutions would be there or
thereabouts. It is strange that this should be so, because both were
failures in the sense that neither achieved the aims of the instigators
– the replacement of an authoritarian and corrupt regime by a more
democratic structure better able to respond to the wishes of 'the
people'. Louis XVI and Tsar Nicholas II were killed and their
regimes were overthrown, but their successors were certainly as
despotic as they were. France had a troubled history in the
nineteenth century and Russia suffered great agony at least in the
last eighty years of the twentieth.

In both cases the ideas which sparked off the revolutions were
noble, in the sense that they were based not on personal material
gain, but on the quest for greater general happiness. And, in both
cases, the revolutions were to end in appalling squalor and slaughter.
The belief that the end justifies the means dominated the minds of
the revolutionaries but the means became part of the end, indeed
eventually subsuming it, as Gandhi was to say it inevitably would.

Marat and Trotsky were idealists and highly intelligent. They
both became utterly ruthless. Their original ideals disappeared in a
welter of blood. As always seems to happen, in both cases the
revolutionary leaders fell out with each other, partly because of

differing policies but also, perhaps to a greater extent, because of personal rivalry. There was much intrigue. In order to bring about a revolution whereby an existing powerful regime is toppled, strong characters are required, able to persist in their aim in spite of enormous difficulties. Strong characters are apt to quarrel anyway, but when there is a jockeying for position and power after a successful revolution, deep antagonisms are inevitable. In very different ways, Marat and Trotsky were both victims of these antagonisms. Both assassinations were highly dramatic – Marat killed in a bath by a woman with a knife and Trotsky in his heavily guarded house in Mexico with an ice pick through his brain.

Jean Paul Marat was born on 24 May 1743 in Neuchatel. His father was a Sardinian Catholic turned Calvinist of remarkably diverse talents, in turn, apparently, a monk, doctor, language teacher and a designer of figures on cloth. He went to Switzerland, where he married a Genevan and had six children, Jean Paul being the eldest. The young Marat (his father's name was Mara – Jean Paul added the 't' in order to seem more French) was brilliant. Leaving home at sixteen, he studied medicine in Bordeaux and Paris before settling in England when twenty-two years old. Although some obscurity still covers his life in England, there is no doubt that he was highly successful in his profession, receiving the honorary degree of Doctor of Medicine at St Andrew's University and publishing two medical tracts, which were of enough value to be republished in 1891 by the Royal College of Surgeons in England. He was awarded the citizenship of Newcastle, where he lived at one stage, probably because of his services during an epidemic. He also wrote a political tract, 'The Chains of Slavery', an acrimonious attack on despotism. However, he did not attack the monarchy as such, believing profoundly that rule by a 'good king was the best form of government'. He also published an 'Essay on Man' whereby he attempted to analyse the reciprocal influence of body and soul. Clearly, he was a very talented and clever young man.

Marat returned to France in 1777 where he became doctor of the bodyguard of the Count of Artois, the king's younger brother and afterwards Charles X of France, a prestigious position which he retained until his resignation in 1783. He built up a wealthy clientele. Between 1783 and the outbreak of the revolution in 1789 he devoted himself mainly to scientific studies, publishing eight books of physical research on fire, electricity, light, optics and other subjects. He won a number of scientific prizes, impressing among others Benjamin Franklin and Goethe. He also published three novels. He was a typical representative of the radical intellectual middle class and he had come under the influence of many of the great Enlightenment thinkers of the time – Rousseau, Voltaire, Montesquieu and others. Perhaps paradoxically, he believed that on the whole the common people were ignorant and that the government should be run by the wealthy, who had more to lose.[1] He published a study of crime and punishment in which he put forward a whole series of radical views while still supporting the monarchy.

It is not the intention here to recount the story of the French Revolution in any detail, but there are one or two points which should be made if one is to understand Marat's assassination and its repercussions. Although the proletariat eventually played a major role in its development, the French Revolution was instigated not by the 'people' but by the bourgeois class of which Marat was a member. The Enlightenment had resulted in the undermining of respect for traditional values and authority. Doubt, religious and political, was in the air, particularly in France. When the unfortunate Louis XVI came to the throne in 1774, the state finances were in a terrible mess. The upper middle class of perhaps half a million and the lesser bourgeoisie of perhaps a million[2] were being heavily taxed in order to try to retrieve the situation, whereas the nobility and the clergy were not. Very naturally, the bourgeoisie felt that this was a most unfair situation. After the failure of the harvest of 1788, appalling hardship was experienced by the poor and this added to the general dissatisfaction. Minor revolutions took place in several provinces and the King was forced to constitute the Estates General, a kind of parliament, for the first time in 175 years. There were three houses – the clergy (the first), the nobility (the second) and the rest (the third). Every house had one vote which meant that the third house, representing some 24,000,000 people, could be outvoted by the other two, between them representing only 300,000 people – an absurd situation. It was at this stage that Marat dropped his scientific studies and began to write political pamphlets putting forward radical views and, in particular, arguing that all the estates should vote together. However, he still did not attack the monarchy itself: Louis XVI was 'a good King, characterized by his love for his people. . . . Blessed be the best of kings.'[3]

After a series of crises the King yielded and the Estates General in effect became a National Assembly. However, the King changed course and gathered troops at Versailles with the intention of using them against this new body. For the first time the populace of Paris took an active part and on 14 July 1789 the Bastille was stormed; its commander and a few soldiers guarding it were massacred. This event is generally seen as the real start of the revolution. Marat did not play much of a part in all this but it was as a result of the events of 14 July that he decided to start a newspaper.

Until shortly before his death Marat's influence on the course of events in France was exerted through his newspaper, which he originally called *Publiciste Parisien* and then, after five numbers, *L'Ami du Peuple* – it was under this name that Marat's powerful presence soon began to be felt. He had strong feelings about the suffering of the poor, but initially he continued to believe that these sufferings would be alleviated if not eliminated by the exertions of decent and liberal members of the bourgeoisie, helped by a beneficent king. It was only when, as he saw it, the stupidities of the middle classes proliferated, together with internal threats of a counter-revolution and external threats of invasion, that he came to urge far more radical measures, including bloodshed.

Marat failed to be elected to the Academy of Sciences, which he suspected was because of nefarious plots against him by lesser men. This added to his general sense of persecution, and he began to see counter-revolution round every corner. However, partly because of the clamour of popular journalism of which Marat was a leading figure, a crowd of Parisians headed by women crying for bread marched on Versailles. Louis XVI and his family were forced to move to Paris, virtually becoming prisoners there. There was a shortage of food in Paris. Marat's articles in *L'Ami du Peuple* became ever more strident and orders were given for his arrest. He was forced into hiding for the first of no fewer than seven occasions. In January 1790 he escaped to England, where he remained until April.

On his return Marat continued with his attacks on many of the leading revolutionary figures in France for their failure to take radical action. Eventually, in November 1790, he turned against the King whom he believed to be planning a counter-revolution by bringing about an attack on France by outside forces, in particular under the auspices of the queen's brother, Leopold of Austria. The King's attempted flight, in June 1791, merely confirmed Marat's fears. To Marat's fury the King was returned to his throne in September on his acceptance of a new constitution – France becoming a constitutional monarchy. At this stage it seemed to many that the revolution was over, the revolutionaries having achieved their aims. Marat bitterly disagreed. He found the constitution totally inadequate mainly because it left far too much power, as he saw it, in the hands of the King, in particular the right to declare war and peace.

Marat lost faith in the National Assembly rightly believing that it was primarily devoted to bourgeois interests. He wrote article after article in *L'Ami du Peuple* attacking almost everything about it. Prices had gone up, there was heavy unemployment, high taxation and food was scarce. Things seemed to be getting worse rather than better and apart from Robespierre and one or two of his supporters there seemed to be nobody in the National Assembly prepared to take any radical action. In disgust Marat returned to England in December 1791.

The danger of war increased as Leopold of Austria called on the rulers of Europe to unite against the 'violent party' in France. The National Assembly had been dissolved to be succeeded by a Legislative Assembly, many members of which, and in particular the radicals led by Brissot, wished for war in order to unite France and snuff out 'traitors'. The King, too, was in favour of war for opposite reasons, as he thought that a victorious war by outside powers would restore him to his previous position as absolute monarch.

Marat returned to France in March 1792 and went through a form of marriage with Simonne Everard, who was his faithful supporter, confidante and, in effect, wife until his death. He opposed hostilities with great vehemence, seeing clearly that war was intended to serve the purposes of the Royalists and the moderates. However, war was declared against Austria and Prussia in April. Marat's invective increased; for instance in *L'Ami du Peuple* he denounced Brissot, who 'apprenticed in chicanery, became a would-be wit, a scandal-sheet writer, an apprentice philosopher, a fraudulent speculator, a crook, a prince's valet, a government clerk, a police spy, publicist, municipal inquisitor, legislative senator, faithless representative of the people, abettor of the ministerial faction and finally henchman of the despot'.[4] The French suffered a series of defeats and the proletariat of Paris invaded the Tuileries, the King narrowly avoiding death. On 10 August the monarchy fell and Louis and his family were imprisoned.

The Legislative Assembly became the National Convention. However, despairing of its apparent failure to bring the Revolution's enemies to trial, Marat advocated the establishment of a Revolutionary Tribunal. He followed this by proposing the creation of a dictatorship. The dictator was to bring the people's enemies to justice and the revolution to a successful conclusion. When this had been done he was to relinquish his office. Possible candidates for the job were Robespierre and Danton and, it was afterwards hinted, Marat himself.[5]

By September 1792 the Prussians and Austrians, having won a series of victories, were almost at the gates of Paris, although in fact never succeeding in entering it. Panic set in. It was feared that the many prisoners in Parisian jails would break out and exert vengeance on the people of the city. As a result there took place what were known as the September Massacres. Between 1,100 and 1,400 prisoners were murdered, including 225 priests.[6] Marat has been blamed for this appalling, cold-blooded slaughter, and evidence for his complicity is strong. For instance, in April he had asked 'the people to rise and let the blood of traitors flow again. It is the only means of saving their Fatherland'. Furthermore, the Committee of Surveillance, of which Marat was a member, sent a circular letter to all the departments expressing its approval of the massacre and exalting them to follow the noble example of Paris.[7] Marat was indeed a bloodthirsty revolutionary.

Marat was then elected to the National Convention which on 22 September 1792 made France a republic. He had changed his views of the monarchy and, with typically wholehearted logic, began to urge the execution of Louis. At this stage he ceased to advocate a dictatorship, having understood that feeling against it was overwhelming. He accepted the establishment of committees of General Security and Public Safety in April 1793.

As seems to be the permanent situation in political affairs, the National Convention, was clearly divided into left, centre and right. On the left were the deputies from Paris including Marat, Danton and Robespierre. These were at first known as the Jacobins since many were members of the Jacobin Club, a radical institution so named because it used to meet at a hall hired from the Jacobin Convent.[8] Later those on the left became known as the Mountain because their seats in the Assembly were physically higher up than the others. On the right were the Girondins representing the department of the Gironde and its neighbours. The rest were known as the Marsh or Plain. They sat in the centre. Neither of the extreme parties could muster a majority, so each would have to get support from the centre.

Marat came to believe that the struggle with the Gironde was a simple matter of patriots against counter-revolutionaries. In practice, of course, matters were not as simple: the Gironde believed that radical change was necessary but in a gradual, peaceful manner. Opinion quickly became polarized, each side believing profoundly in the perfidy and evil intentions of the other. As well as the political differences between the two there was the equally, if not more, emotive element of difference between Paris and its environs (the Mountain) against much of the provinces (Girondists). Matters came to a head when the question of the execution of Louis arose. The Mountain was for immediate execution, the Gironde for a delay or exile. On this occasion the Mountain triumphed and Louis was guillotined.

Leon Bernstein, who adopted the pseudonym Trotsky (after one of his prison guards), was a Russian Jew born on 26 October (according to the old Russian calendar) 1879 in the province of Kherson in the Ukraine. His father, David Bernstein, was a well-to-do farmer. The Jewish population of Russia had been greatly increased by the annexation of eastern Poland and Lithuania at the end of the eighteenth century. Indeed this area contained the densest population of Jews in the world. In 1804 Tsar Alexander I gave these people an escape from the harsh poverty that afflicted them by offering them state lands in the very sparsely inhabited 'New Russia' – the Ukrainian provinces of Kherson and Ekaterinoslav. This inducement to farm, a most unusual activity for Jews of the Diaspora, led to the Bernstein family establishing itself as increasingly successful farmers, culminating in David Bernstein buying a large farm; this was part of a run-down estate given to a Colonel Yakovsky by the tsar, as a reward for his services. Trotsky's father was illiterate but very hardworking and well endowed with native cunning. Although his family lived a Spartan life with few if any frills, the household had a number of servants including, apart from the farm workers, a nurse, a chambermaid, a cook and a steward. To coin a phrase, the family was upwardly mobile. The Jews in Russia continued to be under pressures of various kinds, culminating in 1882, after the assassination of Alexander II, in a

law forbidding them to rent, lease or buy further land. David
Bernstein, however, managed to get round this and continued to
expand his already considerable enterprise.

Trotsky's childhood was typical of his environment, life and times.
That part of his autobiography[9] is worth reading solely as literature
– his insights and powers of description are outstanding. At the age
of seven he was sent to school at a Jewish/German colony two miles
away from home. Here he was taught to read the Bible, translating
it from Hebrew into Yiddish, having to learn both languages.
However, he did, learn to read and write Russian – his normal
language being a Ukrainian patois. His gift for languages was
remarkable: apart from Hebrew, Yiddish, Russian and Ukrainian he
was later to learn German, French and English to the extent that he
could make long extemporary speeches in all seven languages,
together with Italian, Spanish and some Norwegian.

In 1888 Trotsky went to Odessa to be educated, living with his
mother's brother. He went to St Paul's Realschule, a school founded
by German Lutherans. His teachers were German, Russian, Polish
and Swiss – Lutheran, Orthodox, Roman Catholic and Jewish –
cosmopolitan indeed. He immediately became top of every class he
was in. The atmosphere was intellectual and liberal and on his
holidays at home he felt constricted and ill at ease, worrying about
his father's rough treatment of his peasant labourers.

In the summer of 1896, when sixteen, Trotsky went to the town
of Nikolayev to complete his secondary education. Here he lodged
with a family with socialist ideas. He met a number of Narodniks
(Populists), intellectuals with romantic revolutionary ideas but no
clear programme. There was a great deal of talk and little, if any,
action. Although at first opposing Marxism, Trotsky was gradually
converted. He was never to lose a fervent faith in that doctrine,
which came to form the basis of his whole life.

Although neglecting his studies in the later stages of his time at
school, he graduated with first class honours in the summer of 1897
and entered the University of Odessa to study mathematics. He had
a radical temperament, searching for an all-embracing cause to

which he could wholly surrender himself. He found it at Odessa in the Revolutionary Movement. He returned to Nikolayev and started the first trades union in the area – the South Russian Workers' Union. Although only eighteen he was an inspiring leader with inexhaustible energy and drive, a brilliant writer and speaker. Unlike many other Russian intellectuals he believed in action, not just talk. His advice to his followers was in the phrase 'Faith without works is dead'.[10]

His agitation started to have results. Workers began to strike and to take part in sometimes rowdy demonstrations. Inevitably, all this culminated in his arrest. Tsarist Russia did not mollycoddle young revolutionaries. He was put in prison in solitary confinement for two years, at first in appalling conditions with no exercise, heating, chair, bed, newspapers or even interrogation to relieve the boredom. Later his situation improved. However, the only books available, were religious. Although already an atheist, he improved his languages by reading the Bible simultaneously in German, French, English and Italian. He was then exiled to Siberia for four years. On the way there he spent some time in a prison in Moscow where he was introduced to Lenin's writing and from where he began to issue, clandestinely, a continuous stream of essays and pamphlets. He married Alexandra Sokolovskaya, a fellow Marxist, in 1899.

His place of exile was Verkholensk, overlooking Baikal Lake, five thousand miles east of Moscow. Here he embarked on a massive course of reading. His enforced leisure gave him plenty of time and there were no restrictions on books. He continued to read widely all his life, studying the philosophy, history, politics and literature of all the main European countries. In exile he contributed to various journals and became well known as a leading Marxist polemicist – compared to Stalin's gulags, tsarist exile was remarkably free of constraints.

However, in 1902, after two years in Siberia, Trotsky escaped. Following an arduous journey across Russia and Europe he arrived in London in October at Lenin's door. Although they were to have many arguments and political disagreements later, the two men immediately recognized each other's worth.

The history of the Russian émigré community in London, Berlin, Paris and elsewhere at the turn of the century was marked by almost continual violent disagreements and, often, bitterness. Although all were revolutionary, some were more revolutionary than others. The disputes culminated in the second Congress of the Russian Social Democratic Party, as it was then known, in Brussels in July 1903. By this time Trotsky was a famous figure in Russian revolutionary circles, working and lecturing in France, Switzerland and Belgium as well as England. He had also married a new wife, Natalya Sedova, who was to remain his lover, friend and ally for the rest of his life.

The Congress was the scene of extended bitter struggles about a whole series of issues, many of which now appear to be of only esoteric interest. Many delegates, including Trotsky, seemed to change sides with bewildering frequency. All this came to a head in a vote on the apparently minor issue of the composition of the board of the revolutionary paper, *Iskra*. Lenin proposed a small board of only three, his supporters. His opponents favoured a larger, more representative body. Lenin won by two votes. His supporters were known as the Bolsheviks (the Many), his opponents as Mensheviks (the Few). Trotsky, wishing to be a member of the board himself, voted for the Mensheviks.

In fact, of course, the issue was far wider. The Bolsheviks favoured a highly centralized party, directed from the centre with no concessions to other parties or interests. The Mensheviks visualized a more diffuse organization which would cooperate with other parties, adopting a more conciliatory, pragmatic, gradualist approach. Both were Marxist, the Bolsheviks the more extreme and radical in organization and purpose.

Trotsky viciously attacked Lenin, comparing him to Robespierre, adding, however, that the Bolshevik leader was a mere parody of Robespierre whom he resembled as 'a vulgar farce resembles a historic tragedy'. Although of course the situations were very different, there were indeed parallels between the Bolsheviks and the Jacobins (the Mountain) on the one hand and the Mensheviks and the Girondists on the other.

Trotsky now began to fall out with the Mensheviks over the Russo–Japanese War, which he violently opposed. However, he continued to attack Lenin with venom, calling him 'hideous, dissolute, demagogical, malicious and morally repulsive'. One would think that, after this, the two men would never speak to each other again, let alone cooperate. But revolutionaries are accustomed to harsh words and, as we shall see, the two became wholly reconciled.

In January 1905 the workers of St Petersburg marched in a vast, peaceful procession to the Tsar's Winter Palace, led by Father Gapon, a prison chaplain. They carried the Tsar's portraits, holy icons and church banners, hoping to present a petition to the tsar begging him to redress their grievances. However, the Tsar ordered his troops to open fire and many people were killed and wounded. Trotsky sensed a revolution in the making and returned to Kiev in February, moving on to St Petersburg in the spring. Under a false name and in hiding he issued a stream of pamphlets and letters urging a nationwide insurrection. He began to move to the Bolshevik position and away from the Mensheviks, who increasingly favoured liberalism, not socialism.

In October 1905 a general strike broke out in St Petersburg, quickly spreading elsewhere. The first council, or soviet, of workers' deputies was formed. The Tsar began to lose his nerve and to conciliate, promising a constitution, civil liberties and universal suffrage. The strike was called off. There were continual disputes in the soviets and between the revolutionary leaders, Trotsky in fact urging moderation at this stage. However, as revolutionary enthusiasm waned throughout the country, the inevitable happened: the soviet was liquidated and among many others Trotsky was arrested. After a somewhat farcical trial, Trotsky and fourteen others were sentenced to loss of all civil rights and deportation to Siberia for life. They were destined to be sent to Obdorsk on the polar circle nearly a thousand miles from any railway and five hundred from a telegraph station. On the way there Trotsky escaped again, initially in a sleigh driven by a drunken peasant. After a hair-raising journey he managed to return to St Petersburg, where he rejoined his wife.

Again, compared to the Stalinist Cheka, the tsarist secret police were hopelessly incompetent and Trotsky was able to live a comparatively normal life there.

In 1907 there was a massive reaction against the October 1905 Revolution. Courts martial and the gallows dominated the scene as the revolutionary parties were crushed. Trotsky moved to Finland and thence to London where at the congress of the Social Democratic Party, as it was then called, he espoused the theme of permanent revolution, preaching unity and total cooperation between workers and peasants. Although in fact moving towards Lenin's policy of a centralized dictatorship, Trotsky remained unable wholly to throw his lot in with Lenin, partially because his old antagonism had not yet been dissipated.

Unlike many Russian revolutionaries, Trotsky was highly cosmopolitan, perhaps partially because of his 'wandering Jew' background. He called for the Europeanization of the revolution and settled in Vienna, becoming editor of *Pravda* (Truth), a Russian revolutionary journal.

The outbreak of war in 1914 led to a complete split in the Socialist world. As Trotsky saw it, some refused to follow their Capitalist masters to destruction while others, notably the Germans, were enthused by patriotic fervour and gladly marched to death. Trotsky was violently anti-war, which he saw in simplistic terms as a symptom of the disintegration of Capitalist society. He went to Switzerland and then to France, from where he observed the war with cynical aversion. He became editor of the revolutionary journal *Nashe Slovo* (Our Word). In September 1916 *Nashe Slovo* was banned in France and Trotsky was expelled. He escaped over the border to Spain and thence to New York.

In March 1917 bread riots broke out in Petrograd, as St Petersburg had been renamed in 1914. These spread quickly and led to a revolutionary situation, forcing the tsar to abdicate. A provisional Liberal-dominated government under Prince Lvov, followed after a few months by Kerensky, was formed. It tried to halt the revolution in its tracks and initially succeeded, being supported by the

Menshevik-dominated Petrograd soviet. The government was determined to remain in the war and even to take the offensive. From afar Trotsky vehemently opposed the war, arguing that a worldwide revolution was in the making and that Germany would be in the forefront of the event. German workers were friends not enemies of their Russian comrades. 'The Russian revolution represents an infinitely greater danger to the Hohenzollerns than do the appetites and designs of imperialist Russia.'[11]

Trotsky left New York for Russia in a state of exhilaration, which was quickly curbed when the ship dropped anchor at Halifax, Nova Scotia, and he was arrested by the Canadians on British instigation – the British had a major interest in keeping Russia in the war, to which Trotsky was of course strongly opposed. He was taken to a German prisoner-of-war camp. He was released after a month and arrived in Petrograd on 4 May (on the old calendar) 1917.

Lenin had arrived in Russia a month before Trotsky. The Mensheviks and Bolsheviks were still violently opposed to each other, although Trotsky, whose oratory began to have a vast influence on the situation, was moving further and further towards the Bolshevik position of ending the war and establishing a new radical government. There were further disturbances and after Lenin was accused of being in German pay (in fact without any foundation) a counter-revolution was started. Lenin fled to Finland and Trotsky was arrested and sent to prison in Petrograd on 23 July.

The situation became more and more chaotic as a General Kornilov attempted a military counter-revolutionary coup which failed. Trotsky was released. The Bolsheviks seized power in the Petrograd soviet and in other major Russian cities. By now a leading Bolshevik (he had joined that faction on 17 August), Trotsky was elected President of the Petrograd soviet.

Lenin had returned to Petrograd, at first in disguise. After considerable argument, it was decided mainly on Trotsky's initiative to institute a full-scale revolution. On the night of 23/24 October key buildings and positions were seized by the Bolsheviks in Petrograd. Kerensky fled and, without bloodshed, the Bolsheviks became the masters of the capital; the Winter Palace was again taken after bombardment by the battleship *Aurora*, with blanks!

Lenin had been smuggled by the German authorities from Switzerland across Germany in a sealed railway carriage and infiltrated into Russia 'like a bacillus', in Churchill's memorable phrase. Although his presence was undoubtedly decisive, it was in fact Trotsky with his domination of the Petrograd soviet, his drive, his brilliant oratory and his capacity for rapid decision-making who was the real catalyst of the revolution.

At the crucial meeting of the Second Soviet Congress in Petrograd, the moderates called for negotiations with the Provisional Government with a view to compromise. It looked as if opinion was going their way. Trotsky rose:

> What has happened is an insurrection, and not a conspiracy. We hardened the revolutionary energy of the Petrograd workers and soldiers. We openly forged the will of the masses for an insurrection and not a conspiracy. The masses of the people followed our banner and our insurrection was victorious. And now we are told: renounce your victory, make concessions, compromise. . . . A compromise is supposed to be made, as between two equal sides, by the millions of workers and peasants represented in this Congress, whom they are ready, not for the first time or the last, to barter away as the bourgeoisie sees fit. No, here no compromise is possible. To those who have left and to those who tell us to do this, we must say: you are miserable bankrupts, your role is played out: go where you ought to be: into the dustbin of history.[12]

The speech was a triumphant success and the die of radical revolution was finally cast.

Not surprisingly, Louis XVI's execution made no difference to France's fortunes in the war; these had been deteriorating, culminating in the defection of Dumouriez, a French general. Half the deputies were away and the Gironde took the opportunity to arrest Marat and impeach him 'for inciting pillage (sic), murder and other crimes'. A vote was taken as to whether or not Marat should be hauled before the recently established Revolutionary Tribunal. Owing to the many absences the motion was carried. However, by the time the case was heard on 24 April many deputies had returned and Marat was acquitted in some triumph. He seized the occasion to accuse the Girondists of treason and, in the aftermath of his acquittal, the Girondists were expelled from the Convention. Many were arrested and, after a hasty trial in front of the Revolutionary Tribunal, twenty-two were guillotined. Politics was a serious business!

Marat had been becoming gradually iller and iller. He had intense body irritation, probably aggravated by having to live literally underground, sometimes in sewers, in many places of hiding. He also had a lung complaint. In order to find relief from the pain and irritation he had to stay immersed in a bath (in the shape of a shoe), from where he worked and received visitors. The expulsion of the Girondists from the National Convention and the execution of many of the leaders had not ended the matter and many departments including Lyons, Grenoble, Marseilles and the Vendée, were in open revolt. The Girondists were fomenting rebellion in Normandy. It was from there that a young lady named Charlotte Corday came to Paris. Coming from a liberal, near-aristocratic family of local repute, she had been brought up in relative poverty due to the right of primogeniture which had disinherited her father, the great-grandson of the French poet Corneille. She had been a passionate supporter of the revolution in its early days but had been disillusioned and appalled by the excesses which followed, in particular by the September massacres and similar events which had occurred near where she lived in Caen. She had become convinced that the prime instigator of all this evil was Marat. This was compounded by the execution of Louis XVI. She wrote in a letter: 'The most horrible things that can possibly be imagined lie in a future inaugurated by such happenings. . . . All these men, who ought to give us liberty, have killed her. They are nothing but common executioners.'[13] She was a passionate supporter of the Girondists, some of which were her personal friends and had been guillotined in the aftermath of Marat's trial and acquittal. She decided to kill him, come what may, believing that peace and tranquillity would ensue. On 13 July 1793 she went to Marat's house but was refused entry by Simonne Everard. She returned later that day and was about to be sent away again when Marat heard her and instructed Simonne to let her in. She told him that she came from Caen.

'What is going on there?' he asked.

'Eighteen deputies from the Convention rule there in collusion with the Department.'

'What are their names?' She gave them and Marat wrote them down.

'Their heads will fall within a fortnight,' he said.[14]

At that Charlotte plunged a knife she had bought earlier that day into his heart and he died. (A memorable version of the scene was painted by David, himself a revolutionary.) She was immediately arrested. Convinced that she had done a great service for her country, she admitted everything at her trial and, serene to the end, was guillotined.

There was a massive reaction to Marat's assassination. The funeral was lavish, attended by thousands; his body lay in state; memorial meetings took place and busts were unveiled throughout France; the Place de l'Observance became the Place de l'Ami du Peuple; Montmartre became, temporarily, Montmarat; his heart was embalmed and enshrined in a church and on 21 September 1794 Marat was reburied in the Pantheon (again only temporarily). All this was to change in early 1795 when the pendulum swung violently the other way and he was vilified as a bloodthirsty monster.[15]

The assassination had the precise opposite effect to what was intended. Marat's murder led not to a cessation of hostilities but to a belief in a widespread murderous conspiracy of counter-revolutionaries and thence to more and more arrests and executions. The Committee of Public Safety under Robespierre became more powerful, condemning people to death on the flimsiest of excuses, although there are now attempts to rehabilitate him[16] and even to compare him to Jesus Christ.[17] It was not long before the period of 'The Terror' ensued, during which hundreds if not thousands of French men and women were guillotined in a frenzy of killing, finally including even Danton and Robespierre themselves. When the massacres eventually abated, the idealism of the founders of the revolution lay in ruins.

Essentially Marat was not an evil man, although the results of many of his actions and writings were indeed evil. He was touchy, opinionated and suspicious of the motives of anyone who had disagreed with him. He was, especially in his later years, physically ill and ugly and this may have added to his bloody-mindedness. But although his mind was twisted by the certainty that any means, however ghastly, would be justified by the noble ends of the revolution, he was scrupulously honest with himself. Indeed he seemed almost to relish the role of martyr. He did not fit easily into any political grouping or party: he would not compromise, except on one occasion when he gave up the idea of a dictatorship. His ideas were not original. His influence sprung from the extreme and powerful language of his journalism in the organ which he founded – *L'Ami du Peuple* – and because of his consistent championship of the poor and calls for labour and social reform. His political views changed radically from support of the king, through a period when he believed that the poor could only be protected by the bourgeoisie, to an extreme fear and hatred of those, mainly Girondists, whom he saw as counter-revolutionaries. It is impossible to say whether the Girondists would have been defeated if it had not been for the mistake they made in bringing Marat to trial with spurious charges, and whether The Terror would or would not have taken place had it not been for Marat's assassination, which was, indeed, only one, albeit a powerful, factor in the situation at the time. What is certain is that at an important stage in the French Revolution Marat's actions and, above all, his assassination were factors in the developing tragedy and the bloody chaos which was to engulf France.

In the immediate aftermath of the revolution in Russia, the problems faced by the Bolshevik Central Committee were vast. The whole of the enormous creaking tsarist bureaucracy had to be replaced. Lenin and Trotsky and their supporters, none of whom had any government experience, laboured night and day to try to cope with the unprecedented situation. Peace, land and bread had been promised, each of which entailed enormous administrative tasks. Lenin and Trotsky were now totally reconciled, and Lenin appointed Trotsky Minister for Foreign Affairs in charge of negotiations with the Germans at Brest Litovsk in order to achieve the first of these requirements.

Eventually, after a period of 'no peace, no war', and disputes within the Bolshevik leadership because of the stringent terms offered by the Germans, peace was concluded. Trotsky made an enormous impression on the German negotiators. Forceful, articulate, inflexible and incisive, he was apt to dominate any meeting that he attended. However, the terms eventually ratified were draconian. Russia was to cede to Germany the whole of the Ukraine, Latvia, Estonia and Finland and was to carry out complete demilitarization. Lenin, who insisted on acceptance of the terms, was prepared to pay almost any price for a respite to allow the new government to put its house in order. Trotsky did not agree, but eventually voted with Lenin in order to avoid a most damaging public split.

The new Russia was now assailed on all sides – the Americans and the Japanese in the east, the French in the south and the British and Americans in the north. Within Russia there was a civil war, as anti-red (or white) forces tried to restore the status quo or at least to defeat the Bolshevik revolutionaries. White armies succeeded in taking vast stretches of Russia in the north, south, east and west. The Russian capital had been moved to Moscow but Petrograd was nearly overcome. The Germans were still militarily engaged. The tsarist army had completely disintegrated, discipline had vanished, many officers had been murdered and the supply system had become non-existent. Trotsky was made Commissar for War and set about the task of creating a completely new military force – the Red Army. He re-established discipline, succeeded in enticing back no fewer than 40,000 tsarist officers and, giving them the power they needed, albeit each with a commissar beside him, and created a supply system out of nothing. Completely ruthless – the death penalty was common – and untiring, he dominated the highly complex scene and eventually defeated all his enemies, who suffered from the great disadvantage of having no common aim and, after the murder of the Tsar and his entire family at Ekaterinburg, no common focus. He did also have the great benefit of interior lines of communication, while his enemies were spread out on the periphery without any co-ordination worth the name. Furthermore the widespread Allied attacks enabled him to beat the patriotic drum, which was a great help, particularly with the ex-tsarist officers. However, in the circumstances, Trotsky's feat must be seen as almost unique in world history.

While all this was happening, Stalin, who had in fact played a comparatively minor role in the revolution itself, was consolidating his power. Utterly ruthless, a grey, apparently soulless but very able and vastly ambitious man, he was a master intriguer. In Trotsky's absence, he succeeded in establishing himself in a central position in the soviet hierarchy. Lenin was wary of him, but, as with Trotsky, he was happy to make use of his great abilities.

There remained many disputes within the leadership. There were those who believed that a success could only come through world revolution and there were those who believed in 'revolution in one country' first. Trotsky was the former; Stalin the latter. There were those who believed that the workers – the proletariat – should cooperate with the bourgeoisie and others who did not. Trotsky insisted on the latter. There were those who believed in the establishment of a ruthless dictatorship as the only method of success in the early stages of the revolution and others who shrank from the inevitable bloody repercussions of that stand. A bitter argument developed when the Poles under Pilsudski attacked the Ukraine and succeeded in seizing a large part of that very rich territory. They were thrown back by the Red Army but the question then arose as to whether or not the Russians should cross the Polish border. Trotsky was against doing so on the grounds that they were not strong enough and, in any case, a revolution in Poland should come from the people themselves and not be imposed by others. Lenin wished to push right up to the German border, hoping to bring about revolution there. Lenin won the argument but in the event the Red Army was defeated at the gates of Warsaw, had to retreat and peace was signed.

As a result of the war against Germany and the total disruption of administration, which the revolution had caused, the Russian economy was in chaos. Trotsky decided that the only solution to the many problems which existed on all sides was to 'militarize' labour, to enforce rigid discipline and control over everything. The Red Army was put to work in mines, forests and fields. There were many protests but Lenin supported him. However, things went from bad to worse: famine loomed, and indeed occurred, in many areas. Eventually Lenin, with Trotsky's support, changed course and under the New Economic Policy (NEP) allowed the peasants to sell some of their own food, thus increasing production.

In all his many activities during this period Trotsky was never inhibited by any moral doubts about his numerous ruthless actions. These included a successful and bloody attack on the sailors at Kronstadt who had revolted against Bolshevik rule because they lacked any of the necessities of life – 'either you surrender unconditionally or you will be shot like partridges'.[18] Neither did he criticize the Red Terror which followed an attack on Lenin's life on 30 August 1918. Although personally kind, he had a firm belief that the end justified the means. His logic drove him to any measures, however extreme, which he thought essential for the preservation of the revolution, even if these were in complete contrast to the altruistic ideals with which the revolution had been started. The idea of a proletarian democracy was dropped, to be replaced by complete state control over the working classes. Lenin half agreed with him and in 1921 banned all organized political opposition, albeit granting, through the NEP, some economic freedom. The irony was that Stalin, in the thirties, was to adopt Trotsky's ideas in toto and to use them ruthlessly against Trotsky himself and his supporters.

Lenin's death in 1924 was, inevitably, followed by a bitter struggle for power. In theory this struggle was conditioned by differences in principle but in practice it was almost entirely a matter of the personal ambitions of Stalin, a master of intrigue and dissimulation. Trotsky was no match for him in this respect. He was gradually ousted from positions of influence and power and in 1928 he was exiled to Alma Ata, deep in Kazakstan near the frontier with Mongolia. In 1929 Stalin exiled him from the Soviet Union and he moved to Turkey. He then went to France, from where he was expelled in 1935, managing to be accepted by Norway, but whence he was again expelled, moving to Mexico in 1937.

During his exile he suffered a number of personal tragedies, as nearly every member of his family either committed suicide or was murdered by agents of Stalin, although his wife survived. The show trials in Russia by which Stalin gradually eliminated all of his former associates and possible rivals, including the 'old Bolsheviks' Kamenev and Zinoviev who were accused of conspiring with Trotsky to murder Stalin, confirmed Trotsky in the view that he was lucky to be exiled and not murdered. However, in 1929 Stalin clearly did not think himself quite powerful enough to murder a person who, together with Lenin, had been the main leader and instigator of the revolution in 1917.

In all of his havens, Trotsky continued to produce a stream of books, articles and pamphlets putting forward his views and showing how Stalin was betraying everything the Communists (as they were by then calling themselves) had initially stood for. In Mexico he had a number of devoted disciples who guarded him as best they could and his house was fortified. However, Stalin's agents managed to penetrate the defences twice. On the first occasion Trotsky and his wife somehow survived a hail of bullets fired into their bedroom at night. However, on 20 August 1940 a Stalinist agent, Raymon Mercader, having managed to pose as a friend, gained entry into Trotsky's study and plunged an ice pick into his skull.

Whether the assassination was successful in its political aim is open to debate. Trotskyism did survive its founder's death but certainly it suffered a major blow. But this would probably have happened anyway, as the German invasion of Russia in the SecondWorld War had produced an entirely new situation. Stalin's military victory undoubtedly gave him a prestige which would probably not have been dented much, if at all, after the war by a living Trotsky, however articulate. It is certain that the assassination was politically unnecessary. It was Stalin's paranoiac fears rather than any real threat, which impelled him to eliminate Trotsky. The assassination must surely have satisfied his personal need for vengeance and have added to the all-pervading feeling of terror which surrounded him by showing that his writ extended worldwide – even to Mexico. Indeed, this was probably one of Stalin's main motives, and so to this limited extent the assassination did achieve its purpose. But in retrospect the eventual total political, economic and cultural failure of communism in Russia was inevitable, and Trotsky's assassination was irrelevant to this.

As for Marat, his death may well have affected the immediate course of history and even have led to 'The Terror', but that was certainly not what Charlotte Corday intended – very much the opposite.

NOTES

1. L.R. Gottschalk, *Jean Paul Marat*, University of Chicago Press, Chicago, 1967, p. 15.
2. M.J. Sydenham, *The French Revolution*, Batsford, London, 1975, p. 21.

3. Gottschalk, *Marat*, p. 37.
4. A. Cobban, *A History of Modern France*, Vol. 1, Penguin, Middlesex, 1957, p. 195.
5. Gottschalk, *Marat*, p. 117.
6. Cobban, *Modern France*, p. 202.
7. Sydenham, *Revolution*, p. 122.
8. Cobban, *Modern France*, p. 158.
9. L. Trotsky, *My Life*, Penguin, Middlesex, 1975, pp. 1–26.
10. I. Deutscher, *The Prophet Armed*, OUP, London, 1954, pp. 3–5.
11. Ibid., p. 245.
12. R. Segal, *The Tragedy of Leon Trotsky*, Hutchinson, London, 1979, p. 170.
13. Corday, *Charlotte Corday*, translated by Buckley, Butterworth, London, 1931, p. 60.
14. T. Carlyle, *The French Revolution*, Bodley Head, London, p. 607.
15. Gottschalk, *Marat*, p. 186
16. H. Belloc, *The French Revolution*, Williams and Northgate, London, 1911, p. 77.
17. J.L. Carr, *Robespierre*, History Book Club, London, 1972, p. 206.
18. H. Shukman, *The Russian Revolution*, Sutton, Stroud, 1998, p. 88.

CHAPTER 4

LORD FREDERICK CAVENDISH /
ARCHDUKE FRANZ FERDINAND

It may seem to be surprising to link the assassination of Lord Frederick Cavendish in Phoenix Park, Dublin, in 1882 with that of Archduke Franz Ferdinand in 1914. Many people will hardly have heard of the former while the latter's demise at Sarajevo was a world-famous event, said by many to have been the basic cause of the most terrible war in history. This chapter will examine these two events, what led up to them and what the repercussions were. There are, however, some obvious similarities that stand out in even a cursory examination. In both cases the victim was the representative of a regime that claimed sovereignty over an area in which many people, probably a majority, disputed it. In both cases there was much resentment after many years of complicated and bitter history. Neither assassin had thought through the probable repercussions of what they did and, in the event, these were totally different from what they expected. In both cases the assassinations were used by others for their own purposes – in Lord Frederick Cavendish's case the ending of possible cooperation between Gladstone and Parnell, which might well have led to a great improvement of the situation in Ireland, and with Archduke Franz Ferdinand an excuse for an attack on Serbia by Austria/ Hungary. In neither case was the personality of the victim a factor: it was what they represented rather than their individual virtues or vices which was the reason for their assassination. Finally, in both cases chance was a major factor in the deed itself.

Lord Frederick Cavendish was assassinated in Phoenix Park, Dublin, on 6 May 1882. William Gladstone, the Prime Minister and his uncle by marriage, had made him Chief Secretary of Ireland and, together with Lord Spencer (the new Lord Lieutenant), he had just arrived in Dublin. Indeed, he had been sworn in earlier the same day and was walking back to his house through the park when he was joined by Mr Burke, the Under Secretary, when they were set upon by a gang of extremist Irish Nationalists and stabbed to death.

Henry Ford was wrong: history is not bunk. It lies deep, particularly in Ireland where, consciously or unconsciously, it plays a major role in shaping attitudes.

The English connection with Ireland had started as long ago as AD 1170, when the Earl of Pembroke (known as Strongbow) was invited to Ireland by the Irish King of Leinster to help him in a war he was having with a rival. Later Henry II arrived, anxious that Strongbow, who had by that time become King of Leinster himself, was becoming too powerful. Henry II was followed by a series of Norman adventurers, who supported one or other of the permanently warring Irish chieftains, in search of plunder, land or position.

As the centuries passed, the English hold on Ireland waxed and waned. Rebellion succeeded rebellion as successive English punitive measures followed one another, varying in intensity and purpose. The situation became even more complex as the Irish Gaelic nation itself became diluted with English immigrants, beginning with those who had followed Henry II in 1191. This was followed by a number of unofficial attempts at the plantation of English settlers into Ireland in the sixteenth century, the far more successful and numerous official plantation of 1610 and, thereafter, a massive unofficial influx of Scottish Presbyterians into Ulster. The indigenous Irish did not convert to Protestantism. So, to the inevitable conflict between the Irish and their English masters across the sea and between the Gaelic and English or Scottish inhabitants of Ireland itself were added the heady antagonisms of differing religions. However, it would be wrong, to believe, as many do today, that to be Protestant was to be against the Nationalists. Very many Protestants, even in the South, have always been Nationalist: indeed much of the leadership of the Nationalist movement has consistently come from Protestant families.

It is impossible to understand the continuing violent hatred of some Irish people for the English without taking into account the folk memories of what they saw as English aggression, stretching from Henry VIII to Elizabeth I, Cromwell and William of Orange. These memories, also, of course fuelled the Unionist cause, and still do so. Ireland continued as a festering, albeit self-inflicted, sore on the English body politic until the definitive and massively tragic event of the Irish Potato Famine in 1845–9. During these years it has been estimated[1] that about 1,500,000 Irish people emigrated and 1,000,000 died – and this out of a population of about 9,000,000. The figures are appalling and reveal human suffering on a massive scale. Ireland was devastated. Efforts made by Britain to mitigate the suffering were vastly inadequate in spite of many well-meaning individual and collective efforts. The Irish were right in believing that if this, or anything like it, had happened in Britain, the response would have been very different. As a result, anti-English feeling in Ireland – and particularly in the southern counties where the famine was at its worst – was greatly exacerbated.

In essence there were two issues which dominated relations between Britain and Ireland in the nineteenth century – independence and the land. The concept of independence had been invented at the end of the eighteenth century by Protestants led by Wolfe Tone, who wrote of substituting the name of Irishman for those of Catholic and Protestant. It flourished among the Protestant Ascendancy, as the Scots and English who had been 'planted' in Ireland and who controlled the body politic were known. They thought they would be better off in an Ireland which they dominated than if it were joined to the English nation, as they thought England would, in that case, ignore them. Paradoxically, at that time many Catholics were in favour of the union with England for opposite reasons. However, the penal laws enacted against the

Catholics, together with the great persuasive powers of Daniel O'Connell, changed all that.

At their height the penal laws against the Catholics decreed that a Catholic could not hold any office of state, vote, stand for parliament, practice at the bar or, and this was a vital matter, buy land. He could not even hold land on a lease longer than thirty-one years nor could he bequeath any land he did own as he wished. On his death his land had to be divided equally among all his children unless one of them turned Protestant, in which case that child got the lot. At the end of the nineteenth century barely five per cent of Irish land was owned by Catholics.[2] The high Catholic birth rate had meant that the plots of land farmed by the Catholics were constantly diminished in size. Tenants could hardly pay their rent in good times; when the harvest was bad they could not, and were often evicted. If a landlord wished to get rid of a tenant all he had to do was to increase the rent. The situation for a tenant without any security of tenure or system of fixing 'a fair rent' in times of bad harvests was intolerable.

The Catholics began overwhelmingly to support independence. This did not mean that all Protestants changed their views: many continued to fight for independence. The Irish Parliament had been abolished by the Act of Union in 1800 and, although all Irishmen had had the vote since 1793, in the mid-nineteenth century no Catholics were allowed to sit in the Westminster House of Commons. It was Daniel O'Connell who gave the Irish Catholics their self-respect – hence his reputation as 'the liberator'. A Catholic himself, from County Kerry in the far west of the country, he inaugurated two great movements: the first, to achieve Catholic emancipation in all fields; the second, to repeal the Act of Union of 1800 which had abolished the Irish Parliament and united the two kingdoms of England and Ireland 'for ever'. He was largely successful in gaining emancipation, but he failed with repeal of the Act of Union. He died in 1847.

From the eighteenth century until the time of writing, Irish dissent has split into those who would use constitutional means of achieving their aims and those who saw violence as the only way to success. Movements advocating violence have been a fixture in the Irish political scene, beginning with the agrarian secret societies known as the White Boys through the Fenians and the Irish Republican Brotherhood, the Defenders, the Invincibles (who assassinated Lord Frederick Cavendish) to the IRA and, at the time of writing, its various offshoots. The constitutional parties favouring independence, too, have passed through a number of different emanations, including the Irish Party as the movement was known in the House of Commons at the time of Lord Frederick Cavendish's assassination.

In the immediate aftermath of the famine, things quietened down in Ireland owing to the total exhaustion of all concerned. However, this did not last long and the situation worsened, in part fuelled by the Irish who had emigrated to the United States during and after the famine and who had a deep emotive feeling for their mother country. Attempts were made at risings in Ireland and even the invasion of Canada was attempted from the United States in 1866 and 1870. However, informers proliferated and every effort was aborted. It was on this unhappy scene that there emerged the two major figures who between them were to bring about the situation in which Lord Frederick Cavendish lost his life – Parnell and Gladstone.

Charles Stewart Parnell was a Protestant landlord owning some five thousand acres in County Wicklow. His family had been Nationalists since the eighteenth century and he continued the family tradition encouraged by his mother, an American whose father had fought against the British in the war of 1812. The spectre of famine appeared again in the late 1870s as successive harvests failed and cheap American grain flooded into Europe, depressing farm prices and thereby penalizing the small Irish tenant farmer. Michael Davitt, a member of the Nationalist secret society, the Fenians, began to organize the tenants against their landlords. In 1879 he launched a new organization known as the Land League. Parnell, who had entered Parliament and was beginning to make a name for himself as an effective, forceful speaker and parliamentarian, quickly became its President. Many officials in the

Land League had been members of the Fenians and had close connections with the acts of violence that had taken place. Parnell openly disapproved of violence, but was not averse to taking advantage of some of its consequences. Throughout his time in Parliament his attitude towards extremist Nationalists remained somewhat equivocal. His preferred method of opposition to the treatment of their tenants by many landlords was the boycott, an effective ploy of total ostracism used for the first time against a land agent, Captain Boycott.

Parnell was a highly charismatic figure of great political skills and determination. He dominated his party in Parliament and became the central figure of Irish resistance to British rule. At times holding the balance of power in the British Parliament between the Liberals under Gladstone and the Conservatives under Disraeli, he was often able to have a major influence on British political life in the sense that no British Prime Minister could afford not to take his views into account.

Although Gladstone, the 'Grand Old Man' of British politics, may have appeared always to have been old, this was not so! He formed the first of his four administrations in 1868 when aged fifty-nine (middle aged perhaps, but certainly not old). Although he had never been to Ireland he had become increasingly interested in the Irish question because, clearly, its people were not satisfied with their lot, and he had had this thrown in his face by various European leaders when he sought to read lectures to them on their behaviour! Gladstone was a conscientious and fair man by his own lights, which told him that something was very wrong across the sea. He determined to bring in two measures: disestablishment of the Irish Church – the arguments for and against need not detain us – and a Land Act, an attempt to put right the manifold injustices faced by Irish tenant farmers.

His problem was that not only did he face sporadic opposition by the Conservatives, but the Whig grandees of his own party were, almost by definition, landlords with extensive estates in England and viewed with great suspicion any tampering with landlord rights, albeit in Ireland. They feared import into England of measures to their disadvantage. As a result, the Land Bill, which did bring substantial benefits to tenant farmers – notably the right of a tenant to sell or bestow occupancy and the right to compensation if evicted – did not go far enough and substantial injustices remained. As the price of getting acceptance of even this watered-down Act, Gladstone had to agree to a Coercion Act giving special powers to the police and courts to deal with politically motivated crime.

Gladstone's second administration, 1880–5, covered Lord Frederick Cavendish's assassination in 1882. The Grand Old Man was approaching elderly status but still remarkably full of energy and drive. Unlike in 1868, Ireland was not in the front of his mind when he came to office but it quickly forced itself into prominence. There was much distress and unrest in the country. The number of evictions for non-payment of agricultural rent had risen from 483 in 1877 to 1,238 in 1879 and doubled again in the first six months of 1880.[3] In an attempt to ameliorate agricultural distress, Gladstone produced a Compensation for Disturbance Bill, which he managed to force through the Commons with difficulty but which failed dismally in the Lords with many Liberal peers defecting. The Irish Chief Secretary at the time was W.E. Forster, a powerful figure of strong opinions who virtually ruled Ireland single handed. He was so incensed at the failure of the Bill which he had inspired that he decided that the only alternative was coercion.

Meanwhile, the Land League was continuing its very considerable pressures on the administration in Ireland and, indeed, the situation was approaching open civil war. Parnell and thirteen others of its leaders were arrested and tried for conspiracy to prevent the payment of rent, but the jury acquitted them. Parnell and his colleagues were now disrupting Parliament by filibustering and disrupting all government business, and it became clear that the only way to put them behind bars would be by the suspension of habeas corpus. This was effectively achieved by two Acts, the Life and Property Protection Act and the Peace Preservation (Ireland) Act. Parnell was finding himself in an increasingly difficult situation. Poised between the use of violence and constitutional methods in Parliament, he was in danger of falling between two stools. For his part, undeterred by the looming crisis in Ireland, Gladstone persisted with a second Land Bill of 1881. This was a considerable advance on its predecessors, including the three F's – Fair Rent, Fixture of Tenure and Free Sale. It permanently destroyed the absolute power of the landlord. With tremendous and unremitting energy Gladstone, now aged seventy-one, forced it through thirty-two days (and nights) of its committee stage. The Lords approved it on 16 August 1881.

Parnell now courted arrest by making a series of extremely inflammatory speeches – 'The Irishman who thinks that he can now throw away his arms . . . will find to his sorrow and destruction, when too late, that he has placed himself in the power of the cruel and unrelenting English enemy.'[4] Parnell, three other Irish MPs and several hundred other local leaders and organizers of the Land League were put in Kilmainham Gaol near Dublin.

In fact the arrests, together with the increasingly effective Land Act, were temporarily successful in quelling incipient revolt, but it was not long before the trouble started again. Shooting, explosions and cattle maiming were daily occurrences. In the summer of 1882 sixty murders were committed in succession for which no one was convicted.[5] Plainly the Chief Secretary Forster's methods of coercion were not working. Gladstone was determined to find a way out of the deadlock even if it meant the resignation of Forster. From Kilmainham Gaol Parnell broke the ice. He offered to drop his opposition to the Land Act and to 'stop outrage and intimidation' if the government would end coercion and make a settlement of the arrears of rent question. Gladstone and his cabinet agreed. Parnell was freed and Forster resigned. A new era of cooperation between Parnell and Gladstone seemed to be in view, perhaps leading to a permanent ending of hostilities and, even, Home Rule.

The question immediately arose as to who was to succeed Forster as Chief Secretary. The decision had already been taken to replace the ineffective Lord Cowper as Lord Lieutenant by the more forceful and experienced Lord Spencer. The press expected the powerful Joe Chamberlain to be nominated, although Gladstone never had the slightest intention of appointing him. Mr Porter, the Irish solicitor general, was approached but quickly turned it down. Gladstone then turned to Lord Frederick Cavendish and offered him the job.

Cavendish was the second son of the seventh Duke of Devonshire. His elder brother, Lord Hartington, was a leading Liberal politician whom the queen had sent for to form a government on the fall of Disraeli's Conservative administration in 1880. Hartington, a serious, decent mediocrity would clearly have been overshadowed by the brilliant Gladstone and he had advised the Queen to send for Gladstone. Hartington had himself been Chief Secretary of Ireland in the 1870s and Cavendish had visited him there, so he was not wholly ignorant of Irish affairs.

Born in 1836, Cavendish had been educated at home and at Cambridge. He had been private secretary to Lord Granville, who became leader of the House of Lords, and, after entering Parliament as a Liberal in 1865, had become private secretary to Gladstone before entering the government as a junior lord at the Treasury. In his second administration, many thought most unwisely, Gladstone undertook the office of Chancellor of the Exchequer as well as Prime Minister. Cavendish became financial secretary, carrying out much of the day-to-day work at the Treasury in Gladstone's frequent enforced absences as Prime Minister. He married Gladstone's niece, Lucy Caroline. A man of great charm, he was hard working, honest and able. He had many of the virtues of a successful politician but he was a poor speaker and this clearly limited his prospects. However, Gladstone was devoted to him.

Cavendish was appalled at being offered the job of Chief Secretary. He did not believe that he was up to the job and said so: 'I told him [Lord Granville] that I had no tact, no real knowledge of Ireland, no powers of speaking.'[6] His father, the Duke of Devonshire, was horrified. As a landlord he was in any event worried about the direction of Gladstone's policy in Ireland. When Forster resigned he confided to his diary: 'I fear Gladstone is adopting a very rash course of action.'[7] On 3 May he added: 'I hear Gladstone wants Freddie to be Chief Secretary. Freddie seems to have nearly made up his mind to accept. I should have been against it if I had known of the proposal.' And on 4 May: 'I have great misgivings as to him being up to a place of such extreme difficulty at the present time. . . . I fear he is certainly not a speaker of the calibre to deal with the Irish.'

Gladstone was determined to keep the reins of power in Ireland firmly in his own hands. Cavendish had been serving him as private secretary and at the Treasury for some time. He trusted, liked and admired him. He was adamant that he should take the job and, driven by his sense of duty, Cavendish did so in spite of the manifest personal dangers.

Earl Spencer, too, had had doubts about accepting the post of Lord Lieutenant, particularly when Forster appeared to be set on retaining the job of Chief Secretary. But, when Forster resigned, Spencer was much relieved and he and Cavendish left London for Dublin, Cavendish taking the oath as Chief Secretary on the morning of 6 May 1882.

At the end of the nineteenth century the Austro/Hungarian Empire was vast with, as well as Germans, a plethora of different nationalities – Serbs, Croats, Slovenes, Poles, Czechs, Slovaks, Ruthenes, Turks, Bulgarians, Hungarians, Rumanians, Greeks and Albanians. The religions were also varied – Christians (Orthodox, Protestants and Catholic) and Moslem. The edifice was creaky, inevitably so, as national and religious differences, not least the language question, led to turmoil. At the summit of this extraordinarily varied conglomeration sat Emperor Franz Josef, the penultimate Habsburg ruler. He had come to the throne in 1848 at the age of eighteen, a remarkably mature and gifted young man in spite of his many detractors. He died in 1916, after a reign of sixty-eight years, a European record. It is extraordinary not that the Austro/Hungarian Empire broke up in 1918 but that it lasted as long as it did. This was certainly due in part to the mixture of adaptability and firmness shown by the Emperor. As well as coping with his always difficult and often rebellious Empire, Franz Josef had to deal with a number of personal tragedies. His brother Maximillian, who had been foisted by Louis Napoleon of France on the Mexicans as Emperor in 1864, was executed by firing squad there in 1867. His beloved wife, bullied by her mother-in-law, had lived a largely separate life from her husband, finding solace in ceaseless travel including an obsession for fox hunting in England and Ireland. She was assassinated while in Geneva by a young Italian builder's labourer, Lougi Lucheni, an anarchist acting on his own. Franz Josef's son, Rudolph, a gilded youth, full of charm and highly intelligent but frustrated to the point of madness by the failure of his father to give him any kind of role, killed himself at his hunting lodge, Mayerling, in a suicide pact with his mistress, the beautiful Marie Vetsera. To cap it all Franz Josef thoroughly disliked his new heir, his brother's son, Franz Ferdinand.

Franz Ferdinand was a complex character. Like Rudolph, whom he had greatly admired in his youth and who had tried to teach him to relax, he was dangerously frustrated by his impotence in the face of Franz Josef's determination to keep all the reins of power in his own hands. Morose, suspicious, quarrelsome, even violent, he was nevertheless determined to avoid war and, above all, to avoid war with Russia. He fully realized the dangers of confrontation with Serbia and, ironically, was intent to avoid any confrontation with that country. Often a blustering bully, he was driven almost to insanity by seeing his inheritance, the Austro/Hungarian Empire, disintegrate before his eyes while, as he saw it, his uncle, an ageing, remote and intolerant figure, sat in his castle, ignorant of what was really going on and impervious to advice. The deep antagonism between the two men was greatly increased when Franz Ferdinand announced that he intended to marry a girl with the resounding name of the Countess Sophie Chotek von Chotkowa und Wognin. This lady belonged to an old Bohemian family but was not on the list of those considered eligible to marry a Habsburg. Franz Josef was furious and tried to prevent the marriage. However, Franz Ferdinand stuck to his guns and the marriage took place, morganatically. Sophie put up with the humiliations that were heaped upon her and, until she was assassinated, was a marvellous mother to her children and wife to Franz Ferdinand.

Franz Josef had seen, and survived, many catastrophes. His country had been involved in a war against France and Piedmont in 1859, culminating in the massive slaughter at Solferino, a battle in which no fewer than 270,000 men, 40,000 horses and 700 guns were engaged on a fifteen-mile front.[8] Ultimately the French won the advantage but both sides had suffered very great casualties and were equally exhausted. This was followed by the conclusive military defeat of Austria / Hungary by the Prussians under Bismarck in 1866. Franz Josef had narrowly avoided taking part in the Crimean War of 1854–6, but at the expense of unpopularity with Britain and France.

However, it was in the Balkans that the European dance of death leading up to the holocaust of the First World War was to be staged. There were two main problems – the urge to independence of many of the component parts of the Austro/Hungarian Empire and the rivalry and even hatred between the Slavs and most of the rest of Franz Josef's complex domain. There were, of course, many other complications, including the presence of a newly unified Germany, touchy, militaristic and seeking her place in the sun, the re-emergence of Britain into the balance of power in Europe, the looming spectre, as many saw it, of the vast Russian steamroller, intent on gaining an outlet to the Mediterranean and on expiating the disgrace of the Russo–Japanese War, and a France intent on recovering the provinces of Alsace and Lorraine lost to Germany in the war of 1870.

In the late nineteenth century the fate of millions still rested in the hands of a tiny minority. Monarchs, advised by a few ministers who could be dismissed at will, could declare war on each other, thus condemning millions to possible death. Pride was a major factor: face had to be saved; dynasties had to be preserved. The 'people' as such were rarely, if ever, considered or consulted. Alliances were constructed – thus the eventual line-up of Germany, Austria and, initially, Italy on one side and Britain, France and Russia on the other. There were many shifts and nuances in national relationships before the blocks solidified. Britain and Germany dallied with an 'understanding' at the beginning of the twentieth century and Italy, eventually, deserted its alliance. There were valid reasons for every twist and turn in the vastly complicated, and ultimately fatal, minuet danced by the leading actors on the European stage. In the approach to 1914 the tempo of bitter antagonisms hotted up. There were two Balkan wars, in which the leading European nations managed to avoid taking part. There was a war between Italy and Turkey and many scares, including the Agadir crisis of 1911 when a general conflict was only narrowly avoided.

The German Kaiser Wilhelm II with his spiked helmet, waxed moustaches, plethora of medals and long padded overcoat, had in his youth sacked the wise Bismarck. He was jealous of Britain and, in particular, of the British navy. After some dithering he refused to agree to any kind of restricting deal. He struck up a friendship with Franz Ferdinand, who admired him. In December 1912 he told von Moltke, his chief of staff, to prepare for war against Russia and to begin conditioning his people for this event.[9] Franz Ferdinand, for his part, concentrated his antipathies on the Magyars, the Hungarian part of the Empire, whom he saw as potential traitors. He was opposed to the dual monarchy which had been created in 1867 when the Hungarians were granted a parliament of their own, leaving only the common allegiance to the Emperor holding the Empire together. Although nearly all the leading figures in Europe were acutely aware of the dangers of war and often stepped gingerly round issues which might lead to it, the fact was that Europe had become a tinderbox, awaiting ignition. However, the Kaiser, and some of his entourage, saw war in heroic terms – a fatal error for his country and, indeed, for the world.

Although Bosnia had remained nominally under Turkish sovereignty, the Austrians had occupied it in 1878. In 1908 they took a major step by declaring that in future it would be part of the Austro–Hungarian Empire. This was a great affront both to Serbia and to Russia. Deep antagonism between Serbia and Austria had been a major factor in the Balkan situation for many years. The Serbs felt that their fellow Slavs in Bosnia should not, as they saw it, be under the Austrian yoke but be united with them in a greater Serbia. Commenting in a letter of 20 June 1868 to his masters in Vienna, the first Austro–Hungarian diplomatic agent in Belgrade, Kallay, said, 'Bosnia is the centre round which all the wishes and hopes of Serbian statesmen turn. . . . The idea of its possession is the fundamental principle of all Serbian aims'[10] – *plus ça change*!

As far as Russia was concerned, the Austro/Hungarian action aroused deep and sometimes militarily aggressive pan-Slav feelings. The Tsar managed to restrain his extremists who clamoured for war, but had some difficulty in doing so. It was in this situation that it was decided by the Austrian authorities that Franz Ferdinand would, as Inspector General of the Army, attend some military manoeuvres of the Austrian army not far from Sarajevo, the capital of Bosnia. He certainly did not demur: indeed he was enthusiastic about the trip. It was further decided that he would visit the town after the manoeuvres. It was thought that he would be well received. In fact, many Bosnians realized that they were much better off under Austrian sovereignty than they had been under the Turks. The existence of some young extremists was known about, but they were said to be a small minority of little, if any, consequence. The Austrian authorities were warned by the Serbian Government that Franz Ferdinand would be in some danger if he visited Sarajevo but he was no coward and decided to proceed with the visit as planned, together with his wife.

It was later suggested that these manoeuvres were a cover for the invasion of Serbia by the Austro–Hungarian army – and indeed this was used by some as post-facto justification for the assassination of the Archduke. But there was absolutely no truth in this allegation. The manoeuvres were routine and, in any case, nowhere near the

Serb border. On 24 June 1914 Archduke Franz Ferdinand began his tour of inspection in Bosnia, to be followed by a visit to Sarajevo on 28 June.

Almost throughout its history Ireland has been plagued by a plethora of secret and not so secret political movements, groups and societies with a bewildering number of different names. Towards the end of 1881, when most of the Land League leaders were in prison, the torch was taken up by their wives and other female supporters, who formed the Ladies of the Land League. Another, more sinister and terrorist organization came into being in the same period, the Irish National Invincibles – known as 'the Invincibles'. By its very nature, of course, a terrorist group keeps no records and there are varying accounts of how it came into being and how it was organized, as various of its members attempted to give post facto justification for what they had done. About one thing, however, there is no doubt. It was responsible for the assassination of Chief Secretary Cavendish and Under Secretary Burke. The extent of Parnell's contact with the Invincibles is in doubt. Parnell most vehemently denied any association with it and, certainly, was appalled by the assassination. But some of his supporters may have had some kind of link to it. The truth will never be known.

The Invincibles had supporters and members in the United States, in England and of course in Ireland (mainly Dublin). At the end of 1881 the movement decided to follow a policy of assassination in the belief that this would bring about independence. As they saw it, peaceful means had failed: the only answer was violence, which was essential if England was to give up its oppressive domination of their country. A number of efforts were made to assassinate Chief Secretary Forster, but were bungled in one way or another, the last on 19 April 1882 when he was leaving for England.[11] Forster having disappeared from the scene, the decision was made to assassinate Burke, his civil service deputy, a particular object of hatred because he was Irish and a Catholic who, had 'deserted to the enemy'.

On the morning of 6 May Spencer and Cavendish were sworn in as Lord Lieutenant and Chief Secretary respectively at the castle in Dublin, the seat of the Government of Ireland. The Invincibles had a spy (Joe Smith) working there who informed them about Burke's movements and that he would be returning from the castle to his house in Phoenix Park in the early evening. Seven of the Invincibles took up positions in the park. In addition, there were two lookout men and a cab and driver for the getaway.

After the day's work was done Spencer rode to the vice-regal lodge in Phoenix Park with an escort. Cavendish said he would rather walk home and set off alone. Burke followed him on foot some way behind but then took a cab to catch him up. When he did so he left his cab and walked with him. The two men reached the seven Invincibles, who attacked and murdered them with knives, slitting Burke's throat to make sure, and then escaped in the waiting cab. Cavendish was said to have tried to fight back with his umbrella.

The news of Cavendish's assassination was greatly shocking to the whole Establishment in Britain and Ireland. Members of the House of Commons, some of whom had derided the appointment, were deeply affected, half of the membership attending the funeral in Derbyshire. Above all, Gladstone, to whom Cavendish had been almost a son, was devastated. Parnell had just come to an agreement with Gladstone about the immediate future of Ireland and hoped to press on towards Home Rule in the atmosphere of trust that had developed between him and Gladstone. He too was shattered.[12]

As soon as he heard the news, Parnell offered to resign his seat but Gladstone, who still hoped to salvage something from the ruin of his hopes for Ireland persuaded him not to. Parnell's Irish Party in the House of Commons put out a manifesto denouncing the murders:

> On the eve of what seemed a bright future for our country, that evil destiny which has apparently pursued us for centuries has struck another blow at our hopes, which cannot be exaggerated in its disastrous consequences. . . . We feel that no act has ever been perpetrated in our country during the exciting struggles

for social and political rights of the past fifty years that has so stained the name of hospitable Ireland as this cowardly and unprovoked assassination of a friendly stranger. . . . Until the murderers of Lord Frederick Cavendish and Mr Burke are brought to justice that stain will sully our country's name.

Gladstone and Parnell's hopes that they would be able to continue with their new policy of cooperation and movement towards a fairer society, and indeed even to Home Rule were, in the event, vain. There was a great revulsion against Irish Nationalism and a new Coercion Bill was passed. Contact between Gladstone and Parnell was continued through various intermediaries; one of the principal ones was a Captain O'Shea who, together with his wife Katharine (Parnell's mistress) had been playing an important, though subsidiary, role in the move towards reconciliation. But the atmosphere in England and in Parliament had changed as a result of the assassination and there was no question of any further move. Gladstone, despairing of Ireland (though he later reverted to the attempt to bring in Home Rule) turned his attention to other problems. Katharine O'Shea continued her efforts on Parnell's behalf for some time, but when he was cited as co-respondent in the divorce case taken against his wife by Captain O'Shea, Parnell was disgraced and died shortly afterwards, in 1891.

The question as to whether Cavendish's murder was premeditated, or whether it was pure chance as he happened to be accompanying Burke, has never been satisfactorily decided. The chance theory was, at first, widely accepted: it was to the advantage of almost all concerned that it should be. The consciences of both Parnell and Gladstone and his supporters would be less severely tested if the murder was a mistake. Lucy Cavendish was convinced that her husband was such a blameless character that no one in their senses would wish to murder him. Of the two principal Invincibles who 'told all', one (Tynan) said that the act was deliberate and that the assassins knew exactly whom they were attacking and the other (Carey) insisted that they had no idea their second victim was Cavendish.

It took the police in Ireland some time before they were able to bring the assassins to justice, but eventually several Invincibles, including Carey, turned queen's evidence and five were executed. Now in great danger, Carey was given an assumed name and, together with his wife and child, secretly put on board a boat sailing for South Africa. However, the Invincibles, discovered the secret and managed to get one of their number, a Patrick O'Donnell, on the same boat. As it approached Natal, he shot Carey dead. O'Donnell was arrested, brought back to England, tried and, in his turn, executed.

It is impossible to be sure what would have happened in Ireland if Cavendish had not been assassinated. What is certain is that the process of reconciliation and movement towards Home Rule was stopped in its tracks and many bitter years were to pass before Ireland, split into two, was to become independent. It is quite possible that had Parnell and Gladstone been left to bring about a process of slow but sure movement towards Home Rule they might have succeeded without the need for partition – after all Parnell was himself a Protestant. Certainly the assassins did not achieve their objective – an immediate English retreat from Ireland. As the last words of the book *The Phoenix Park Murders*[13] put it:

> The men of sane vision on both sides, the men who believed in a new Ireland to be made by Irish men working in co-operation with English men, were given no chance, however slight, to work out their plans. That this was so, that the momentary glimpse of a harmonious future for Ireland so quickly vanished, was a result of the actions of the Irish National Invincibles and of the murders in Phoenix Park, a classic demonstration of the utter futility of assassination as a political weapon.

The population of Bosnia/Herzegovina was very mixed. Less than half were orthodox Serbs, a third were Moslems – Serbs and Turks – and a quarter were Roman Catholic Croats.[14] The Croats and the

Serbs had a longstanding dislike of each other. Unsurprisingly, the Serbs wished for union with Serbia, although comparatively few were fanatical about it. The Moslems wished to remain as they were, under Austria / Hungary.

As in Ireland, in the Balkans secret societies abounded. One such, 'Young Bosnia', was dedicated to Bosnian absorption into Serbia. It was closely involved with a Serb organization mainly comprising dissident army officers called 'Union or Death', more generally known as the Black Hand. A group of young Bosnian Serbs dedicated themselves to the assassination of a prominent Austrian dignitary involved in the government of Bosnia. They were led by Gavrilo Princip, a nineteen-year-old student. He was joined by Damilo Ilik, a 24-year-old school teacher turned journalist, Vaso Cubrilovic, Cvjetko Popovic, students of seventeen and eighteen respectively, two other friends, Cabranovic and Grabez, and a Moslem, Mohammed Mehmedbasic. Almost certainly without official sanction, the Black Hand were financed by the Serbian secret service under the control of Colonel Dragutin Dmitrievic, known as Apis. The original plan was to assassinate General Potiorek, the military governor of Sarajevo, but they learnt in March 1914 that Franz Ferdinand himself was coming to Sarajevo in June and their plan changed to the killing of the heir to the throne of Austria / Hungary.

To be a young student in the Balkans in 1914, and particularly so in Bosnia/Herzegovina, was, almost by definition, to be a revolutionary. Princip and his friends certainly did not think through the probable political consequences of what they were about to do. They were fed up with what they saw as the pusillanimity of their political leaders in the face of Austrian aggression against their country, and were determined to take violent action of some sort. Franz Ferdinand's arrival in Sarajevo was a perfect opportunity to show their mettle and strike a blow for freedom.

There is no doubt that Apis was in close touch with the assassins. He was responsible for training Princip, supplying him with arms, and was totally privy to the plan – indeed he may have inspired it.

The question which became of the utmost importance later, however, was whether the Serbian government itself was involved: indeed it was on this very matter that the fate of the world appeared to hang during the period after the assassination and before the world war began. There is no doubt, now, that it was not: indeed an enquiry set up by the Austrian Government after the event concluded that the Serbian Government was not involved and it is difficult to see any advantage to Serbia in Franz Ferdinand's assassination. Quite apart from anything else, the Serb army was totally unprepared for conflict. Apis probably instigated the assassination using the young student Nationalists in Serbia for his own purposes without the knowledge of his government or indeed of most of the leadership of the Black Hand. Indeed, as we have seen, the Serbian Prime Minister, Nicola Pasic, informed the Austrians through his ambassador there that there was a plan to murder Franz Ferdinand on his visit to Sarajevo. He would hardly have done so if it were he who was responsible for the plot. He was himself bitterly opposed to the Black Hand but did not have enough internal support to ban it or to arrest its members, many of which were army officers.

The assassination itself was a haphazard affair. A bomb was thrown at the Archduke's car by Cubrilovic. Franz Ferdinand was able to divert it on to the ground behind the car, where it exploded, wrecking the following vehicle and severely wounding Potiorek's adjutant. The car continued past Cabranovic, Popovic and Grabez, who all lost their nerve. The Archduke and his wife, acting with great courage, continued on their way to the City Hall where they received a welcome from a very chastened mayor. Franz Ferdinand responded with anger about his treatment. They then set off for lunch. However, the Archduke insisted on going to see the wounded adjutant and it was on their way to the hospital that, having taken the wrong turning, the car began to turn round, by an extraordinary coincidence, just where Princip was standing. He took out his revolver and fired two shots, one killing Franz Ferdinand and the other Sophie – a remarkable feat in the circumstances.

The events of the following month have been covered in hundreds of publications detailing the exact movements and activities of all the major participating figures almost minute by minute. It seems that very few, if any, of the leading figures really wanted war. Some Austrian politicians and soldiers probably did, seeing the assassination as an excuse to silence the 'cocky' Serbs once and for all. Franz Josef's attitude appears initially to have been wariness of war. But he was a very old man and his powers of resistance to the influential war party in Vienna were not great. The Kaiser, one minute posturing and aggressive, the next appalled by the results of his own actions, changed his mind constantly. The Serbs, the Russians, the French and, certainly, the British – whose foreign secretary, Grey, was only too well aware of the appalling consequences of conflict – were all intent on avoiding the holocaust if they possibly could.

The key moment came when the Kaiser gave his full support to whatever the Austrians decided, indeed at one stage urging them to attack Serbia.[15] The peace party in Austria/Hungary was outflanked and war became inevitable. The Austrians knew perfectly well that the Serbs had not instigated the assassination – indeed their own enquiry said so – but, nevertheless, an ultimatum was sent to Serbia detailing a number of actions the Serbs would have to take in order to avoid war, which any self-respecting government would have to reject. However, the Serbs accepted nearly all of these, except one which they insisted should be sent to the International Court of Justice for a decision. This was not good enough for the Austrians, who declared war on Serbia. The Russians began to mobilize, followed by the Germans and the French. The speed of mobilization then became a major factor in the developing crisis. The Germans had adopted a plan by a previous Commander-in-Chief, von Schlieffen, which called for a rapid invasion of France via Belgium in order to attain a victory within forty days; the German army could then turn to meet and defeat the Russians, whose mobilization, given the vast size of the country, would take much longer. The fact that Prussia had with

Britain been a signatory to the Treaty of London of 1832, guaranteeing Belgium independence, was ignored. The consequent German invasion of Luxembourg and Belgium triggered the entry of Britain, which declared war on Germany. The stage was therefore set for general war.

The question now inevitably arises as to whether it was the assassination of Franz Ferdinand which brought about war or whether a major European conflict was inevitable and the assassination was merely the particular event which started it off. By its very nature this question is impossible to answer. However, it is reasonable to argue, and many do, including the author of this book, that the fears, antagonisms, prejudices and deep-rooted jealousies in Europe at that time would inevitably have resulted in armed conflict sooner or later. Whatever the truth of this, it is certain that, not having been properly consulted in any way, the peoples of Europe greeted the onset of war with euphoria. The streets of London, Berlin, Vienna and St Petersburg were thronged with patriotic citizens delighted at the onset of war; millions flocked to the colours, and to death.

To return to the comparison between the assassinations of Archduke Franz Ferdinand and Lord Frederick Cavendish, in neither case did the assassins achieve their aims. As we have seen, if anything the Phoenix Park murders delayed rather than hastened Home Rule for Ireland and indeed might perhaps have prevented the eventual achievement of a united Ireland. As for Sarajevo, the Serbian extremists were rewarded not by a greater Serbia, including Bosnia/Herzegovina, but by the invasion and occupation of their country by Austria/Hungary.

Defeat of the central powers in 1918, followed by the emergence of a Serbian dominated Yugoslavia, may indeed have pleased those who supported Princip's action at the time if they were still alive. But the conspirators certainly did not envisage a general war, with something like nine million deaths, in order to achieve it. Furthermore, the Serbian domination of its neighbours has not survived. At the time of writing, Bosnia remains detached from its neighbour Serbia and this particular story is very far from reaching its end. Indeed the future of Kosovo is, tragically, obscure.

NOTES

1. R. Kee, *Ireland*, Macdonald, London, 1980, p. 101.
2. Ibid., p. 54.
3. R. Jenkins, *Gladstone*, Macmillan, London, 1995, p. 474.
4. T.H. Corfe, *The Phoenix Park Murders*, Hodder and Stoughton, London, 1968, p. 128.
5. Ibid., p. 150.
6. As quoted in Lady Frederick Cavendish's Diary, 3 May 1882, Murray, London, 1921.
7. The Seventh Duke of Devonshire's Diary, 2 May 1882, Chatsworth Archives.
8. E. Crankshaw, *The Fall of the House of Hapsburg*, Longman, London, 1963, p. 162.
9. M. Gilbert, *A History of the Twentieth Century, 1900–33*, HarperCollins, London 1997, p. 218.
10. Quoted in Seton-Watson, *Sarajevo*, Hutchinson, London, 1926, p. 64.
11. Corfe, *Phoenix Park*, p. 145.
12. The Seventh Duke of Devonshire's Diary, 12 May 1882, Chatsworth Archives.
13. Corfe, *Phoenix Park*, p. 226.
14. Crankshaw, *The House of Hapsburg*, p. 380.
15. It is now accepted by many historians that Germany, and in particular the Kaiser, was largely responsible for the First World War. This had been asserted in Article 231 of the Treaty of Versailles, which read:

> that Germany alone among the nations was prepared for a Great War; that Germany, the only disturber of peace for decades, had prepared a war of aggression and conquest; that Germany had deliberately unchained this war in 1914 in order to obtain 'predominance in Europe', and to carry out her 'plans for universal domination'; – whereas the allies only desired 'to preserve their liberty'.

However, in a remarkable document, 'An Appeal to British Fair Play', in 1924, signed by no fewer than 120 leading German academics, politicians, journalists, clergymen, industrialists and writers (including Thomas Mann), this thesis is vehemently disputed, arguing that the responsibility for the slaughter was far more widely spread.

CHAPTER 5

TSAR ALEXANDER II /
ABRAHAM LINCOLN

The history of every country is, of course, unique. But, somehow, the history of Russia seems to be 'more unique' than others. Cut off from the rest of the world for centuries until Peter the Great forced it, reluctantly and often against its better judgement, into the European orbit, it nevertheless retained much of its obscurantist and feudal way of life until late in the nineteenth century. Only in the United States, surprisingly in view of its origin as a refuge for the 'huddled masses' across the ocean, was there anything approaching the almost unbelievable contrast in human conditions that existed in Russia. It is true that the Southern estate owners lived in luxury, but it was of a different order to the glittering and sophisticated opulence of St Petersburg. But in one respect the two regimes were the same: slavery/serfdom existed in both. Two men were responsible for changing the laws of their country in order to outlaw this state of affairs where one man could own another – and his wife and children – Tsar Alexander II in Russia and Abraham Lincoln in the United States. Although in both cases those in perpetual servitude became free, in both cases also the legal and other changes left a most unsatisfactory state of affairs with a great deal remaining to be done before the achievement of any kind of equality before the law, let alone in opportunity and way of life. But a start was made in both countries in the face of enormous difficulty. In the United States there was a civil war: in Russia there was great determination in the face of powerful and continuing opposition. In both, too, the originators of freedom were assassinated.

In 1855 when Alexander II became Tsar, of the 60 million inhabitants of European Russia there were some 50 million peasants. Nine-tenths of the people lived in the villages. The roads were appalling and there were only 650 miles of railway. In 1859 10.7 million male serfs lived on land belonging to the hereditary nobility and 12.8 million lived on state-owned land.[1] The serfs were allowed to cultivate a part of the estate where they lived for their own use, but had to pay for this either in labour or in cash: the landlord could decide which. There were about 1.5 million house serfs who worked directly for the landowners. The owner had almost total control over his serfs. For any offence committed against him the owner could, by law, exert a punishment not exceeding forty lashes with a birch or fifteen blows with a stick. Flogging was a permanent part of life. But far worse than this, the owner could present any serf to the authorities either for transportation to Siberia or as a recruit for the army. This latter fate entailed a period of twenty-five years' service in the hardest of conditions, with flogging almost to death a common punishment. Her husband having joined the army, a recruit's wife was left to cope on her own and was legally allowed to remarry after three years. The threat of being sent to join the army must have been enough to bring even the most recalcitrant of peasants to order. Furthermore, no serf could marry without the owner's consent and, if the owner wished, he or she had to marry the person selected by him. On the other hand, many, perhaps most, landowners may well have been kind to their serfs and behaved properly towards them – but there were undoubtedly some who were not, and the constant peasant revolts made this clear.

Russia was beset by bureaucracy. There were over half a million officials of one sort or another and many were corrupt. As in some Third World countries today, the officials were badly paid and as a result corruption was endemic. The law was equally corrupt: the law courts were staffed by officials who were wide open to bribery. Proceedings were secret; lawsuits dragged on for years; there were no juries.

Discussion of these abuses was forbidden by the censors. Nicholas I, Alexander II's father, came to the throne of this extraordinary country in 1825. His father, Paul I, had been murdered. His elder brother, Constantine, had refused the crown. Nicholas's accession was marked by a revolt by over a hundred young members of the nobility with support by some army units. However, this was easily quelled. Five of the so-called Decembrists were hanged and the rest sent to lifelong penal servitude in Siberia (later released by Alexander II). The net result of the revolt was to confirm Nicholas I in his view that the only way to govern Russia was by complete autocracy. Although initially he made some moves thought to show a more liberal attitude, this did not last long and he reverted to total absolutism. For instance, no one was allowed to smoke, even in the street, because he disliked the smell of tobacco. Only guards officers were allowed to wear moustaches but these had to be black, dyed if necessary, because this was what he preferred. Once he dismissed the head of a school because pupils in the sickbay had stared at him out of the window with unshaven faces.[2]

While the corruption and gross maladministration of the state persisted, the glitter and absurd opulence of life for the nobility in St Petersburg continued. The Emperor gave a ball every Monday night, Nicholas, a man of great personal charm, presiding with military precision. Furthermore, the wedding of the heir apparent, Prince Alexander, was celebrated by a fancy-dress ball at the Winter Palace attended by many thousands of people.

Nicholas maintained a tight grip on the country imposed by the Secret Service, with universities under police supervision, foreign travel prohibited, public meetings banned and intellectuals subjected to arbitrary imprisonment and exile. Somewhat paradoxically, he did attempt to free the serfs. However, in the face of powerful opposition by the nobility no progress was made. In pursuit of an exit into the Mediterranean through Constantinople he found himself embroiled in the Crimean War, a disastrous foray as far as Russia was concerned as the shortcomings of the Russian military supply system became apparent to all. Nicholas died of a chill just before the fall of Sebastopol, the Russian naval base on the Crimean peninsula, in 1855.

Alexander II came to the throne amid widespread hope that the new Tsar would make massive changes for the better. These hopes were not to be disappointed, at least in the early stages of his reign. His first problem was the war in the Crimea. The Russian army had been shown to be even more incompetent than its enemies, the British and French, certainly as far as its lines of communication were concerned. France under Napoleon III was fed up with the continuing struggle. Austria, too, although not itself involved, wished for peace. Only England wished to continue the fight to obtain total victory. Alexander favoured peace and, in spite of the comparatively harsh terms on offer, the peace was signed in Paris on 30 March 1856.

Alexander then concentrated on bringing in a whole series of reforms with the emancipation of the serfs as the most famous, although in practice, perhaps, not the most important. He set up a series of commissions and committees in an attempt to involve the landowners themselves in the process. He showed remarkable persistence and courage in continuing against great obstruction. Although he had a number of allies both in his own family and among some of the nobility, it took him four years to achieve his aim. It was not a simple matter. Freedom for the serfs was one thing, but how were they to exist thereafter? Should they be given all the land they cultivated without any compensation for the owners? If so, what would the owners live on? If compensation was to be paid, who was to pay it? Eventually compromises were arrived at whereby, in general, the serfs received their own homesteads and about half of the land on which they worked; for this they would pay compensation over a series of years. The whole extremely complex document, containing sixteen Acts with over a thousand sections, was enacted and signed by the Tsar on 3 March 1861. It really was a massive achievement by Alexander. He was in truth the protector and champion of the serfs against a high proportion of the landowners, a 'little father' to the peasants.

However, there remained a whole series of other reforms which were necessary in order to achieve anything approaching a fair system of government in Russia, and Alexander began to implement some of them. Censorship was vastly toned down, universities were opened up to all and allowed to develop without police supervision, the whole legal system was overhauled, trials were open to the public, juries were established for criminal cases, the judiciary was separated from the executive, elected local government was instituted with powers over a whole range of matters including education, roads, hospitals and food, travel abroad was permitted and, perhaps most important, conscription was introduced, with a ballot system whereby all classes had an equal chance of being called up. New banks were established all over Russia and a system of credit was instituted whereby new businesses could be started up, coinciding, particularly in the south of the country, with the emigration of many ex-serfs to the towns in search of work. The whole financial system was overhauled and proper budgeting was introduced. The transformation and liberalization of the governmental system in Russia was, in theory, and indeed to a considerable extent in practice, almost total.

However, and this was the tragedy of Russian history in the nineteenth century, although reform had in many areas improved the lives of millions, it also led to greater unrest and thence to violence. The reactionary view that 'the more they had the more they wanted' was true. The new freedom of thought in the universities and the students who returned from abroad hot with revolutionary ideas resulted in an atmosphere of revolution which pervaded intellectual Russia. Echoes of the French Revolution and the more recent series of European upheavals in 1848, together with the writings in London of the famous Russian, Herzen, and others, pervaded the atmosphere. Two attempts were made on Alexander's life and, consequently, he began to retract some of his reforms and to revert to some repressive policies. He had appalling problems in Poland, then a Russian province, with its extreme, and understandable, nationalist yearnings. As he saw it, Poland needed a firm hand, which in the event entailed much bloodshed and cruelty. However, he managed, to deal with similar problems in Finland, also then a part of Russia, without bloodshed and that country remained comparatively free from Russian interference.

Not surprisingly, the students were not disposed even to attempt to understand Alexander's difficulties. After emancipation, many of the peasants were, in practice, not much better off, if at all, than they had been as serfs and there was great unrest. Many students thought that the answer to Russia's problems was to 'go to the peasants' and try to inculcate in them the revolutionary ideas they had learnt in Europe. This so-called 'Narodnik' movement was a dismal failure. The peasants did not understand what they were being told and, in some cases, handed the students over to the authorities for punishment.

A further complicating factor in the Russian scene at the time was the enmity between the 'Westerners' and the 'Slavophiles', the former wishing to adopt a Western European ethos while the latter believed in establishing a separate Slav identity, perhaps involving a new Pan/Slav Empire to include all European Slavs.

On top of all this, Alexander had great personal problems. In 1839, when twenty years old, he had toured Europe in search of a suitable wife and had fallen hopelessly in love with the fifteen-year-old Princess Marie, the daughter of Prince Alexander of Hesse – and she with him. But there was a problem. Marie was rumoured, probably correctly, to be illegitimate and Alexander's father, the Tsar, forbade the engagement, ordering his son to return to Russia immediately. However, Alexander showed the same determination he was later to demonstrate in his liberation of the serfs. He refused to back down and the Tsar eventually relented, the marriage taking place in the spring of 1841. Marie shared Alexander's liberal views and was a constant companion and wife to him, bearing no fewer than six sons and a daughter. However, the Romanovs had a reputation for philandering, and he was no exception. In 1864, when forty-six, he fell deeply in love with an eighteen-year-old girl, Princess Catherine Dolgoruka. Marie came to accept the situation, but some of her children and other courtiers did not, particularly when Alexander, fearful for his mistress's life, moved her into a suite of rooms in his palace. When Princess Marie died, Alexander insisted on marrying his mistress forty days after his wife's death, an event which caused great scandal and even hatred. In spite of the contentment he received from his affair with Catherine, who bore him three children, towards the end of his life Alexander was a deeply unhappy man on personal as well as political grounds.

Although Alexander had persisted with his internal reforms, his powers were not unlimited, particularly on overseas affairs. As was the case internally, he sought peace and stability abroad, but was unable to achieve it. Against his will, the military establishment extended the Russian Empire in central and east Asia by military means, and the Slavophiles forced him into another war with Turkey over the status of Bulgaria, Bosnia and Herzegovina. An armistice was agreed on 31 January 1878, followed by the Treaty of San Stephano under which the three territories became autonomous while still in theory under Turkish suzerainty.

As we have already seen, the students' attempt to stir the peasants into revolution had failed. A new secret revolutionary society – 'Land and Liberty' – was formed, based in St Petersburg, with a well-organized and widespread structure. Its object was to bring about an economic revolution from below by militant methods,[3] but its activities led to more repression. The vicious circle that Alexander had attempted to break was, tragically, resumed. Education was restricted by laws insisting on the teaching of Latin and Greek in schools at the expense of other, more liberal studies. Censorship was reintroduced and students studying abroad were made to return to Russia. This latter move was particularly self-defeating since revolutionary ideas inevitably became more widespread as a result. An attempt was made on the Tsar's life, when a train in which he was scheduled to travel was blown up on 1 December 1879: he was not on it.

Land and Liberty was divided between those who advocated terrorist methods, following the exhortations of the anarchist Bakunin (mentioned in the Introduction), and those believing in peaceful propaganda. In the spring of 1879 Land and Liberty was dissolved, splitting into two – 'Black Partition' and 'People's Will', favouring peaceful propaganda and terrorism respectively.[4] On 7 September 1879 the latter condemned Alexander to death.

Of all the major figures in the United States since the death of George Washington, Abraham Lincoln stands supreme. His fame rests not so much on his achievements – his rise from log cabin to the White House, victor in the civil war, the emancipator of the slaves, the matchless power of his oratory – as it does on his character. He was honest almost to a fault, forgiving, selfless, determined, at once self-confident but with a pervading humility and, its companion, an ever-present sense of humour.

His qualities were well summed up after a speech in New York in 1860 in which he made the simple point that slavery was wrong and that it was idle to seek for common ground with men who said it was right. It was his first appearance before a sophisticated intellectual eastern audience and was a major factor in his being adopted by the new Republican Party as their presidential candidate. One of his audience, a prominent New York lawyer, a Mr Rufus Choate, had a vivid recollection of that evening:

He appeared in every sense of the word like one of the plain people among whom he loved to be counted. At first sight there was nothing impressive or imposing about him; his clothes hung awkwardly on his giant frame; his face was of a dark pallor without the slightest tinge of colour; his seamed and rugged features bore the furrows of hardship and struggle; his deep set eyes looked sad and anxious. His countenance in repose gave little evidence of the brilliant power which raised him from the lowest to the highest station among his countrymen: as he talked to me before the meeting he seemed ill at ease. But when he spoke, he was transformed; his eye kindled, his voice rang, his face shone and seemed to light up the whole assembly. For an hour and a half he held his audience in the hollow of his hand. His style of speech and manner of delivery were severely simple. What Lowell called 'the grand simplicities of the Bible', with which he was so familiar, were reflected in his discourse. . . . It was marvellous to see how this untutored man, by mere self-discipline and the chastening of his own spirit, had outgrown all meretricious arts, and found his way to the grandeur and strength of absolute simplicity.[5]

Abraham Lincoln's father, Thomas, was the third son of a pioneer who had moved to Kentucky from Virginia and become a comparatively rich and well-respected figure with about six thousand acres of land in the richest area of the state. When he was killed by Indians, his eldest son inherited everything under the primogeniture rules then applying and Thomas was left to fend for himself. He worked hard as a labourer and carpenter and eventually bought his first farm. He then moved to Knob Creek where, in 1809, his son Abraham was born. He had married Nancy Hanks, a frontierswoman who, Lincoln later said, was the illegitimate daughter of a Virginian gentleman. It may well be true that Abraham's brilliant intellectual gifts came from this liaison. If heredity played a part in this, they were unlikely to have sprung from his father.

Nancy died when Abraham was eight years old. After a year Thomas married again, Sarah Johnston, a widow. She was illiterate, but Abraham adored her and looked up to her for the rest of his life. Thomas moved from farm to farm with his family until, at the age of twenty-one, Abraham started on his own independent life, initially at New Salem in Illinois. Abraham had lived the hard life of a son of a pioneer, helping in cutting down trees, erecting fences, clearing the land and generally taking his full share of the necessary chores. Two attempts were made to send him to school, where he learnt the alphabet, a little reading and writing and some arithmetic, but his formal education totalled just under one year, remarkable indeed for a future President.

Abraham was very tall and strong, ungainly but affable and intelligent beyond his station. He tried a number of different careers

The death of Julius Caesar. (Photo: AKG London)

Thomas à Becket, murdered in Canterbury Cathedral, 1170. (Photo: AKG London)

Gandhi arriving at No. 10 Downing Street, for a meeting with Ramsay Macdonald, 1931. (*Illustrated London News*)

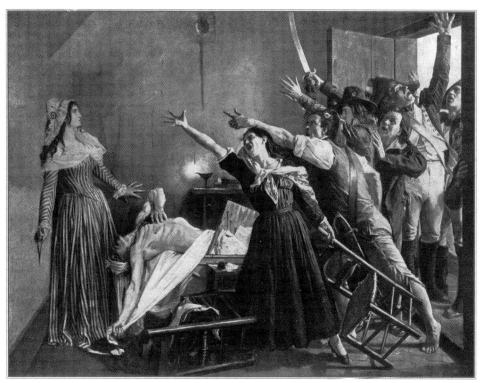

The murder, by Charlotte Corday, of Jean Paul Marat, 1793. (Photo: AKG London)

Leon Trotsky, *c.* 1920. (*Illustrated London News*)

Lord Frederick Charles Cavendish, Chief Secretary for Ireland, 1882. (Private Collection/Bridgeman Art Library)

Photographed a few minutes before their deaths, the Archduke Franz Ferdinand and his wife in Sarajevo, 1914. (*Illustrated London News*)

Tsar Alexander II. (Private Collection/
Ken Welsh/Bridgeman Art Library)

Abraham Lincoln, 1863, President
of America from 1861 to 1865.
(*Illustrated London News*)

Sir Henry Wilson. (National Portrait Gallery, London)

Michael Collins, Irish soldier and nationalist politician in the uniform of the Irish Free State, 1922. (Hulton Getty)

Anwar Sadat, President of Egypt, 1977. (Photo: AKG, London)

The Israeli Premier, Yitzhak Rabin, 1974. (Hulton Getty)

Martin Luther King's 'Dream Speech', 1963. (Hulton Getty)

Malcolm X.

– carpenter, riverboat man, store clerk, soldier, merchant, postmaster, blacksmith and surveyor – but, not surprisingly, was unhappy with all of them and he eventually decided to become a lawyer. He also began to have political ambitions and managed to get himself elected to the Illinois State Legislature at the second attempt, appearing in the State House at the capital, Vandalia, for the first time on 8 December 1834. He borrowed two hundred dollars and spent sixty of them to buy his first suit for the occasion. He was an amusing, convivial companion, full of funny stories and quips, and he was a popular figure both in New Salem and in the legislature. He studied hard for the law and began to make a statewide political impact. He was a Whig, a minority party in the state which was largely Democratic. There were indeed some differences between the parties – the Whigs were in favour of more federal intervention than were the Democrats – but personality was more important than policy in the United States in those days (as perhaps now?).

Lincoln was re-elected on three occasions (elections were held every two years). The state capital was moved to Springfield, a small town of 1,500 inhabitants, and Lincoln, still a very young man with alternating moods of deep depression and boundless optimism, moved there. He was shy with women, and had a sad love affair with a woman who died. But then he married Mary Owen, the daughter of a well-to-do Kentucky farmer. During one of his hiccups on the way to the marriage he delivered himself of the quip: 'I have now come to the conclusion never again to think of marrying; and for this reason: I can never be satisfied with anyone who would be blockhead enough to have me.' (This was later plagiarized by Groucho Marx, talking of a club rather than marriage.)

Handsome, often gay (in the original sense!), intelligent but incurably moody and sometimes very difficult, Mary Owen played a major role in his life thereafter, eventually suffering ten long hours of agony as Abraham died after the fatal shot in the theatre.

Lincoln became a partner of a leading lawyer in Springfield and began to make his way in the law, working very hard and beginning to gain a reputation for his sagacity, energy and honesty which was to stand him in good stead as he began to rise up the political ladder. He became the leader of the Whigs in the Illinois State Legislature until, feeling that there were no new worlds to conquer in that assembly, he did not seek re-election in 1842.

Lincoln's eyes were now on Congress, and he was elected as a Whig to the House of Representatives in 1847. His two years there were not notable. He did speak against the war with Mexico, an inglorious chapter in American history whereby the United States acquired California and all the territories belonging to Mexico to the east of it. The Whig policy, to which Lincoln adhered, was to vote for supplies but to protest against President Polk's action in declaring a war which, they said, had no legal or moral justification. Lincoln became unpopular in his home state because of his stance, which was attacked as treachery to the soldiers already fighting. Lincoln was not politically naive, even at that stage: he knew perfectly well that his actions might well prevent him being reselected as Whig candidate, but regarded it as absurd to expect him to 'tell a lie' on this or any other matter. Partially because of this he was not reselected. He was offered the governorship of Oregon Territory but, spurred on by his wife who saw a glittering political career in front of him, he turned down this, not very prestigious post. He reverted to his legal practice, working very hard but not turning his back on the political scene.

In the middle of the nineteenth century in the United States slavery was fast becoming a predominant issue. To our modern eyes it is a simple matter, but it certainly was not in those days in the United States. Almost all Americans believed that the forcible abduction of blacks from Africa, followed by their shipping over the Atlantic Ocean to the United States, was wrong. Indeed, this had been abolished by federal law in 1808, the penalty for slave traders being death by hanging. (Lincoln, when President, was to refuse to commute the death penalty for Nathaniel Gordon, the first American slave trader to be convicted and hanged).[6]

The question was, what was to be done with the slaves who were already in the United States? The cotton trade, as it had developed in the South, was largely dependent on slave labour. Slavery was legal in the southern states, but illegal in most of the North. How about the slaves who escaped from the South and went to the North? Were they to be forcibly repatriated? They were subject to state laws in the southern states which had voluntarily joined the Union on the understanding that their laws were to be respected. Was the North to renege on its commitment to observe southern state laws? How about federal territories such as the District of Columbia (Washington) and any new territory which might adhere to the Union? Were they to adhere to any federal law which might be made on this matter, or were they to be allowed to make up their own minds? The political structure was not designed to cope with these problems.

There were those in the South who abhorred slavery and those in the North who supported it, and many people were not convinced one way or the other. There were many abuses of slaves in the South. Slave families were split up on the death or bankruptcy of their owners, and men and women were sold like cattle. On the other hand many owners behaved in an exemplary fashion to those slaves whom they owned, impressing even some of those Europeans who visited the southern states expecting, and sometimes determined, to see nothing but unhappy degradation.

The Whig Party attempted to straddle these differences by avoiding adherence to any principle one way or the other. Clearly this was impossible in the long term and the Whigs were replaced in 1854 by the Republican Party which Lincoln joined soon after its foundation. The Republican Party was composed of a majority of the former Whigs in the North and many northern Democrats who had deserted their former party.

The Republicans had a simple policy on slavery: there should be no extension of it in the present or future territories of the United States. Democratic policy, on the other hand, was to hand those decisions to the people of the territories themselves. Neither party was in favour of abolition by federal law in the existing slave states of the Union. Slavery was a major issue in the Presidential election of 1856 – the first to be fought by the Republican Party. Buchanan, the Democratic Party candidate, was elected, but the Republican Party did surprisingly well. They were, however, shattered by a ruling of the Supreme Court of the United States, known as the Dred Scott case, to the effect that the exclusion by federal law of slavery from any part of the federal territories, including the District of Columbia, was unconstitutional.

Lincoln now decided to try for a seat in the Senate. He was selected and ran as Republican candidate for Illinois, his opponent being Stephen Douglas, a highly experienced, well-known and respected figure in the Democratic Party. A series of seven public debates was held between the two men, receiving great publicity. The debate centred on Douglas's sponsorship of the Kansas/ Nebraska Act which allowed the settlers in the territories themselves to decide for or against the admission of slavery. Lincoln, while refusing to support the abolitionists in their aim of abolishing slavery throughout the United States, argued passionately against an extension of what he saw as a wholly evil practice. In one of his major speeches he said:

> I think . . . that it is wrong in its direct effect, letting slavery into Kansas and Nebraska – and wrong in its prospective principle, allowing it to spread to every part of the wide world, where men can be found inclined to take it. . . . This declared indifference, but as I must think, covert real zeal for the spread of slavery, I cannot but hate. I hate it because of the monstrous injustice of slavery itself. I hate it because it enables the enemies of free institutions, with plausibility, to taunt us as hypocrites – causes the real friends of freedom to doubt our sincerity and especially because it forces so many really good men amongst ourselves into an open war with the very fundamental principles of civil liberty – criticizing the Declaration of Independence and insisting that there is no right principle of action but self interest.

He went on, with typical moderation:

> Let me say I think I have no prejudice against the southern
> people. They are just what we would be in their situation. If
> slavery did not now exist amongst them, they would not
> introduce it. If it did now exist amongst us, we should not
> instantly give it up. This I believe of the masses North and
> South. Doubtless there are individuals, on both sides, who
> would not hold slaves under any circumstances; and others who
> would gladly introduce slavery anew if it were out of existence.
> We know that some southern men do free their slaves, go North
> and become tip top abolitionists; while some northern ones go
> South and become most cruel slave masters. When southern
> people tell us they are no more responsible for the origin of
> slavery than we, I acknowledge the fact. When it is said that
> the institution exists and that it is very difficult to get rid of it
> in any satisfactory way I can understand and appreciate the
> same. I surely will not blame them for not doing what I should
> not know how to do myself. If all earthly power were given me,
> I should not know what to do as to the existing institution. . . .
> When they remind us of their constitutional rights,
> I acknowledge them, not grudgingly, but fully and fairly; and
> I would give them any legislation for the reclaiming of their
> fugitives which should not . . . be more likely to carry a free
> man into slavery than our ordinary criminal laws are to hang an
> innocent one. Equal justice to the South, it is said, requires us
> to consent to the extending of slavery to new countries. That is
> to say, inasmuch as you do not object to my taking my hog to
> Nebraska, therefore I must not object to you taking your slave.
> Now I admit that this is perfectly logical if there is no
> difference between hogs and Negroes. . . . The doctrine of self-
> government is right — absolutely and eternally right — but it
> has no just application as here attempted or perhaps I should
> rather say that whether it has such application depends on
> whether a Negro is not or is a man. If he is not a man, why in

that case he who is a man may, as a matter of self-government, do just as he pleases with him, but, if the Negro is a man, is it not to that extent a total destruction of self-government to say that he too should not govern himself? If the Negro is a man, why then my ancient faith teaches me that 'All men are created equal' and that there can be no moral right in connection with one man's making a slave of another. . . . Our Declaration of Independence says – 'We hold these truths to be self-evident: that all men are created equal; that they are endowed by their creator with certain inalienable rights; that among these are life, liberty and the pursuit of happiness.'[7]

This speech has been quoted at some length because it exemplifies many of Lincoln's qualities which led him to his great achievements and thence to his assassination – his eloquence, his rigorous self-examination and honesty, his refusal to compromise on his principles and his essential humility. In the event, in spite of Lincoln obtaining a majority of the state votes, Douglas was elected because of the vagaries of the electoral system of the time. However, Lincoln's stock was rising fast.

By now Lincoln had been bitten by the political bug and was permanently addicted to it. Although continuing to work hard at his legal practice, he made a number of speeches across the United States including his oration in New York in February 1860 already mentioned on page 111. He was a stickler for the law. In October 1859 John Brown, at the head of a large party of abolitionists and Negroes, invaded the slave states and seized the federal arsenal at Harper's Ferry in Virginia. He was soon defeated by federal troops under Robert E. Lee (on his last engagement before changing allegiance to the Confederacy), captured, condemned to death and hanged (in fact for murdering sentries at the arsenal). In spite of his vehement views on slavery, Lincoln's reaction was unequivocal. He regarded lawlessness and slavery as twin evils:

That affair [John Brown's raid], in its philosophy, corresponds with the many attempts related in history at the assassination of kings and emperors. An enthusiast broods over the oppression of a people till he fancies himself commissioned by Heaven to liberate them. He ventures the attempt, which ends in little else than his own execution.

The similarity to his own assassination is uncanny.

Lincoln's views of the Negroes, as Afro-Americans were called in those days, may be somewhat bizarre to us now. Although accepting the Declaration of Independence, with its strange and clearly inaccurate announcement that 'all men are created equal', he certainly did think that some were more equal than others. He said, 'There is a natural distrust in the minds of nearly all white people at the idea of an indiscriminate amalgamation of the white and black men.'[8] He by no means took it for granted that equality in political power must necessarily and properly follow upon emancipation of the slaves. He toyed with the idea of black colonization – a return of the Negroes to Africa. During one of his debates with Douglas he had made it clear that he felt the blacks could never be the moral or intellectual equals of whites.[9] Later, when President, on 14 August 1862 he addressed a deputation of free blacks in the following terms:

> You and we are different races. We have between us a broader difference than exists between almost any other two races. Whether it is right or wrong I need not discuss, but this physical difference is a great disadvantage to us both, as I think your race suffer very greatly, many of them by living among us, while ours suffer from your presence. In a word we suffer on each side. If this is admitted, it affords a reason at least why we should be separated. . . . Even when you cease to be slaves, you are yet far removed from being placed on an equality with the white race. . . . Go where you are treated the best, and the ban is still upon you. It is better for us both, therefore, to be separated. . . .

Surprisingly perhaps, there are clear similarities in these words to the views of Hendrik Verwoerd, which we will discuss in a later chapter.

Lincoln was chosen as Republican Presidential candidate for the 1860 election. 'I must in candour say I do not think myself fit for the Presidency', he wrote to the editor of the *Rock Island Register* and to other of his supporters.[10] He had no administrative experience of any sort, he had never been a state governor or even a mayor, he had only served one less-than-successful term in the House of Representatives and in the last ten years he had held no public office. On the other hand, unlike many of his competitors for the Republican nomination he had nothing against him, while his character and brilliant oratory were beginning to be felt across the land. There were five candidates and five hundred delegates at the Republican Convention, which was held at Chicago in Lincoln's home state. During the campaign Lincoln had travelled the most widely of any of the candidates (four thousand miles and twenty-three speeches in 1859). He won on the fourth ballot, defeating William Seward, the front runner from New York, after doing a deal with Simon Cameron of Pennsylvania by promising him the Treasury Department in return for his support. Horse trading in American politics has a long pedigree!

The Democratic Party was hopelessly split on the issue of slavery and in fact fielded two candidates – Douglas (the North) and Breckenridge (the South) – thus in practice forfeiting power for the next twenty-four years. There was a fourth candidate, John Bell of Tennessee, who represented the old Whigs and stood for the constitution of the country, the union of the states and the enforcement of the law – not a very arresting platform. With this plethora of candidates, on 6 November 1860, Lincoln, who as was the custom of the time played no personal part in the election, was elected on 40 per cent of the vote – an example of the vagaries of the electoral system. If the Democratic Party had been united they would undoubtedly have won the Presidential election, and the history of the United States might well have been very different.

Lincoln's election gave rise to immediate concern amounting in some cases even to panic in the South. Shortly after his victory, one Virginian called him 'a cross between a sandhill crane and an

Andalusian jackass – vain, weak, puerile, hypocritical, without manners, without moral grace'.[11] In spite of his repeated promises that he would not interfere with the existing southern laws on slavery, the southern states felt that by his policy of preventing the extension of slavery, Lincoln was inserting the thin end of a wedge which would eventually destroy the system throughout the United States. To be fair, Lincoln agreed with this, believing that the whole concept of slavery would die a natural death if it was halted in its tracks. Whereas an overwhelming majority of southern whites thought that, given the circumstances of the time, slavery was a perfectly reasonable way of life, nearly all northerners thought it was evil and had no moral justification.

The other issue was, of course, that of the Union. The North believed profoundly that, once in the Union, states could not be allowed to secede. The South, as a whole, believed that, just as they had themselves decided to join, they could themselves leave if they wished to. Lincoln believed deeply in the sacred nature of the Union which he had sworn to uphold. He never gave any hint that he might waver in that view. Indeed, when President, he said, 'My paramount object in this struggle is to save the Union, and is not either to save or destroy slavery. If I could save the Union without freeing any slave I would do it; and if I could save it by freeing all the slaves I would do it; and if I could save it by freeing some and by leaving others alone I would also do that.' It must also be said that, as well as the differences over slavery and the Union, many southern leaders saw themselves as aristocratic gentlemen as opposed to the rough, tough, vulgar North. The election of Lincoln, the archetypal backwoodsman as President, merely confirmed them in that view.

It was not only the slave owners who favoured slavery. There were some 6 million southern whites who had no direct interest in slavery: they owned no slaves. There were already 262,000 freed slaves in the South and the poor whites were afraid that emancipation would lead to many more blacks seeking their jobs. Many southerners, too, thought that the North's moral indignation about the institution of slavery was spurious and based on mean economic motives. As Jefferson Davis, the Confederate President, put it: 'You . . . are not interested in slavery at all . . . you desire to weaken the political power of the southern states. Because you want by an unjust system of legislation to promote the industry of the north-east states, at the expense of the people of the South and their industry.'[12]

The state of South Carolina started the rot. Four days after the Presidential election, its legislature convened a specific convention to decide on the question of secession. On 20 December the convention passed a formal 'ordinance of secession'. Six other southern states quickly followed. In the end there were eleven Confederate States with a population of 5,449,467 whites and 3,521,111 slaves. Nearly 1 million of the white males served in the Confederate army, of whom 300,000 were casualties – an incredibly high ratio. There were nineteen Union States with a population of 18,936,579 and four border states with 2,589,533 plus 429,401 then slaves, over 100,000 of whom served in the Union army, which numbered 1,600,000. During the war nearly 1 million further immigrants arrived in the North, of whom 400,000 served in the Union army.[13]

There can have been few leaders in any country who have been faced, immediately after being elected, with such an appalling problem. When South Carolina announced its secession Lincoln had hardly chosen his cabinet, let alone stamped his authority on Congress and the nation. Under the American system, although elected he did not actually become President until 4 March 1861. There were those who urged him to take forceful military action as soon as he assumed power in spite of the fact that his military resources were very limited, and there were those who opposed any such initiative which would certainly lead to civil war. Throughout his Presidency Lincoln was a cautious man. He always waited to see clearly what was developing, what support he had and what the result of any definite action would be before he took it. The seceding states of the South had convened a congress on 4 February, and the new Confederacy had decided to take over the military forts and other federal properties within its boundaries. The issue narrowed to that of Fort Sumter which was besieged by Confederate forces. Should it be evacuated or relieved by an expeditionary force of some kind? Eventually, after his inauguration, Lincoln decided with typical caution not to do either, but to send provisions to the garrison, telling the Governor of South Carolina that if this was unopposed no further action would be taken. Lincoln was determined to avoid any charge of provocation and wished that, if there was to be a civil war, it would be clear to all that the originator of this calamity would be the South and not the North. In the event, the Confederates opened fire on Fort Sumter on 13 April 1861 and the war was started.

It would be tedious to cover the course of the civil war in detail here. As so often seems to be the case, both sides thought the war would be over very quickly. In fact it lasted a tragic four years. The original seven states seceding – South Carolina, Mississippi, Florida, Alabama, Georgia, Louisiana and Texas – were followed, after Lincoln's inauguration, by the bulk of Virginia, North Carolina, Tennessee and Arkansas. Maryland, Kentucky and Delaware were in some doubt but eventually decided to stay with the Union.

On taking over as President, as well as attempting to cope with the problems of secession, Lincoln found himself besieged by seekers after office. The American system adopted since the early days of the Union meant that every official post from cabinet minister to postmaster was up for grabs when the Presidency changed (there was no permanent trained civil service to give continuity). Quite apart from the tradition that the President should be available to see anyone wanting to see him, he found himself besieged by those who expected rewards for their efforts to help him in his campaign and many others.

There was clearly an immediate need for large numbers of soldiers and all the accoutrements of war. Lincoln also had to select generals. The first was not such a problem as there was considerable enthusiasm for maintaining the Union, and thousands joined the colours. As far as the latter was concerned matters were not so simple. During the course of the war Lincoln found himself in the hands of a series of incompetent commanders, in great contrast to the genius of Robert E. Lee, who had been a general in the Federal army, but had joined the Confederates not because of his adherence to the southern policy of secession (he himself believed in the Union) but because he conceived that his first duty was to his home state of Virginia. Another, almost legendary Confederate commander was 'Stonewall' Jackson, who was a brilliant commander until he was killed in May 1863.

The North was vastly superior in resources, so in theory it should have won quickly, but it did not. It was not fighting for its life whereas the South felt that it was. The first real battle at Bull Run on 21 July 1861 was a startling and massive victory for the South. It was followed by a series of southern victories and an invasion of Maryland; this was checked by a battle at Antietam which, although not decisive, was on the whole a northern victory. As the months and years went by, Lincoln found himself increasingly drawn into the actual conduct of the war, because he considered (and he was probably right) his commanders were inefficient and lacking in offensive spirit.

Some of Lincoln's subordinate commanders used methods which were illegal and certainly against the spirit of the American Constitution. In many cases, but not all, Lincoln supported them, and he suspended habeas corpus, occasioning heavy criticism. However, he brushed these criticisms aside, pleading military necessity in time of war. Of course Lincoln also had to cope with the normal problems of any President – the shifting sands of public opinion and of the members of his cabinet who varied greatly in competence and loyalty.

Lincoln's views on slavery were changing. Although totally committed to the rule of law in normal times, he saw that he needed support from the southern Negroes, many of whom had escaped to the North. Many of these were enlisted into the army and used both for garrison duties and sometimes for actual fighting, in which they often distinguished themselves. In order to allow this to happen, Lincoln delivered himself of the famous 'Proclamation of Emancipation' on 22 September 1862: 'That on the first day of January in the year of our Lord one thousand eight hundred and sixty three, all persons held as slaves within any state, or designated part of a state, the people whereof shall then be in rebellion against the United States, shall be then thenceforward and forever free.'

As he saw it, the proclamation was an act of war as Commander-in-Chief of the forces and Lincoln only claimed legal force for his proclamation in so far as it was an act of war. It certainly helped the Union cause: by the end of the war no fewer than 180,000 ex-slave troops were under arms for the North. In the event the proclamation made it a political certainty that by one means or another slavery would be ended if the North won. Lincoln had in fact drafted the proclamation many months before but decided he should wait until he had a victory (Antietam) to announce it, thinking, quite rightly, that after the series of defeats which the North was suffering, such a proclamation would appear absurd and actually do the North harm.

At one stage when the South again invaded the North, the situation was saved by the successful battle of Gettysburg on 1–3 July 1863. The National Cemetery was dedicated there on 19 November 1863 and it was at this ceremony that Lincoln delivered perhaps his best-known speech:

Four score and seven years ago our fathers brought forth on this continent a new nation, conceived in liberty and dedicated to the proposition that all men are created equal. Now we are engaged in a great civil war, testing whether that nation or any nation so conceived and so dedicated, can long endure. . . . The brave men, living and dead, who struggled here have consecrated it far above our poor power to add or to detract. . . . It is rather for us to be here dedicated to the great task remaining before us – that from these honoured dead we take increased devotion to that cause for which they gave the last full measure of devotion; that we here highly resolve that these dead shall not have died in vain;

that this nation, under God, should have a new birth of freedom; and that government of the people, by the people, for the people, shall not perish from the earth.

After many vicissitudes, Lincoln found a general, Grant, who began to deliver victories. He made him Commander-in-Chief of all the Federal armies and the situation was gradually transformed.

A Presidential election was due in November 1864. As it approached, the North was suffering a further series of defeats and Lincoln's popularity was low. However, before the election the military situation was transformed, and Lincoln was duly elected in a landslide, such were the vagaries of public opinion. The question of slavery was again the principal issue. It was clear that only an amendment to the constitution would ensure that slavery was illegal throughout the United States. Lincoln pushed hard in Congress for what was the thirteenth amendment to the constitution, and a joint resolution by the two Houses was passed and received the Presidential signature on 31 January 1865. In fact it could have no effect until many months later when the requisite majority of states had ratified it (which they duly did).

Lincoln's second inaugural address was yet another major and universally known speech. Although he had not joined any Church, unable to accept the dogmas attached to organized religion, he had a profound faith in God. After his death his wife said, 'Mr Lincoln never joined a church, but still as I believe he was a religious man by nature.'[14] He read the Bible avidly (and incidentally Shakespeare, whom he quoted constantly). Although the war was not yet over, it was clear that the end was close. Lincoln was determined that the North should not demand revenge and that North and South should be peacefully and happily united as far as possible without recrimination. Victory should not bring exaltation but reconciliation. 'Judge not that ye be not judged,' he said and ended with the following famous words:

With malice towards none; with charity for all; with firmness in the right, as God gives us to see the right, let us strive on to finish the work we are in; to bind up the nation's wounds, to care for him who shall have borne the battle, and for his widow, and his orphan – to do all which may achieve and cherish a just and lasting peace among ourselves, and with all nations.

Efforts were made by the South to conclude a compromise peace, but Lincoln continued to insist on retention of the Union and on emancipation of the slaves. Grant won more victories and on 9 April 1865 Lee surrendered to Grant at Appomattox. On 14 April the Union flag was hoisted again on Fort Sumter. The war was clearly at an end, although a Confederate army was still in existence under General Johnston; this surrendered to General Sherman a few days after Lincoln's assassination.

Lincoln was faced by a massive task as he assembled his cabinet on 14 April. The country, North and South, was in a bad state, economically, politically and in every other way. Above all there were, inevitably, deep and bitter antagonisms and much hatred. Arguments raged about the reconstruction of state legislatures in the South. There were calls for punitive action which Lincoln rejected:

We must extinguish our resentments if we expect harmony and union. There is too much of a desire on the part of some of our very good friends to be masters, to interfere with and dictate to those states, to treat the people not as fellow citizens; there is too little respect for their rights. I do not sympathize in these feelings.

These were Lincoln's last recorded words on public affairs. On the evening of that day he decided to go to the theatre.

On the evening of 17 February 1880 the dining room of the Winter Palace in St Petersburg was blown up. The royal family were late for dinner and survived. In the room below, forty Finnish soldiers of the guard were killed. Alexander realized that something new must be tried: things were going from bad to worse, the country was in turmoil and it was clearly only a matter of time before he himself would be murdered. He determined to revert to a more liberal policy while at the same time rooting out terrorism, if necessary by extreme means. He appointed General Loris-Melikov as supreme commissioner with control over ministers, a virtual dictator. Melikov stated that he regarded the support of the public as the principal means of restoring normal conditions. He started off by abolishing the secret police (the Third Section established by Nicholas I). He gave the press more freedom, and appointed a liberal minister for education and another liberal to the Ministry of Finance. He then produced a plan for involving locally elected representatives in legislative matters, an obvious, although perhaps modest, approach to constitutional rule. This coincided with the arrest of a revolutionary, Goldenburg, who began to inform on all the details of the revolutionary organization, the 'People's Will'. The remaining conspirators began to be isolated from the people as a whole since Melikov's reforms were proving to be very popular.

The conspirators realized that unless they acted quickly it would be too late: their moment would pass. They had mined a number of streets in St Petersburg, waiting for Alexander to pass. On 17 March 1881 Alexander signed a decree embodying Melikov's project of involving elected representatives of the people in lawmaking. After reviewing some troops he drove down one of the roads which were mined. The leader of the gang, a young woman, Sofia Perovskaya, gave a signal and a young conspirator, Ryssakov, threw a bomb at his carriage. The Tsar was not touched and dismounted to speak to some of the Cossacks of his suite who were wounded. At this moment another assassin, Grinevitsky, a Polish student, threw a second bomb between his feet. His legs were crushed, his stomach torn open and his face terribly mutilated. He could only say 'Home to the Palace, to die there', which he did an hour or so later.[15] The assassin, Grinevitsky, was also killed in the explosion.

Five other conspirators, including the girl Perovskaya, were arrested, tried, condemned and hanged in public.

The liberals, realizing the damage the assassination would do to their cause, were appalled. Alexander's son, Alexander III, became Tsar, and all liberalizing progress was halted. Autocracy and repression were reintroduced. Russia went back almost to where it had started on Alexander's accession. It is true that the serfs were not re-enslaved, but the approach to constitutional rule was ended.

Alexander II was a great man in his way. He was no intellectual and was, inevitably, conditioned by his background. But he did try, with some success, to redress some of the more obvious abuses of Russian life, and he persisted against great opposition. As a French diplomat said at his funeral:

> He loved his people and his solicitude for the humble and the suffering was unbounded. . . . Remember the reforms he introduced. . . . Think of all the resistance he had to overcome to abolish serfdom and restore the foundation of rural economy. Think that thirty million men owe their enfranchisement to him. . . . And his administrative reforms! He aimed at nothing less than the destruction of the arbitrary bureaucracy and social privilege. In the judicial sphere he established equality before the law, assured the independence of the magistrates, abolished corporal punishment, instituted the jury. And this was done by the immediate successor of the despot Nicholas I.[16]

Furthermore, it was in his reign that the flowering of Russian culture really took off, with Turgenev, Dostoievsky, Tolstoy, Mussorgsky and Rimsky-Korsakov writing and composing their masterpieces. He deserved a better fate.

Did the assassins achieve their aim? The answer must be that they did not, certainly in the short term. Russia, poised as she was on the edge of constitutional rule and other freedoms which were in general taken for granted in the West, lurched back towards the Middle Ages. It was not until after the failed revolution in 1904 that the move towards liberalism was resumed – and that led to the 1917 revolutions with the rigid obscenities which were to follow. Alexander had tried to change course and was in part successful: he was, justly, known as 'the Liberator'. But in the end the task was too much for him, and he was removed from the scene at a crucial moment. In this case, assassination brought about the precise opposite of what the assassins had hoped for.

Lincoln's assassin, John Wilkes Booth, came from a theatrical family. His father, Junius Booth, and a brother, Edwin, were great actors, another brother was a producer and a brother-in-law was a noted comedian. John was brought up on a farm in Maryland to which his alcoholic and mentally unstable father returned in-between bouts of acting. He was handsome, vain and flamboyant. As a boy he used to charge through the woods on horseback holding a lance and shouting battle cries. He hated cats and killed all on the farm, much to his father's dismay.[17] From the age of seventeen he was constantly on the stage, eventually graduating to leading roles in *Richard III*, *Romeo and Juliet*, *Hamlet*, *Macbeth*, *Othello*, *The Merchant of Venice* and *Julius Caesar*.

Unlike the rest of his family, from the beginning of the civil war, he supported the South. He said of slavery that it was 'one of the greatest blessings both for themselves [the slaves] and us that God ever bestowed upon a favoured nation. Witness heretofore our wealth and power. Witness their elevation and enlightenment above their race elsewhere.'[18] In 1859 he became a member of the Virginia militia which took part in the arrest and execution of John Brown. He saw the civil war as a simple struggle between tyranny and freedom, as did the North, though with the roles reversed.

Although not actually enlisting during the civil war – he had promised his mother not to do so – he was determined to play a major role in the struggle in some way. He gathered round him a band of others of like mind. At the end of 1864 he conceived a plan to kidnap the President, forcibly taking him to Richmond and keeping him as a bargaining counter either to end the war or, at least, for an exchange of prisoners. His first idea was to capture him at Ford's Theatre in Washington on 18 January, binding him and lowering him from the box to the stage and then carrying him off. Not surprisingly, this hair-brained scheme came to nothing. His second plan was to capture Lincoln when he was out riding on 17 March, but the President did not turn up. Finally he decided on assassination. On 11 April Booth heard the President recommend in a speech suffrage for blacks who were educated or who had served in the Union armies. 'That means nigger citizenship,' he muttered and added – 'that is the last speech he will ever make.'

A plan was made whereby on 14 April Booth would assassinate Lincoln in his box at Ford's Theatre. One of his associates, Atzerott, was to murder the Vice-President, Johnson, in his room at a hotel. Another associate, Payne, was to assassinate the Secretary of State, Seward. All three murders were to take place at 10 p.m. Atzerott lost his nerve, but Payne got into Seward's house and badly wounded him.

During the morning of 14 April Booth entered Ford's Theatre and prepared a contrivance so that the door could be barred from the inside to prevent entry from the outside after he had shot the President. He spent much of the day drinking brandy and preparing himself mentally for what he considered to be a noble act. Later he was to compare himself with Brutus in his heroic killing of the tyrant Caesar, complaining that even some of his Confederate allies did not see him in that light. To what extent reality and play-acting were mixed up in his fevered mind will never be known.

As a well-known actor, he had no difficulty in entering the theatre and going upstairs to the President's box shortly after 10 p.m. The policeman on duty had gone off to have a drink, and the White House footman at the door let him in. The play, *Our American Cousin*, a creaky farce about an American bumpkin who goes to England to claim a fortune, had just reached the point where the American says, 'Don't know the manners of good society, eh? Well, I guess I know enough to turn you inside out, old gal – you sockdologizing old man trap,' which always led to much laughter. This almost covered the sound of the shot which hit the President in the head. Drawing a knife, Booth slashed at one of the President's companions, who attacked him, and then jumped from the box on to the stage shouting, '*Sic semper tyrannis*' (the motto of the state of Virginia) and 'The South is avenged'. However, he caught a spur in the drapery lining the box and fell, breaking a small bone in his leg. He struggled across the stage, leaving by the stage door, where he mounted a horse and rode away. He was joined by an associate, Herold, and they went to the house of a Dr Mudd, a sympathizer, who set his leg. After a series of adventures over fourteen days, during which they crossed the rivers Potomac and Rappanoch, they managed to reach the farm of a Richard Garrett in the State of Virginia on 23 April. They slept in a barn, where they became surrounded. When they refused to come out the barn was set on fire. Herold came out and surrendered. It is not certain exactly how Booth died but he probably shot himself.

All the accomplices were captured and tried. They were accused of conspiring with Jefferson Davis, the Confederate President and Confederate officials in Canada to murder the President. The trial was a travesty. The authorities were determined to show that the Confederacy was involved which, in fact, it was not. Witnesses were intimidated and evidence was suppressed, including Jefferson Davis's diary which would have negated the charge of conspiracy. Furthermore, there was no firm evidence to show that Mrs Surratt in whose house the plot was hatched, knew anything about it. However, Herold, Payne, Atzerott and Mrs Surratt were executed. The rest received life imprisonment but were later pardoned. Jefferson Davis, against whom there was virtually no evidence, spent two years in prison but was never brought to trial and died many years later, in 1889. Lincoln was carried to a house opposite where he lay for some ten hours before dying. His wife was totally shattered and later died insane.

Lincoln was succeeded by the Vice-President – Andrew Johnson. Johnson came from Tennessee, a state which had joined the

Confederates. His father was a bank porter. He was another self-made man, but without Lincoln's genius. At the age of ten he was apprenticed to a tailor and learned to read and write. He became a local mayor and was elected as a Democrat to the House of Representatives from 1835 to 1837 and 1839 to 1841. He was a senator from 1841 to 1845. From 1853 to 1857 he was Governor of Tennessee and from 1857 to 1862 again a senator. He was the only southern senator to declare for the Union, hence his value to the Republican Party. He was a man of no very great consequence, who was found to be dead drunk during Lincoln's second inauguration ceremony and had to be pulled down by his coat tails. But he had had the guts to stand up for the Union in a wildly anti-Unionist state, and Lincoln admired him for this.

On Lincoln's death Johnson tried to carry on Lincoln's policies of reconciliation. He issued a general amnesty proclamation granting full pardon to all ex-Confederates (except certain leaders) who would take an unqualified oath of allegiance to the United States. He arranged that the southern states would have conventions and elect senators. However, when Congress assembled in December 1865, this overwhelmingly Republican body refused to admit the senators from the rebel states in the South. The Republican radicals in the Senate demanded that the late slaves be granted the right to vote and that a sufficient number of ex-Confederates be disenfranchised to ensure Republican majorities. Johnson refused to yield. In 1867 Congress threw aside the work of restoration and proceeded with a bill of its own involving the restoration of military control, the enfranchisement of the Negroes and the disenfranchisement of many ex-Confederates. Johnson vetoed it but it then passed again with a two-thirds majority, thus becoming law. Relations between the President and Congress worsened and, over the President's veto on 2 March 1867, Congress passed the Tenure of Office Act prohibiting him from dismissing from office any officer appointed by and with the consent of that body unless the Senate agreed. Johnson then sacked the Secretary of War, Edwin Stanton. The House of Representatives brought articles of impeachment against the President (a unique occasion in American political history, until Clinton's escapade). But, when the matter came to a vote in the Senate Johnson escaped by one vote (35 to 19), a two-thirds majority being necessary. On 4 March 1869 he left the Presidency a beaten and embittered man.

In conclusion, the assassination of Lincoln by Booth, a violently pro-southern partisan devoted to the cause of slavery and secession, led to the precise opposite of what he and his friends had hoped to achieve. Slavery was ended and the Union was maintained. Furthermore, the South was greatly damaged because, if Lincoln had not been assassinated, reconciliation between North and South would certainly have been achieved much earlier. With the vast prestige he had accumulated during the previous four and a half years, he would certainly not have allowed Congress to block his efforts at reconciliation. In effect his assassination was as much a disaster for the South as it was for the North, perhaps even more so. Lincoln's political skills, his moderation, his humility and his devotion to justice and truth, let alone his sense of humour, were greatly missed by the whole nation in the years to come. He is, now, rightly revered across virtually the whole of the American political spectrum.

In practice, therefore, in both cases examined in this chapter, assassination as a political weapon was a total failure. However, the assassins were, by their own lights, idealists in that their acts were not motivated by personal gain but by what they saw as a noble cause. To coin a phrase, idealism was not enough.

NOTES

1. W.E. Mosse, *Alexander II and the Modernisation of Russia*, English University Press, London, 1958, p. 12.
2. V. Cowles, *The Russian Dagger*, Collins, London, 1969, p. 18.
3. B. Pares, *Russia*, Penguin, London, 1940, p. 427.
4. Mosse, *Alexander II*, p. 164.
5. Charnwood, *Abraham Lincoln*, Constable, London, 1916, p. 155.

6. D. Donald, *Lincoln*, Pimlico, London, 1995, p. 342.
7. From a speech by Lincoln at Peoria on 16 October 1854 in the series of debates with Stephen Douglas.
8. Charnwood, *Lincoln*, p. 123.
9. Donald, *Lincoln*, p. 176.
10. Ibid., p. 236.
11. Ibid., p. 280.
12. P. Johnson, *A History of the American People*, Phoenix, London, 1997, p. 442.
13. Ibid., p. 471.
14. Ludwig, *Lincoln*, Putnam, London, 1930, p. 171.
15. Pares, *Russia*, p. 441.
16. Mosse, *Alexander II*, p. 180.
17. *Dictionary of American Biography*.
18. Donald, *Lincoln*, p. 586.

CHAPTER 6

FIELD MARSHAL
SIR HENRY WILSON /
MICHAEL COLLINS

Ireland has always been assassination-ridden. It is not the intention of this book to probe national psychologies but, for all their charm and many other qualities, the Irish do at times seem to kill each other, almost with relish, to a greater extent than do many other nationalities, certainly more than the English who, for some reason or other, do not go in for that particular form of violent behaviour. There have been a few failed attempts, but, apart from Spencer Perceval, a rather dull Prime Minister who was killed by a madman with a personal grievance in 1812, it is difficult to think of any important English figure actually assassinated in England by an Englishman in the last two hundred or so years.

In the early 1920s in Ireland assassination really did become a way of life or, perhaps more accurately, of death. War broke out between the southern Irish and the British, but this was war not with armies, drums and fifes, advances and retreats and the usual paraphernalia of military conflict, but war with solitary and furtive assassinations of picked individuals interspersed with occasional widespread slaughter of guilty and innocent alike. As the southern Irish saw it, the British were occupying their country. As the British, or perhaps more accurately the English Establishment, saw it, the Irish in the south were rebelling against legitimate authority. The eternal question – terrorist or freedom fighter? – recurred with fiercely different replies.

As we shall see, the situation deteriorated into chaos, with the additional complication of Ulster adding considerable fuel to the already scorching flames. In any book about assassination it would be wrong to ignore Ireland in the 1920s and, in particular, Michael Collins, the undoubted hero/villain of the scene. It would also be wrong to ignore Field Marshal Sir Henry Wilson, a most remarkable man who, in many ways, personified the deep opposition to the abandonment of the union with Great Britain and who found himself Chief of the Imperial General Staff when the fighting began. Both men were assassinated, Wilson shortly before Collins. Wilson was shot on the steps of his house in London, Collins in an affray in the wilds of Cork. Coming from very different backgrounds, they were both victims of the deep-rooted hatreds of the tragic island of Ireland. To add to the tangled story, one of them (Collins) probably ordered the assassination of the other (Wilson), before he too was assassinated by his own people in the Irish Civil War.

Henry Wilson was the second son of James Wilson, the owner of a comfortable estate in County Longford in the South of Ireland. Like so many others, the family had come to Ulster from the southern lowlands of Scotland. Having made money in a shipping concern in Belfast, they had moved to the South and were, like many others in the south, staunch Unionists and Protestants. They felt themselves both Irish and English, and Henry was destined for the British army after education at Marlborough. Most surprisingly for a future Field Marshal, in spite of extra cramming he failed the entry examinations twice for Woolwich and three times for Sandhurst. He, and presumably his father, was nothing if not persistent and he entered the army through the back door, the militia, joining his regiment, the 1st Battalion the Rifle Brigade, in India in 1885 as a commissioned officer.

Although a brilliantly successful soldier, in his career Wilson had very little experience of personally leading soldiers in battle, as his detractors never ceased to point out. Not long after arrival in India, however, when searching for bandits in Upper Burma, he was hit on the head with an axe wielded by one of those he was searching for. He had to return to England and suffered from severe headaches for the rest of his life as a result.

There were resemblances between Wilson and Collins. They were both acutely intelligent, very tall (Collins was known as the 'Big Fellow'), boisterous and full of humour, their speech often punctuated by amusing quips. Neither of them suffered fools gladly, they both had an eagle eye for detail and were men of outstanding determination and character. They both despised equivocation and hypocrisy and followed the truth as they saw it. Michael Collins had more of the schoolboy about him: he delighted in wrestling on the floor with his friends and indulging in practical jokes and horseplay, sometimes to the amused despair of those around him. However, Collins was hero-worshipped by his associates whereas Wilson did not evoke this kind of emotion, perhaps because he did not have a 'cause' in the same way as did Collins; indeed after his childhood and early youth, Collins's whole life was devoted to what he believed to be long overdue – Irish freedom.

Wilson was very ambitious. After his sick leave in England when he was due to return to his regiment in India, he decided that this would not further his career, quite apart from being rather tedious. He avoided this posting by passing into the Staff College and at the end of his course, when ordered to rejoin his regiment east of Suez, he found another officer to take his place (that was possible in those days!). He managed to get himself into the Intelligence Department at the War Office and in May 1895, at the age of thirty-one, became the youngest staff officer in the British army. Then, pulling every string he could, he went to South Africa in the Boer War as brigade major to the Light Infantry Brigade, commanded by Brigadier General Lyttleton of the cricketing family, and distinguished himself as a staff officer during the disastrous battles that ensued. Towards the end of the war, Wilson, whose intelligence and efficiency were clearly outstanding, was transferred on to General Roberts's staff, in which appointment he returned to Britain in 1901.

It was at this stage that Wilson began to move into political circles and started to gain his reputation as a political, not a fighting, soldier, an accusation which dogged him for the rest of his army career. In South Africa he had become friends with Bron Herbert and Leo Amery, both then writing for *The Times*, and through them he met Balfour, Churchill, Asquith and other leading political figures in England. Although still only a lieutenant colonel, he became a key figure in Whitehall as the army underwent massive reforms, emerging on 1 January 1907 as commandant of the Staff College and then director of military operations. It was at this stage in his career that he was described as 'lanky, horse faced, arrogant, at forty-six with a reputation for insubordination, intrigue and strongly held opinions'.[1] In his biography of Haig, Duff Cooper adds to this when describing a later period of Wilson's life: 'Faced with the problem of how to be loyal to Lloyd George and Haig at the same time, he solved it by being loyal to neither.'[2]

When commanding the Staff College, Wilson had visited his counterpart at the French École de Guerre, General Foch, and had struck up a friendship with him. Indeed, they ended up as firm friends, a most important relationship in the war which was to follow. Wilson was certain that war with Germany was imminent. As director of operations he realised that very little, if anything, had been done to prepare the British army for intervention in Europe. His diary records his impressions: '. . . very dissatisfied . . . no rail arrangements . . . no arrangements for horse supply . . . a scandalous state of affairs! . . . no train arrangements to ports, no staff arrangements to port, no naval arrangements . . . absolutely no medical arrangements . . . horse difficulty has not been solved . . . absolutely nothing exists, which is scandalous! . . . unpreparedness disgraceful'.[3]

With great dynamic energy he transformed the situation, albeit without proper authority. He personally toured the French–German and Belgian frontiers by bicycle and other means and had many staff talks with the French military commanders. In August 1911 at a key meeting of the Imperial Defence Committee, chaired by Prime Minister Asquith, Wilson, in a brilliant display of coherent and taut argument, persuaded the committee to adopt a policy of sending six divisions to France on the outbreak of war to take up positions on the French left. Under various guises and with varying official support, staff talks with the French continued and, eventually, after much argument and often abrupt changes of policy, when war came the British did indeed send an army to France, which played a crucial role in averting an immediate German victory.

During the whole of the First World War Wilson was a permanent fixture at the summit of Anglo–French decision-making in various official positions. Unlike in the Second World War, when Winston Churchill reigned supreme, the British leadership in the First World War was beset by intrigue as the politicians and, indeed some soldiers, sought to outwit their rivals and to foist themselves into positions of authority. Furthermore, the scene was complicated by the difficulties, inherent to any joint venture, of Allied command and control. This was particularly so since the French contribution to the Allied force in Flanders was, at any rate in the early stages, vastly superior in numbers to that of the British and there were constant questions of command which had to be addressed. Wilson had the great advantage of speaking fluent French, thanks to a succession of French governesses in his early youth and of friendship with many of the French general staff including Foch. He played a part in the ousting of Asquith and his replacement by Lloyd George, in the replacement of General French by General Haig and in the eventual shifting of General Robertson as Chief of the Imperial General Staff to be succeeded by himself. He did command a corps for a short period, not actively concerned in the fighting at the time, but it was as a ubiquitous go-between, adviser and often pourer of oil on troubled waters that Sir Henry Wilson spent virtually the whole of the war. He was greatly disliked by some, notably General Haig, and greatly admired by others, in the early stages by Lloyd George, but in any case he could not be ignored.

During this period, certainly until 1916, Sir Henry Wilson was not hugely, if at all, concerned by Ireland and he would never have heard of the young man who was to play a prominent part in his death.

Michael Collins was born on 16 October 1890, the eighth and last child of his father – also Michael Collins. The family were tenant farmers at Woodfield in West Cork. They were Roman Catholic and had survived the Great Famine, eviction and emigration. Michael's early life was close to the earth: his family was self-sufficient. They drank their own milk, ate home-baked bread from their own corn, ate their own potatoes and vegetables, wove their own linen from their own flax, spun their own wool and made their own clothes. Michael's father made their furniture and his own farm gates and cow stalls. The young Michael greatly admired his father who, like the whole small community, was a fervent Nationalist, and unquestioning Nationalism was the background in which Michael was brought up. There was a puritanical element, too, in his upbringing: their house was always spick and span, debts were always paid and Mass was a part of life. Michael's rural Irish background was an essential element in his whole life, to which he returned whenever possible. After going to the local school at Clonakilty, Michael took the British Civil Service examination, passed it and went to work in London at the Post Office Savings Bank, staying with one of his sisters who was already working there. He stayed with this sister in London for the next nine and a half years. He left the Post Office after four years, moving to a stockbrokers' firm, thence as a clerk at a Labour Exchange and finally to the London office of the Guaranty Trust Company of New York.

During his time in London, Michael educated himself by reading widely through European literature, became a member of the Gaelic Athletic Association and joined the Irish Nationalist movement Sinn Fein (We Ourselves), which was founded in 1905 by Arthur

Griffith, destined to become Michael's closest political colleague and mentor. Michael's enthusiasm, intelligence and fervent Nationalist feeling brought him to the attention of the Irish Republican Brotherhood, a secret oath-bound society devoted to the cause of Irish independence, which they believed could only be achieved by physical force. Michael was sworn in as a member in November 1909 – a definitive moment in his progress as a leading revolutionary figure. This movement, which had organized a failed rising in Ireland in 1867, was revived on the return from the United States of Thomas Clarke. A fervent Nationalist (or Fenian) who had suffered fifteen years' imprisonment, Clarke was to play a leading part in the Easter rising of 1916, and was to be executed after it.

The Gladstone Land Acts, which had undoubtedly improved the lot of Irish tenant farmers, were followed in 1909 by two further Land Purchase Acts. Under these, 11 million acres changed hands from landlord to tenant, to be followed by a further 2 million acres, in total by far the majority of the land in Ireland, although much of the best land remained in the hands of landlords. As a result of this, discontent in the rural areas in the early years of the century had greatly diminished. However, the slums in Dublin were the worst in Europe. There were strikes, which led to even greater poverty. Larkin and Connolly, two Trades Union leaders, formed an armed militia – the Irish Citizen Army – which was later to play its part in the 1916 rising.

In Britain, the Irish Nationalists led by Redmond held the balance of power in the British Parliament and the way was open for the Liberal Government at last to bring about Home Rule for Ireland. The abolition of the veto of the House of Lords in 1911 removed the final obstacle and it was clear that Home Rule was imminent. However, this was bitterly opposed by the Conservative Party with its links to the Ulster Unionists, and the reaction in the Protestant areas of Ulster was immediate. An Ulster Unionist Council was formed under the dynamic leadership of Sir Edward Carson, an Irish Protestant barrister, Member of Parliament for Dublin University and a prominent Conservative politician. A series of gigantic meetings was organized by Sir James Craig, a self-made whiskey millionaire, culminating in a demonstration in Belfast by no fewer than 100,000 people. The leader of the British Conservative Party, Bonar Law, took the salute and pledged, 'There will not be wanting help from across the Channel when the hour of battle comes.' At a meeting in England in 1911 he said, 'There are things stronger than parliamentary majorities. . . . I can imagine no length of resistance to which Ulster will go, in which I will not support them.' This appeared to be an invitation to revolution and indeed there can be no other explanation for it – a most surprising ploy for a 'Conservative' politician. An Ulster volunteer force was formed, initially of 100,000 men, drilling at first with dummy rifles but later real arms were obtained. No government could afford to ignore opposition of this nature and a compromise was canvassed whereby some of the Ulster counties would be excluded from the Bill. The result of this, however, was that a rival force, the Irish Nationalist Volunteers, was formed in the South, dedicated to preserving the original Bill under which 'Ireland would not be mutilated' and would remain one country. In fact the initiative behind this venture came from the secret Irish Republican Brotherhood (of which Michael was a member), who wished to use it later for their own purposes.

As Director of Military Operations, Wilson, whom Bonar Law called 'the cleverest man in England', was inevitably involved in the situation whereby, as well as the British army elements stationed in Ireland, North and South, there were two volunteer armies, both clearly illegal but openly drilling and arming themselves. On top of this there was an Act of Parliament which had passed through the parliamentary process and which, if enforced, would lead to war with one of them and if not enforced might well lead to war with the other. A further problem for the Liberal Government was that if they did not enforce the Act they would lose their parliamentary majority since Redmond and his Irish Party in coalition with them would desert them. King George V, who was to play an important and extremely sensible part in this whole affair, was very worried, as was the army leadership. Wilson was passionately devoted to the Ulster cause and thought of resigning if Ulster was forced to join an independent Ireland. Together with French, the Chief of the Imperial General Staff, he tried to convince the government that to press the issue would have disastrous consequences, that the army would be hopelessly split and that the result would be bitter and bloody chaos. Wilson urged Carson to avoid any provocation but, after a visit to Belfast, told Colonel Seely, the Minister of War, that the Ulster Volunteers were well organized and would fight if pushed to it. Winston Churchill, in an unguarded but typically forthright speech, added fuel to the fire by saying that, if Ulster was determined to challenge the authority of Westminster, 'there might be nothing for it but to go forward together and put these grave matters to the proof'.[5]

There followed what became known as the 'Curragh Mutiny' of March 1914, whereby, most unwisely, the officers of the 3rd Cavalry Brigade stationed at the Curragh barracks, just outside Dublin, were asked point blank if, in the event of them being ordered to fight against Ulster, they would do so or whether they would resign. Brigadier Sir Hubert Gough, later to be an army commander in the First World War, asked the officers of his brigade what they would do in those circumstances. Having done so, he told General Paget, the Commander-in-Chief in Ireland, that he and nearly all his officers would resign if ordered to take up arms against their compatriots in Ulster. (A similar situation nearly arose as a result of the Rhodesian Unilateral Declaration of Independence in 1965.) This was clearly a threat of near-mutiny in the event of war with Ulster. Wilson was heavily involved, supporting Gough to the hilt. The government backed down. It was clear that Ulster had won: there could be no question of the Protestant counties of Ulster being forced against their will under the control of an independent Ireland. From that moment onwards Wilson was seen by the Irish Nationalists as a powerful and constant enemy.

The outbreak of war in August 1914 pre-empted further decisions on the problem of Ireland and Redmond agreed that Home Rule should be deferred for twelve months or until the war ended, whichever was the later, and that an Amending Bill would be introduced at that time to deal with Ulster, allowing the six counties to opt out at least for a period of years. In view of this, believing that Home Rule was at last certain for the bulk of his country, Redmond pledged the Volunteers for war service in the British army in order to fight the Germans and no fewer than 200,000 Irishmen did so. However, the extremists, including the Irish Republican Brotherhood, in Ireland, bitterly opposed Redmond's gesture. They saw the British Government's difficulties not as an opportunity to show their support for the British defence of Belgium – a small country like Ireland – but as an opportunity to press their case, by violence if necessary, in order to obtain independence.

The Irish Easter Rising in 1916, when Yeats's 'terrible beauty' was born, was the most remarkable affair. It did not have the slightest chance of success, it did not have the support of the mass of the Irish people, it was hopelessly bungled from start to finish – and yet it was a turning point for Irish Nationalism. The war in France had taken a vast and tragic toll of British manpower by the end of 1915 and conscription of the whole of Great Britain, including Ireland, was mooted. This was dynamite in Irish Nationalist circles in London and there was heady talk of a rising in Ireland. Collins packed his bags and returned to Dublin on 15 January 1916, the day before the Conscription Act came into force (in fact it was never enacted in Ireland). While awaiting the call to arms which he was sure would be forthcoming he obtained a job looking after Countess Plunkett's property accounts – Count (a hereditary papal title) Plunkett was a prominent Nationalist.

A flavour of the contradictory, and to the outsider perhaps baffling, nature of the Irish character is apparent in a passage in the short book *The Insurrection in Dublin*, by the well-known Irish poet James Stephens.[6] Stephens was living in Dublin at the time and gives a gripping day-by-day account of what happened from the point of view of an apparently non-committed and astonished bystander. He says in the foreword:

If freedom is to come to Ireland – as I believe it is – then the Easter Insurrection was the only thing that could have happened. I speak as an Irishman, and on momentarily leaving out of account every other contribution. If, after all her striving, freedom had come to her as a gift, as a peaceful present such as is sometimes given away with a pound of tea, Ireland would have accepted the gift with shamefacedness, and would have felt that her centuries of revolt had ended in something very like ridicule. The blood of brave men had to sanctify such a consummation if the national imagination was to be stirred to the dreadful business which is the organizing of freedom, and both imagination and brains had been stagnant in Ireland this many a year. Following on such tameness, failure might have been predicted, or, at least feared, and war (let us call it war for the sake of our pride) was due to Ireland before she could enter gallantly on her inheritance. We might have crept into liberty like some kind of domesticated man, whereas now we may be allowed to march into freedom with the honours of war.

The Irish Republican Brotherhood had organized an arms shipment of some twenty thousand rifles from Germany through the fervent Nationalist Sir Roger Casement, a famous former British consular official, and it was due to arrive in a neutral ship, the *Aud*, just before Easter. Casement had been disillusioned by the small amount of help the Germans were prepared to give and landed from a German submarine on a lonely beach in County Kerry in order to tell the Nationalists to call off their rising. However, on landing, Casement was immediately arrested. The *Aud* was intercepted by the Royal Navy and scuttled by her German crew.

The rising had been due to start on Easter Sunday under the cover of so-called 'manoeuvres' that only the leadership knew were to be the real thing. The authorities in Dublin had not taken the

Volunteers seriously and many people laughed at what they saw as their childish and ineffectual posturing. The official leader of the Volunteers, Eoin MacNeill, a professor of early Irish history, was only told at the last minute that the manoeuvres were for real. Much against his better judgement, he was persuaded to support the intended insurrection. However, when he heard that Casement had been arrested and the arms ship sunk, he lost his nerve and placed an advertisement in the *Sunday Independent* cancelling the manoeuvres. Nevertheless, the rest of the leadership decided to go ahead, twenty-four hours late, on Easter Monday. The result was great confusion as some Volunteers turned up and some did not and many of those who did had not realized that the rising was to be in earnest.

The plan was to seize a number of prominent buildings in Dublin and hope that the insurrection would spread throughout the country. There was even a rumour that the Germans would land and come to their aid. In the event the General Post Office was seized, together with some other buildings. Collins, passionately devoted to the cause, was part of the rebel 'garrison' of the Post Office. There followed a week of heroic, if desperate, defence. There was also some looting as the poorer people of Dublin took advantage of the situation, while the bulk of the population looked on in astonished non-belligerence. Then the Nationalist Volunteers, including the Citizens' Army which had joined them, had to surrender. The last to do so was the garrison at Bolands Mill under the command of Eamon de Valera, a largely unknown mathematics teacher.

The total Nationalist force in the rising comprised about 1,600 Volunteers and 300 Citizens' Army. Most of the rank and file, including Collins, were sent to internment camps in Britain but the leaders were court-martialled. Seventy-seven were condemned to death but only fifteen were in fact executed. Although there was clearly a cast-iron case for the death sentence and, after all, Britain was itself suffering massive casualties in its life-and-death struggle with Germany, the actual executions were unwise. They created martyrs, some of whom still excite Irish passion. Many Irish people who had condemned the rising at the time now began to feel that the cause must be worthy if so many Irishmen had been prepared to die for it and fifteen had actually done so.

Wilson, deeply involved in the higher military and political direction of the war in Flanders was not concerned with these matters. Lloyd George made him Chief of the Imperial General Staff in February 1918 and it was not until after the war that he had heavy responsibilities with regard to Ireland.

Together with two thousand other internees, Michael Collins found himself in a camp at Frongoch, North Wales. Vastly enthusiastic, cheerful, athletic and determined, albeit with a hair-trigger temper, he began to emerge as the leader of the extreme Nationalist element. Frongoch became in effect a Nationalist university, the mornings being spent in military drill, the afternoons in lectures about Irish history and language and the evenings in the study of the strategy and tactics of what all believed to be the future revolution. Collins looked for recruits to the Irish Republican Brotherhood and began to build up an intelligence organization throughout the South, and particularly in Dublin, which he was to develop and use to devastating effect later. Together with all other internees he was released on 22 December 1916.

On arrival in Dublin, Collins became secretary to the Volunteer Dependants' Fund, an organization set up by Mrs Clarke, the widow of Tom Clarke who had been executed after the 1916 rising, in order to help those men and their families to whom the aftermath of the Easter Rising would have meant destitution. Although it had a real humanitarian purpose and, with American financial help, was to be extremely effective in that way, the fund was also a centre and focus for the Nationalist cause. Collins was tireless and very effective. He seemed to have a magnetic energy about him and he became extremely well known in Irish Nationalist circles throughout Ireland.

At this stage in Irish politics there were three Irish Nationalist strands of opinion. Except in Ulster, a considerable majority believed in an independent Ireland. The Parliamentary Irish Party, led by Redmond, thought this could be obtained by constitutional means through the Parliament at Westminster. Secondly, Sinn Fein, led by Griffith, were convinced that membership of the Westminster Parliament was not the way forward: they believed in standing for that body but not taking up their seats, and campaigned in every way short of violence for a separate Dublin Parliament. Finally, there was the Irish Republican Brotherhood, which believed that only violence would achieve their aim. The latter body, of which Collins was an enthusiastic member, supported the moderate Sinn Fein, seeing this as only an interim step on the road to full statehood. De Valera, who, because of his American nationality was the only leader of the 1916 rising not to be executed, was elected President of both Sinn Fein and the Volunteers. He began to shift Sinn Fein to a more radical stance.

Collins started to climb the ladder of the Nationalist leadership, becoming Adjutant General of the Volunteers, the military arm of Sinn Fein. The Royal Irish Constabulary, and in particular the detective, or G, division of the Dublin Metropolitan Police, began to take more than a passing interest in him and he was arrested on 2 April 1918. He took bail and left prison on 20 April, the last occasion on which he was to be behind bars.

Although never in fact implemented in Ireland, the announcement of conscription led to an immediate hardening of the Irish Nationalist position. The Irish Party left the Westminster Parliament, and Irish recruiting for the British army came almost to a standstill. (180,000 Irishmen had already volunteered for war service and by the end of the war no fewer than 49,000 of these would be killed.[7]) Many young Irishmen joined the Volunteers and Sinn Fein completely supplanted the almost defunct Parliamentary Irish Party. When a German plot to assist the militant Nationalists was suspected, the government in Dublin Castle decided to arrest the whole of the Sinn Fein leadership. But by now Collins's intelligence network was extremely efficient and he had three agents in the castle ostensibly working for the government. As a result he had foreknowledge of who was to be arrested and they were warned.

Nevertheless, seventy Sinn Fein members were put in jail including De Valera and Griffith. Nationalist affairs then came under the control of two men – Harry Boland, a close friend of Collins, for Sinn Fein, and Collins himself for the Volunteers.

Peace with Germany brought no lessening of tension. Collins redoubled his efforts, perfecting his intelligence network and organizing his army. In the 1918 General Election for the Westminster Parliament a few weeks after the Armistice, Sinn Fein won all the Irish seats, except for those in Unionist areas. It had seventy-three members, of whom thirty-five were in prison, three had been deported and six were on the run. There was no question of any of the Sinn Fein members taking up their seats at Westminster and it was decided to set up an illegal Irish Parliament (Dail Eireann) which would be attended by as many of the newly elected as possible. It met on 7 January 1919. De Valera was in prison but an acting President, Brugha, subsequently a bitter enemy of Collins's, was elected and a cabinet was formed in which Collins was designated Minister for Finance. From now on Irish affairs were reduced to near farce. Collins organized the escape of De Valera from Lincoln Jail. This was followed by the escape of a Sinn Fein leader, Barton, from Mountjoy Jail in Dublin, succeeded by a mass breakout, also organized by Collins, from the same prison of no fewer than twenty Sinn Fein members. The Dail Eireann continued to meet in secret and the so-called cabinet continued to function, while Collins was extremely successful in raising over £250,000 worldwide for the Nationalist cause.

The Irish Republican Brotherhood was the inspiration behind radical Irish Nationalism and Collins was elected President of its Supreme Council. Many of the Royal Irish Constabulary, as the law-enforcing body of the hated English Government, were becoming unhappy about the situation whereby merely to be a member of that body occasioned automatic hatred by many fellow countrymen. Collins decided to attack the G division of the Dublin Metropolitan Police, who were devoting more and more of their time and energy to following and arresting Sinn Fein members. He formed what was essentially an assassination squad, known as the twelve apostles, out of the extreme membership of the Volunteers and decided to kill those whose names were given to him by his spies in Dublin Castle as being particularly active and effective. He was very successful in this venture and by January 1920, fourteen Irish policemen had been assassinated.

At this stage Collins was leading a most extraordinary life. He refused to adopt disguise of any sort and walked and bicycled around the streets of Dublin apparently without let or hindrance. He was the most wanted man in Ireland with £10,000 on his head, dead or alive. Advance information from his spies in Dublin Castle about plans to arrest him, together with astonishing luck and a nose for approaching danger, enabled him permanently to escape arrest – a Pimpernel if ever there was one. On one occasion he even managed to get into the record room of G division, where he spent the night recording all the details of the RIC intelligence system. He read with amusement his own file saying that he came from 'a brainy Cork family'.[8] He escaped out of windows, on to roofs and by barefaced bluff on many occasions, often joining in a search for himself. Once, for instance, he was to meet his sister off the train in Dublin and the police were given warning of this, together with information that his sister would be wearing a brown overcoat. However, as luck would have it, on the way, at Athlone, a friend lent her a fur coat against the cold. On arrival all the passengers on the train were held while they were closely interrogated. Collins met her and began to complain loudly about her arrest, as she pretended to be ill. He stormed up to the officer in charge, asked why they were all being held and on the reply that the police were searching for Michael Collins he responded, 'That damned Collins again! This is the third time today I have been held up on that damned blackguard. Look at that poor lady. She is obviously very ill. What possible use can there be in detaining her?' Seeing her fur coat the officer let her, and Collins, go.

Collins was a brilliant leader. As Robert Kee has put it, 'Of all the many rebel leaders who shine out of Irish history only one stands out as a really effective revolutionary: Michael Collins . . . He was a sort of Irish Lenin. He took hold of a potentially revolutionary situation in Ireland and made it work.'9

The violence escalated, with houses being burnt down by both sides all over Ireland. There were many reprisals. The Lord Mayor of Dublin was murdered and the Lord Mayor of Cork, Terence MacSwiney, died on hunger strike in Brixton Prison. New recruits for the police were found in England, named, because of the colours of their uniform, after a famous pack of foxhounds in Tipperary – the Black and Tans. Many of them were of doubtful background who joined purely for the money. Eventually, there were 7,000 of them. A special force, known as the Auxiliaries, was also recruited, made up of British officers, of whom many had fought in the First World War. They were paid at twice the rate of the Black and Tans. These two bodies had no scruples about their methods of reprisal. They shot people, often at random, burnt houses suspected of harbouring Nationalists and paid little if any regard to the rule of law. Eventually they burnt down the whole of the centre of Cork. There were many pitched battles in the countryside – on one occasion the Nationalists killed a whole party of eighteen Auxiliaries. On 21 November 1920 Collins organized the simultaneous killing of fourteen undercover British Intelligence officers (known as the Cairo gang) in Dublin, many of them in front of their wives and children. In reprisal the Auxiliaries opened fire on the crowd attending a football match between Dublin and Tipperary, killing twelve people including one of the Tipperary players. In May 1921 the IRA, as it was by then called, seized the Dublin customs house. On this occasion the Auxiliaries and other government forces succeeded in surrounding them and 120 surrendered. But in general, as Frank Owen put it, 'The Irish Civil War was a murder duel in the dark between two Secret Services.'10

The country was in a state of almost total chaos. Large areas, particularly in the west, were virtually under the control of the Nationalists, who had formed an administration, including the installation of courts of justice, which operated and imposed their own fines and other penalties. De Valera, who had been in America fund-raising and drumming up support for Irish Nationalism (although he failed to persuade Woodrow Wilson to allow Irish representation at the Versailles Peace Conference), returned to Ireland and, as president of Sinn Fein, made contact with the British Government on 9 July 1921. Two days later a truce was signed covering all the Crown forces and the IRA.

On the ending of the First World War, Wilson as Chief of the Imperial General Staff was confronted by a host of problems, not least the advice he was constantly being asked for during the Versailles Peace Conference. He had conceived a vast distrust and dislike of the Prime Minister, Lloyd George, and he was constantly intriguing with Bonar Law, the leader of the Conservative Party in the governing coalition, who had similar views to his own on the question of Ulster. Wilson was bitterly opposed to Home Rule, writing in his diary in November 1919 that 'If England goes on like this she will lose the Empire'.[11] However, he was appalled by the lawlessness of the Auxiliaries and Black and Tans and called for martial law to be imposed over the whole of Ireland. There were two alternatives, as he saw it. Either Britain must rule and impose her will under the rule of law – if necessary, by 'shooting by roster'[12] (the compiling of a list of the principal opponents of British rule and then executing them in turn!) – or get out altogether (less Ulster), which would be disastrous as a free Ireland would be utterly opposed to its old master, Britain. On 28 June 1920 Wilson wrote in his diary: 'I don't see any determination or driving power in the cabinet and I really believe we will be kicked out [of Ireland].'[13]

In January 1919 Lloyd George had introduced his Bill for the Better Government of Ireland (eventually passed on 23 December 1920), under which separate parliaments were to be set up for the twenty-six southern counties and the six north-eastern counties with authority to create a Joint Council of Ireland. There would be no question of a republic and Ireland would be represented in the

Imperial Parliament. Considerable powers were reserved for Westminster. Conservative Unionists accepted this but the southern Irish did not, voting heavily against it in the local elections on 15 January 1920. At one stage in the negotiations leading up to a truce De Valera was invited by Lloyd George to come to London and discuss matters. Wilson wrote in his diary on 27 June: 'I told Churchill this morning that in my opinion inviting Valera over was pure cowardice and if a man committed a sufficient number of murders he was qualified to be asked to breakfast at 10 Downing Street. . . . The way to get England on our side was to expose the murderers and not to breakfast with them.'[14] He said later, 'If I met Valera I would hand him over to the police.'[15] On 11 September, Wilson's diary read: 'Valera is now firmly established thanks to Lloyd George and has a government and ministers and judges and magistrates and police and army and money. . . . Valera now dictates terms – as I said he would.'[16]

The truce had been signed on the understanding by both sides that negotiations would take place in order to attempt to find a solution to the problems of Ireland, North and South. De Valera, the President of both Sinn Fein and of the Dail Eireann, had to decide whom he would send to London for the negotiations. The British had a top-level team including Prime Minister Lloyd George, as leader, Austen Chamberlain, the Foreign Secretary, Winston Churchill, Minister for War, and Lord Birkenhead, Lord Chancellor. De Valera decided not to go himself, but sent Griffith, the highly respected founder of Sinn Fein and cabinet minister, as leader, with Collins and three other lesser figures as members. The exact powers of the delegation were never precisely defined – in particular whether or not they had full plenipotentiary authority. In retrospect, it was a great mistake by the British to accept any delegation without the participation of De Valera in it. It was essential that De Valera should be personally tied to whatever agreement was made, and this could only be achieved by his signature on a document which he had negotiated. Indeed, that probably explained De Valera's absence.

The negotiations were extremely difficult. Nevertheless, the two parties got on with each other surprisingly well. Collins and Birkenhead struck up a real friendship, while Winston Churchill began to appreciate the true stature of Collins and vice versa. The Irish delegation was not united and communications with Dublin were far from perfect. Griffith and Collins returned to confer with De Valera on several occasions, but when the final moment for signature came on 6 December 1921 the document had not been cleared with De Valera and that was fatal.

In essence, the treaty gave the constitutional status of the Dominion of Canada to twenty-six of the thirty-two counties of Ireland. They were to be called the Irish Free State and were to have complete control over their own affairs at home, with their own army and navy, subject only to membership of the British Commonwealth and an oath of loyalty to the King. As far as Ulster was concerned, the six counties would be included in the Free State unless they chose to opt out within one month: if they did opt out (and they did so) a Boundary Commission would be set up to adjust the border 'in accordance with the wishes of the inhabitants'. Collins and some other Nationalists had thought that two of the six counties, Tyrone and Fermanagh, which probably had Catholic majorities, would vote against opting out and would therefore join the Free State. But in the event there were, inevitably, great arguments about the status and operation of the Boundary Commission and existing boundaries were left as they were except for some small changes to the border between Donegal and the new Northern Ireland.

On the Irish delegation's return to Ireland it was clear that the treaty was very far from being unanimously acceptable. The mass of the Irish people were greatly relieved that the 'war' was at last over but there were many who saw it as a sell-out, including the vital figure of De Valera, who refused to accept any oath of allegiance, however carefully phrased, to the King. Collins had, of course, appreciated the difficulties this would cause and had managed in the negotiations to have the word 'allegiance' placed as far away as

possible from the word 'King' – but that was not good enough for
De Valera. In circumstances of high drama and after days of debate
the Dail eventually voted in favour of the treaty by sixty-four votes
to fifty-seven and this was confirmed in a general election in June
1922. The essential difference between those who accepted and
those who did not accept the treaty lay not in the partition
argument but in the failure of the treaty to accept Republican status
for the South. The fact that Collins, the great revolutionary leader,
had signed the treaty was, of course, a major factor. It also made him
into a hate figure for die-hard Republicans, who saw him as having
betrayed what they had fought for all their lives.

In early 1922 rioting broke out in Northern Ireland, the Protestants
fearing that the Boundary Commission would undermine the new
State. Catholics were attacked and many left as refugees for the South,
where civil war was breaking out. Collins found himself in the
position of arming and directing the new Free State army against the
anti-treaty forces in the South while providing arms, some of which
he had procured from the British, for the anti-treaty IRA in the
North in order to protect the Catholics there.

Relations between Wilson and Lloyd George had now
deteriorated to the point where they rarely spoke to each other and
Wilson's advice was seldom sought. He decided not to accept an
offer to renew his term of office when it expired in February 1922.
He had always hankered after political life and was elected
unopposed as Member for North Down in Ulster, making his
maiden speech in the House of Commons on the army estimates on
15 March 1922.

Wilson had been asked by Sir James Craig to advise the Northern
Ireland Executive as to what action they should take in the near
chaotic situation they faced there. Deaths in communal violence in
the six counties in the first six months of 1922 amounted to 264
(two-thirds of them Catholics).[17] He answered in a letter:

You have asked me for my opinion and advice on the present
and the future. Here they are.

Owing to the action of Mr Lloyd George and his government, the twenty-six counties of south and west Ireland are reduced to a welter of chaos and murder, difficult to believe, impossible to describe. A further consequence of the course pursued by Mr Lloyd George is seen by the state of unrest, suspicion and lawlessness that had spread over the frontier into the six counties of Ulster.

The dangerous condition which obtains in the twenty-six counties will increase and spread unless:

1. A man in those counties rises who can crush out murder and anarchy, and re-establish law and order. With a thousand years of Irish history to guide us, it is safe to predict that this will not happen.

2. Great Britain re-establishes law in Ireland. Under Mr Lloyd George and his government this is frankly and laughably impossible, because men who are obviously incapable of holding the Empire, are still more incapable of regaining it.

He went on to recommend that a general and staff should be secured to superintend the constabulary, that the Royal Irish Constabulary at present existing in Northern Ireland should be disbanded, that a force of three thousand Royal Ulster Constabulary with five regular officers to each thousand should be raised to take their place, that stringent regulations should be introduced and enforced in respect to the carrying of arms and that the law should be strengthened in various ways for dealing with men found guilty of outrage.[18]

Wilson become more and more bitter. He worried about the lives of British army men who were still in the South and about the faithful Royal Irish Constabulary there who were clearly in great danger. In a speech in the House of Commons he spoke forcefully of the incompetence and cowardice of the government. He was in despair.

Wilson had been asked by the Chairman of the Great Eastern Railway Company to unveil the war memorial that was set up at the entrance to Liverpool Street station. After the ceremony he returned to his house in Eaton Place and began to walk up the steps. Two young men were loitering at the street corner. One of them drew a revolver and shot at him, but missed. Wilson turned round and drew his ceremonial sword, whereupon both men opened fire and he fell, mortally wounded. As the two men made off, both were pursued by workmen and others. One of them had a wooden leg, which slowed down their escape, and eventually, after wounding two policemen and a civilian, they were overpowered. They gave false names but were soon identified as R. Dunn and J. O'Sullivan, Irishmen and Roman Catholics, both with connections to the IRA. It is not certain under whose orders they were acting. Collins had indeed ordered the assassination of Wilson before the truce, and it is possible that by mistake he had not cancelled the order; however, it is more probable that he had renewed it.[19] The truth of the matter was never clearly established. Collins tried to save the lives of the assassins but, in due course, they were both hanged.

In June 1922 open civil war broke out between the anti-treaty Republicans and the pro-treaty Free State army. The Republicans had seized the Four Courts building in Dublin and, partly in response to the assassination of Wilson, Churchill, speaking for the British Government, insisted that Collins should take action; if he did not, the treaty would be abrogated. After a few days Collins borrowed two field guns from the British and forced the occupants of the building to surrender by sustained shellfire at short range. Collins set about the anti-treaty Republicans with determination, borrowing ten thousand rifles from the British Government and filling the ranks of the new Free State Army with ex-soldiers of both the British and American armies. After eight days' fighting in Dublin, during which sixty people were killed, including Brugha, and three hundred wounded, all the anti-treaty Republicans in Dublin surrendered. The city of Cork was recaptured from the Republicans and pressure on the Republican army (the IRA) began to mount.

A week after the reconquest of Cork, Arthur Griffith, who had become President of the Dail Eireann, died of a heart attack, a shattering blow for the new Irish Free State. Collins, whose responsibilities seemed endless, decided to visit some of the units of his victorious army in Cork. He hoped to bring about the recovery of some £120,000 (a very large sum of money in those days), which had been stolen from Customs and Excise at the point of a gun by the IRA and laundered through some London banks. More importantly, he hoped to open peace negotiations with prominent Republicans.

He was advised not to go by many of his associates, including his director of intelligence, Joe McGrath, who told him that it was extremely foolhardy to go to County Cork, where IRA activity was at its height. But he was convinced that the people of Cork, although perhaps unanimously anti-treaty, would not lift a finger against one of their own.[20] He was wrong.

His movements were being closely monitored by the IRA and, as his little convoy drove along a small country road at Beal na mBlath near Clonakilty, his vehicles were stopped by a road block. Shots were fired at them from the hillside. Collins picked up a rifle, jumped out and began to fire back, while standing up. However, his luck at last deserted him and he was shot through the head, dying shortly afterwards. It has never been clear who fired the fatal shot.

The civil war continued with increased ferocity. Bank robberies, destruction of buildings and the killing of individuals increased. The Dail passed a new Emergency Powers Act which enabled the shooting of any Republicans found carrying arms. No fewer than seventy-seven of these executions took place in six months, including Erskine Childers, a well-known Nationalist and the author of *Riddle of the Sands*, who had been secretary to the Irish delegation in the treaty negotiations with the British Government. Ironically he had fought for the British in the First World War in the Royal Naval Air Service, being decorated with the Distinguished Flying Cross. The anti-treaty Republican command ordered the shooting of any member of the Dail who had voted for the Emergency Powers Act. This was followed by the immediate execution by the Irish Free State Government of the four leaders of the Republicans who had seized the Four Courts, including the famous Rory O'Connor. The pace of murder on both sides increased. The IRA eventually collapsed and De Valera, as the Republican political leader, ordered the dumping of arms.

The Irish Free State Government had won. It was led by William Cosgrave, who had been condemned to death but reprieved, after the Easter Rising. No fewer than 13,000 Republicans were in jail – many undertaking long hunger strikes. De Valera himself was behind bars for a year, refusing to take any part in government because he was not prepared to take the oath of allegiance. Eventually he changed his mind, formed a new party in 1926 (Fianna Fail), accepted a euphemistic form of words for the allegiance oath, and triumphed in the General Election of 1932. The IRA, although illegal, continued in existence and canvassed heavily for Fianna Fail. The new government amnestied many IRA fighters and enlisted some in the Free State Army. Before long, however, the IRA began to murder some of its enemies. It was, again, declared illegal and indeed four IRA men were executed. De Valera and Fianna Fail remained in power until 1948, when they were succeeded by Cosgrave's old party (Fine Gael) under John Costello, who finally declared Ireland a republic in that year.

So what had these two assassinations of Wilson and Collins achieved? Wilson's death certainly did not alter the pattern of antagonism or change the status quo very much. If anything, it reinforced the determination of the British Government to see that the treaty was observed by both sides. As far as partition was concerned, the six counties had already in effect won their case. Ulster was to be permanently (or at least so far) excluded from the Irish Free State. The conclusion is that Wilson's assassination was unnecessary. It changed nothing and proved to be merely an irritant at a difficult moment, if anything stiffening the resolve of the assassins' enemy, Great Britain.

As regards Collins, he had certainly been a great revolutionary leader. The fact that he, of all people, had been party to the treaty with Britain had a great deal to do with its acceptance by the bulk of the Irish people in spite of the powerful opposition of De Valera and his Volunteers. The Irish Free State did survive and it was not until nine years later that Cosgrave's government was voted out of office, to be succeeded by De Valera himself and his Fianna Fail party. The assassination of Michael Collins, although a shattering blow for many Irish people at the time, did not in fact alter the general situation. Even without him, the Irish Free State Government won the civil war against the Volunteers and it must be most unlikely that Michael Collins, if he had lived, would have been able to prevent the eventual return to power of De Valera as the political pendulum swung in his direction.

Both men were accorded state funerals. Henry Wilson was buried in the crypt of St Paul's Cathedral after a solemn progress by his coffin on a gun carriage from his home in Eaton Square, followed by an immense cortege of troops and viewed by large crowds in the street. The funeral was attended by virtually all the military and political Establishment. Michael Collins was given a stupendous state funeral in Dublin. The cortege was over three miles in length. A host of Irish, British and foreign dignitaries attended and hundreds of thousands lined the streets. He was much loved.

Seventy-five or so years later Henry Wilson has largely faded from the national consciousness of both Britain and Ireland. What does remain, however, is the vision of the brave, devil-may-care, highly charismatic and effective figure of Michael Collins, young, attractive and with compelling leadership qualities, a romantic icon still for very many Irish men and women.

NOTES

1. W.G.F. Jackson and E.N.W. Bramall, *The Chiefs*, Brasseys, London, 1992, p. 45 quoting Samuel Williamson, 'The Politics of Grand Strategy'.
2. Duff Cooper, *Haig*, Faber and Faber, London, 1936, p. 328.
3. Barbara Tuchman, *August 1914*, Papermac, Constable, London, 1962, p. 50.
4. R. Kee, *Ireland*, Macdonald, London, 1980, p. 146.
5. Collier, *Brass Hat*, Secker & Warburg, London, 1961, p. 145.

6. J. Stephens, *The Insurrection in Dublin*, Maunsell, Dublin, 1919, p. xii.

7. M. Forester, *Michael Collins*, Sidgwick and Jackson, London, 1971, p. 86.

8. J.A. Mackay, *Michael Collins*, Mainstream, London, 1996, p. 128.

9. Kee, *Ireland*, p. 175.

10. Owen, *Tempestuous Journey*, Hutchinson, London, 1954, p. 559.

11. Caldwell, *Sir Henry Wilson*, Cassell, London, 1927, p. 216.

12. Ibid., p. 237.

13. Ibid., p. 246.

14. Ibid., p. 297.

15. Ibid., p. 298.

16. Ibid., p. 305.

17. Kee, *Ireland*, p. 195.

18. Caldwell, *Wilson*, p. 333.

19. Forester, *Collins*, p. 317.

20. Mackay, *Collins*, p. 281.

CHAPTER 7

KING ABDULLAH /
ANWAR SADAT /
YITZHAK RABIN

King Abdullah, Anwar Sadat and Yitzhak Rabin came from very different backgrounds, yet they had much in common. They were all in their time leading figures engaged in the Arab/Israeli conflict and they were all assassinated by extremists from their own side because they were seeking peace. In order to understand why these assassinations occurred, it is necessary to examine the historical circumstances leading to the creation in 1948 of the State of Israel. Great passions have been, and still are, aroused on this matter. Both sides are quite certain that they are right, historically, morally, politically, economically and in every other way. There is no simple panacea: if there were, the problem would have been solved long ago.

The political history of the Children of Israel, as they came to be known, up to AD 135 is a long chronicle of wars and military disasters interspersed with occasional successes, and dominated by the two exiles in Egypt and Babylon both of which ended in a return to the land of Canaan (or Palestine as it came to be known). The two great political facts that emerge are, first, the feeling of nationhood which came to dominate the outlook of the twelve tribes and, secondly, the great attachment to the Promised Land and in particular to Jerusalem. Subsequent history tended only to confirm these two convictions in spite, or perhaps because, of their final expulsion from Palestine by the Romans in AD 135 and their spreading over much of the world often in conditions of extreme misery and isolation. The constant persecution which the Jews had suffered in many lands led, naturally enough, to a longing for some permanent haven.

Unlike many refugees, the Jews were not, in general, assimilated in their host countries. This is partly because, unlike for instance the Huguenots, they did not flee voluntarily owing to persecution by their own nationals, but were expelled by aliens – the Romans – as a result of a persistent refusal to behave themselves and to accept Roman hegemony, material and spiritual. They did not 'vote with their feet' but were pushed out by 'foreigners'. Unlike the Huguenots, the Jews had no reason to embrace a new identity as a reaction against their own country.

However, probably the main reason for the fact that the Jews remained a separate body of people in their Diaspora, easily identified and therefore ideal scapegoats, lies in their religious beliefs. The two essential elements of Judaism, elements which have not changed at all since Abraham, are, first, that the religion is monotheistic and, secondly, their belief that the God thus worshipped made a covenant with a certain people – the Jews – and promised them rewards on earth if they obeyed His orders. The main reward was to be the land of Canaan, the brightest jewel of which came to be the city of Jerusalem, or Zion as it is sometimes called. The failures of the Children of Israel to adhere to the commandments of their God came to be directly associated in their minds with their earthly failures, defeats and setbacks in their struggle to reach and secure their Promised Land. The closer they kept their law (The Torah) the closer they came to their longed-for home. There was, therefore, always a perfectly clear explanation for miseries, which to their contemporaries might have seemed to be the unexplained visitations of a chaotic and cruel universe.

With this firm and enduring belief, they were sure that they were indeed the chosen race and must remain so. God, the Almighty Creator, would not allow them to disintegrate. Their feeling of uniqueness was, if anything, increased by tribulations which could easily be explained by the visitations of a jealous Creator on His erring children.

The Zionists' dream of a return to the land of Canaan is, therefore, as old as the religion itself and, during the whole of the Diaspora, it remained for the majority of Jews a dream, a mystical vision of a distant and presently unobtainable future. Some Jews indeed were in Palestine, very often in great need and supported by the alms of their dispersed compatriots. For centuries there was, however, no question of a general return to Palestine and the establishment of a Jewish state there.

During the nineteenth century, the first rumblings of the volcano of modern Zionism were to be heard in various countries, initially diffident and weak in volume but gradually becoming more insistent until eventually erupting in the great founder of modern Zionism, Theodore Herzl, and his book *Der Judenstaat* published in Vienna in 1896. This was followed by the first Zionist conference in Basle in 1897. The Basle programme produced there defined the purpose of the Zionist organization as 'the creation in Palestine of a home for the Jewish people secured by public law'.

As far as the Zionists were concerned, the turn of the century was marked by a great persecution of Jews in Russia and this lent urgency to their programme. The Zionist leaders had to convince non-Jewish statesmen and politicians of their credentials as representing world Jewry as well as convincing them of the justice of their cause. This meant that it was comparatively easy for Jews who disagreed with any aspect of the Zionist programme to kill it at birth by merely throwing doubt on the Zionist claims to represent Jewry without even bothering to argue about the programme itself. There were many Jews, often from the higher echelons of society, who opposed Zionism. They wished to be fully accepted as citizens of their host country and not to be continually thought to be looking elsewhere with disloyal eyes. There was in most countries of the Diaspora a strong anti-Zionist Jewish lobby. However, Zionism received a boost as persecution of the Jews in Russia worsened, until in 1903 the news of a particularly brutal pogrom at Kishinev burst on the world. In this bloody incident forty-five men, women and children were killed, more than a thousand were wounded and fifteen hundred houses and shops were destroyed. This took place just before the sixth Zionist Congress, at which Herzl produced a letter from the British Government signed by the Foreign Secretary, Lord Lansdowne, offering the Jews an autonomous territory in East Africa. The prospect of lifting thousands, perhaps hundreds of thousands, of Jews out of their present misery and starting them afresh in the new country was dazzling. However, the question was – should the Zionists accept any country but Palestine? The debate was long and very bitter. Eventually, after the death of Herzl, the offer was rejected at the seventh Zionist Congress in 1905.

All these controversies and many others came to a head when the First World War shattered the general peace of Europe for the first time since Napoleon. It soon became clear that the Zionists would have to make up their minds as to which country was to be their principal ally. Jewish feeling about the outcome of the war was mixed. It is one of the ironies of history that there were very many German Jews who were convinced that their permanent home lay in Germany, a country for which they had a deep emotional affection. Furthermore, Germany's opposition to the hated Russia inclined the Jews towards the central powers. On the other hand they had a great regard for the generally liberal and humanitarian outlook of Great Britain and, later, America, together with a dislike of the mildly anti-Semitic and repressive regime of Turkey. With the increasing success of the British action against Turkey in the Middle East, it became clear that Britain, as the probable occupier of Palestine, was the country best suited to assist in the achievement of the Zionist aim. Partly as a result of this, there emerged as undisputed leader of the Zionists a man who had deliberately identified himself with Great Britain – Chaim Weizman. He was a remarkable man with great influence over some British politicians, including Winston Churchill who was stirred by his romantic vision.

The First World War was indeed providential for the Zionist cause. The Ottoman Empire in 1914 still stretched right across

Syria and Palestine and, indeed, nominally included Egypt although the connection between Egypt and Turkey was by then tenuous. In any event, it was obvious that the status quo would not be resumed in the Middle East after an Allied victory, particularly as a large slice of the Arab world had joined in the Arab revolt engineered by the British in order to help them in their Palestine campaign. Here at last was an opportunity for the Zionists to achieve their aims with a minimum of disturbance during a general redistribution of territory. Furthermore, an essential third element could be shown to be present, in addition to the Zionists longing to return to Palestine and the opportunity presented by the dissolution of the Turkish Empire. This was the identity of interests between the Zionists and Great Britain.

The initial heavy British opposition to the digging of the Suez Canal had dissolved very quickly, to be replaced with disarming hypocrisy by a proprietary interest in the venture which was strengthened in 1875 by the acquisition of the Khedive Ismail's shares, sold to prevent bankruptcy. Communications were vital to a world Empire and, of course, through the Suez Canal lay the main route to that brightest jewel in the Imperial Crown, India. Even before the discovery of Middle Eastern oil, the British sensitivity to any danger in the Suez area was acute. The entente cordiale, in spite of its spectacular results in Europe, had not penetrated as far as Franco–British relations in the Middle East. Furthermore the Egyptians had not taken at all kindly to British domination over their country, ungrateful though they may have appeared to British eyes for that honour. What better safeguard could the British have for their interests in the Suez Canal than a young and vigorous nation, passionately pro-British because of the British responsibility for its existence, poised close to the canal and sandwiched between that waterway and the likely French area of influence or control in Syria and the Lebanon?

In fact in May 1916 Britain had signed a secret agreement with France (the Sykes–Picot pact) under which after the war Britain would have hegemony in the Baghdad and Basra provinces of

Mesopotamia, France would have hegemony in Syria and Lesser Armenia in Turkey, there would be an international zone in Palestine and the rest would be constituted into an independent Arab state or federation divided into British or French zones of influence.[1] A pro-British Jewish state in part of Palestine would undoubtedly help to contain any French ideas of expansion to the south. Furthermore, by 1917 the situation in Europe was dark, with little hope of it improving. The first Russian revolution had brought great anxiety for the Allies: there was fear that the Russians would desert the war altogether (as of course they did, later). It was feared that the large Jewish element in Russia, because of its hatred of the tsarist regime, might throw its weight on the side of a quick end to the war. The United States' entry into the war did not seem to be making much difference and there was a feeling in Britain that the Americans were dragging their feet. A great gesture to the Zionists, such as the declaration that Great Britain would support Zionist aims, would, it was argued, have a great effect both in Russia and the United States. There was also the possibility that Germany might jump the gun by making some similar declaration itself, thus producing great embarrassment to the Allies in both Russia and America.

Chaim Weizman and his friends put all these arguments to the British Government with charm and vehemence and, finally, after great opposition from the anti-Zionist Jew Montagu, a cabinet minister, there emerged the Balfour Declaration. This took the form of a letter from Balfour, the foreign secretary, to Lord Rothschild, a leading British Zionist, dated 2 November 1917. His letter read as follows:

Dear Lord Rothschild,

I have much pleasure in conveying to you, on behalf of His Majesty's Government, the following declaration of sympathy with Jewish Zionist aspirations which has been submitted to, and agreed by, the Cabinet.

His Majesty's Government view with favour the establishment in Palestine of a National Home for the Jewish people, and will use their best endeavours to facilitate the achievement of this object, it being clearly understood that nothing shall be done which may prejudice the civil and religious rights of non-Jewish communities in Palestine, or the rights and political status enjoyed by Jews in any other country. I should be grateful if you would bring this declaration to the knowledge of the Zionist Federation.[2]

Zionists were for the first time being taken seriously by a great nation. Furthermore, it must be remembered that not only were the British the only Allies engaged in fighting in the Middle East and therefore with an overriding moral authority for that area, but Great Britain in 1917 still had that enormous significance in world affairs which sprang from the dynamic vitality of its Victorian heyday. American power was of course growing rapidly but American claims to influence in any Middle Eastern settlement were stunted by the fact that the United States had not declared war against Turkey.

A further complicating factor, entirely of British making, was the correspondence between the British High Commissioner in Egypt, Sir Thomas McMahon, and Hussein, the Sharif of Mecca and the hereditary head of the Hashemite clan. In this correspondence Hussein agreed to lead a revolt against the Ottoman Empire and in return was told that, subject to certain modifications, 'Great Britain [was] prepared to recognize and support the independence of the Arabs in all the regions within the limits demanded by the Sharif of Mecca'. The modifications referred to the land 'lying to the west of the districts of Damascus, Homs, Hama and Aleppo'. As no part of Palestine is to the west of these districts the Arabs believed that Palestine should have been included in the area in which Britain had promised an independent Arab government.

The letters were indeed extremely vague, probably deliberately so, couched in the flowery language believed to be beloved by the Arabs. For instance, Hussein was addressed as

The excellent and well born Sayid, the descendant of Sharifs, the Crown of the Proud, Scion of Mohammed's Tree and Branch of the Koreishite Trunk, him of the Exalted Presence and of the Lofty Rank, Sayid son of Sayid, Sherif son of Sherif, the Venerable, Honoured Sayid, His Excellency the Sherif Hussein, Lord of the Many, Emir of Mecca the Blessed, the Lodestar of the Faithful, and the cynosure of all devout Believers, may his Blessing descend upon the people in their multitudes.[3]

The upshot was that the Arabs thought that Palestine had been pledged to them: the British were to argue that that was not so. This must have been difficult to sustain, as was the British claim later that a national home for the Jewish people did not imply the creation of a Jewish state.

Accusations of double dealing by the British are difficult, if not impossible, to refute and the situation thus created undoubtedly was a major factor in the assassination of all three leaders considered in this chapter. The only defence possible is that Britain was engaged in a life and death struggle in France at the time and the temptation to take every opportunity of improving the situation, even if it meant making contradictory promises impossible to fulfil, must have been great. The horrors of the carnage in the trenches in France were such that any effort to alleviate or end them must have appeared to have an overriding justification. However, the truth of the matter was succinctly summed up by Sir John Chancellor, the British High Commissioner in Palestine from 1928 to 1931, in a despatch to his government as follows: 'The facts of the situation are that in the dire straits of the war, the British Government made promises to the Arabs and promises to the Jews which are inconsistent with one another and incapable of fulfilment.'[4]

Among the many problems that the Versailles Peace Conference had to address, one of the most difficult was the dismantling of the Ottoman Empire. There were many vultures picking over the carcass, notably Britain, France, the Zionists and various Arab potentates, all claiming sovereignty over some or all of the area on offer. Sherif Hussein, the King of the Hejaz – the western region of what was to become Saudi Arabia – was represented at Versailles by his third son, the Emir Feisal. He was accompanied by Lawrence of Arabia, by then a very famous figure. Feisal asked that 'the Arabic speaking peoples of Asia . . . be recognized as independent sovereign peoples under the guarantee of the League of Nations'. In that highly sophisticated and vastly experienced gathering he was an ineffective figure and he failed to achieve any of his objectives. Indeed, he was ejected by the French from his throne in Damascus, which he had entered with Allenby at the end of his campaign.

The Peace Conference decided that Hussein should be confirmed in his sovereignty over the Hejaz, while France was given a mandate over Syria and Lebanon. The Zionists were to have a National Home in Palestine, although what that meant remained obscure, and Britain was to have a mandate over Palestine, Iraq and Transjordan. All this was very vague and, clearly, greater definition was necessary. As appeared to be almost always the case from the Boer War to the end of the Second World War, when major decisions were pending, Winston Churchill burst on the scene, this time in the guise of the British Colonial Secretary, romantic, decisive and inventive as ever.

He called a conference in Cairo in 1921 attended by 'practically all the experts and authorities in the Middle East', as he put it – including Lawrence and the formidable Gertrude Bell. He was heavily influenced by the romantic aura attached to Lawrence, who had been devastated by what he saw as the betrayal of his Arab friends and allies, the Hashemites. With a stroke of a pen Churchill created two new states – the Kingdom of Iraq and the Emirate of Transjordan, both with Hashemite rulers – Feisal in Baghdad and his brother Abdullah as Emir of Transjordan (a territory into which the latter had in fact already marched). Their father, Hussein, retained his sway over much of the Hejaz until he was defeated by Ibn Saud, who took his place and created the state of Saudi Arabia in 1932.[5]

Abdullah had been born in Mecca in 1880. He had been educated in Constantinople where he had also received some military training. From 1912 to 1914 he was deputy for Mecca in the Ottoman Parliament. He had a profound faith in the destiny of his Hashemite family, descended as they were from the Prophet's daughter Fatima. He saw them as eventual rulers of an independent Arab Empire. He was politically ambitious, astute and charming. He had played a powerful role in the Arab revolt, although it was his younger brother, Feisal, who had received the glory.[6]

As a result of Churchill's decisions Abdullah found himself ruler of the largely barren and certainly unviable territory of Transjordan, initially a mandated territory but which had become nominally independent by the treaty of 1928. However, he was dependent upon a British subsidy and British expertise in various forms — notably the formation of the army and police force. He undoubtedly saw his role of ruler of Transjordan as one stage on a ladder which would lead to greater things, at least for his family if not for himself. He resented the growing Jewish presence in the neighbouring mandated territory of Palestine, but accepted that it was a fact and he would have to deal with it. It was this attitude of *real politik*, together with his liking for and dependence on the British, and his aspirations to hegemony over a greater Syria including Syria, Lebanon, Transjordan and Palestine, which was to make him so vastly unpopular with his fellow Arab leaders and was to lead to his assassination.

In between the two world wars Great Britain, as mandatory power, was saddled with the impossible task of creating a 'National Home for the Jewish people whilst not doing anything to prejudice the civil and religious rights of existing non-Jewish communities in Palestine'. It was certain that either the Jews or the Arabs or, more probably, both would be upset. The touchstone was to be the question of Jewish immigration.

After the initial impetus given by the Balfour Declaration, the number of Jews arriving in Palestine began to decline and in fact in 1928 there were more Jewish emigrants than immigrants. However, the rise of anti-Semitism in Europe and in particular in Germany in the 1930s, led to an almost overwhelming increase of Jewish immigration, to 45,000 in 1934 and 66,000 in 1935.[7] There were great pressures on the Arabs to sell their land to Jewish immigrants, and many did so. Resentment grew fast and a series of Arab revolts took place, culminating in the Palestinian Arab rebellion of 1937/8. The Palestinian Arabs themselves were divided, not in their opposition to the growing Jewish influx, but on the tactics to be used. Haj Amin al-Husseini, whom the British, to their later vast regret, had chosen to build up as the Grand Mufti of Jerusalem, believed in all-out opposition without cooperating in any way with the mandatory power. The mayor of Jerusalem, Raghib al-Nashashibi, was in favour of more subtle ways of achieving their objectives. He and his followers were prepared to cooperate with the British if they saw advantage in doing so. Abdullah found himself allied to the Nashashibi family while soon becoming the enemy of the Husseini clan. Although there were exceptions, on the whole the Nashashibi were landowners and merchants, the Husseinis intellectuals, fervent religious believers and other extreme Nationalists.

The Arab rebellion was partly prompted by the recommendations of a British Royal Commission which in July 1937 had favoured the partition of Palestine. Galilee was to be given to the proposed Jewish state in spite of the fact that it had an Arab majority. Jerusalem, Bethlehem and a corridor to the sea were to remain under the British mandate and the rest of Palestine was to be united with Transjordan. The Nashashibi family and their supporters were prepared to accept this plan as the best obtainable in the circumstances whereas the Husseinis were not. The British eventually put down the rebellion at the cost of some twenty thousand Arab casualties.

Britain then decided to change course and the White Paper of 1939 proposed a limitation of Jewish immigration to an average of 15,000 a year for five years and offered an outline of an independent, bi-national state in Palestine by 1949. This was bitterly opposed by the Jews, who insisted on unlimited Jewish immigration and the creation of a purely Jewish state. When the war intervened, the

Jewish Establishment agreed to postpone their struggle and support the British in the fight against Hitler. Ben Gurion coined the phrase – 'We will fight the white paper as if there was no war and the war as if there was no white paper.'

When Abdullah had been installed as Emir of Transjordan he had agreed to coordinate its foreign policy with London and to allow the stationing of British troops on its soil. In February 1928 Transjordan formally entered into a treaty with Britain and a British resident was appointed, by whose advice Abdullah agreed to be guided. Abdullah announced his full support for Britain on the declaration of war and reiterated this, in Britain's darkest hour, in 1940. Cynics argue that, subsidized and supported by Britain as he was, he had no alternative. His supporters, on the other hand, hailed this as a heroic gesture, arguing that Transjordan was the only ally Britain had in the world apart from her Commonwealth and Empire. Transjordan acquired independence in May 1946. Abdullah assumed the title of King and renamed the Emirate of Transjordan as the Hashemite Kingdom of Jordan.

Anwar Sadat was different to Abdullah in almost every way. He was born in Mit Abul Kum, a village in the Nile Delta of Egypt in 1918. Britain had occupied the country in 1882, declaring it a Protectorate on the eve of the First World War. The British recognized it as a sovereign state in 1922 but maintained a military presence. There was considerable Nationalist feeling against the British occupation and its interference in Egypt's internal affairs, a feeling which was fully shared by Sadat as he grew up. Sadat's father was a clerk in the military hospital; his mother was the daughter of a Sudanese fellah, or peasant. According to his wife,[8] his village had no electricity or plumbing. His grandmother acted as the village healer, treating sickness with ancient concoctions of herbs. They had very little money. At the Quranic teaching school where he and the other village boys learnt the 114 chapters of the Quran by heart, Sadat's only meal consisted of bread crusts and dry cheese. When

not at school he would take the cows and the water buffalo to drink
from the village canal, drive the oxen pulling the thresher through
the fields of wheat and help to harvest the dates and cotton. At
night he would often listen to his mother and grandmother, whom
he particularly admired, tell bedtime stories of modern Egyptian
heroes standing up to the British. Sadat believed that his village was
a major determining factor in his life: 'I learned [in Mit Abul Kum]
. . . the fact that wherever I go, wherever I happen to be, I shall
always know where I really am. I can never lose my way because
I know that I have living roots there, deep down in the soil of my
village, in that land out of which I grew, like the trees and plants.'9
However, when he was seven he moved to Cairo. There he lived in a
four-roomed flat together with his grandmother, his two brothers,
his sister and his father and mother. His father took another wife
from the village and she bore him nine more children, all of them
living in the four rooms.

The British–Egyptian Treaty of 1936 allowed the Egyptian army
to expand and, for the first time, to open the officer corps to the
lower classes. Sadat, clearly a bright lad, joined the Royal Military
Academy and graduated with the rank of second lieutenant in 1938.
Among the other graduates was Gamal Nasser. Sadat was a
passionate Nationalist and, as such, in the Egypt of his youth,
violently anti-British. He saw the British occupation of his country
and their power over its internal affairs as an insupportable affront
to Egyptian, and therefore his, dignity. The Second World War was,
to him, an opportunity to get rid of the hated British. He formed a
secret organization, The Free Officers Organization, and contacted
the Germans, who were approaching Egypt across the desert, in
order to offer Egyptian military help in return for independence. He
was contacted by two German spies, who gave him a wireless
transmitter. His house was searched but the radio was not found.
Nevertheless, he was sent to the Aliens Jail in the summer of 1942.
He escaped twice, on the first occasion returning to prison
voluntarily in order to humiliate the British. When the war ended
and martial law was lifted he joined a secret organization with the

objective of ridding Egypt of collaborators with the British. He was arrested in January 1946 and charged with the assassination of Amin Osman, the Egyptian minister of finance. It took two and a half years for his case to come to trial, during which time he languished in the extremely uncomfortable Cairo Central Prison; nevertheless, in Cell 54 he claims to have found peace of mind. At his trial he was acquitted, although his wife was to say later in her autobiography that 'It was Anwar, I later learned, who had taken the men who did it into the desert and told them to shoot.'[10] Indeed, in his own autobiography Sadat freely admits to a leading part in the plot.[11]

On his release, Sadat tried to earn his living as a businessman, but he had no head for figures and he and his wife, whom he had married in May 1949, came near to destitution. By pulling strings with a member of King Farouk's staff,[12] Sadat managed to get himself reinstated in the army with his old rank of captain. He was posted to Rafah in the Sinai, where he once more came into contact with Nasser.

Yitzhak Rabin was born in Jerusalem in 1922. His father and mother both came from Russia, his father via the United States, and they were both passionate Zionists. His mother was a particularly powerful character, becoming a leading figure in the Haganah – the Jewish defence organization. Rabin and his sister lived a puritanical and very earnest life where achievement was all; there were few frills. Rabin was clever and was offered a scholarship at the University of California. However, he felt that his duty lay in the Zionist cause. He joined the Haganah and when war broke out graduated into the Palmach, the official military arm of the Zionist Organization. Although illegal in British eyes, it cooperated with the British in a reconnaissance into the Lebanon in June 1941, in which Rabin took part.

When the war ended and it became clear that the British were not going to deliver a Jewish state, the Haganah and the Palmach turned to armed resistance. Rabin rose quickly, becoming a brigade commander by 1948, aged twenty-six.

Among its many problems in 1945 Great Britain found itself lumbered with a vastly unpopular occupation force in Egypt and the even more unpopular mandate for Palestine. The horrors of the holocaust had led to massive worldwide sympathy for the Jews left alive in Europe, and Britain found herself trying to prevent many of them from emigrating to Israel in order not to exceed a quota imposed to keep some kind of balance of population and to restrict Arab protests to a minimum. There were many unpleasant incidents. Jewish freedom fighters/terrorists (depending on your point of view) launched a major assault on the British army in Palestine. The Irgun Zvai Leumi under Menachem Begin, subsequently to become Prime Minister of Israel, blew up the British headquarters in Jerusalem, the King David Hotel (narrowly missing the author of this book!). Another group, the Stern gang, had murdered Lord Moyne, the British Minister of State in the Middle East, in Cairo in November 1944. The Haganah had dissociated itself from this latter action, but after the war armed attacks increased and Ernest Bevin, the British Labour Government Foreign Secretary who, incidentally, had come under heavy criticism for being pro-Arab, eventually decided to place the issue before the General Assembly of the United Nations.

Under heavy United States pressure the United Nations produced a plan whereby a Jewish state was to be established in Palestine to include nearly 60 per cent of the country (with under a third of the population). There were to be more Arabs than Jews in this state, and Jerusalem was to be internationalized. The rest of Arab Palestine was to be set up as a separate state. All this would clearly have to be enforced by military means, which Britain was not prepared to exert. The final date for British withdrawal was fixed as 15 May 1948.

It was argued that a Palestinian state on the lines proposed would be an unviable entity and Abdullah prevailed upon Ernest Bevin to give at least tacit support to its union with Transjordan. After secret negotiations with Golda Meir, the head of the Jewish Agency's political department dealing with foreign affairs, the Israelis agreed. However, this was anathema to the rest of the Arab world, which refused to accept partition at all; they were highly suspicious of Abdullah, whom they regarded as a British lackey, becoming far more powerful and adding to his pretensions as leader of the Arab world ruling over a greater Syria.

Nevertheless, Abdullah was given nominal command of an attack on the new state of Israel by the Arab League, an organization of Arabic-speaking states finally set up in March 1945 after an earlier British initiative in September 1944. However, the air force was woefully inadequate in numbers, training, weapons and coordination. The only military contingent of any real value was the Arab Legion, Abdullah's Transjordan army set up in 1921 under the British Peake Pasha and later commanded by Glubb Pasha – also British. All the other Arab forces – Egyptian, Iraqi, Lebanese and Syrian – were defeated or retreated from the scene. There were a number of cease-fires and the war ended with a series of armistice agreements whereby Israel, which had declared itself to be a sovereign state on 14 May 1948, acquired considerably more territory than the United Nations had allocated to it. However, a large area of the West Bank of the River Jordan, including the eastern part of Jerusalem, was occupied by Jordanian forces and later annexed by Jordan. The only countries to profit from this war were Israel and Jordan, both of which greatly increased their territory. Abdullah openly despised the efforts of his Arab partners[13] and the hatred of him in virtually the whole of the Arab world, except in his own country, intensified.

Yitzhak Rabin played a major part in the Arab–Israeli War of 1948 (during which, incidentally, Anwar Sadat was still in prison, a very frustrated man). The new Harel Brigade of the Palmach which Rabin was commanding, aged twenty-six, was deployed on the Jerusalem front. At first it fought to secure the main road to Tel Aviv, the lifeline for Jerusalem. The fighting was heavy, but after many vicissitudes the road was eventually secured. The brigade then moved to Jerusalem but failed in its attempt to take the Old City, which was defended by the Arab Legion. Rabin blamed this failure on what he saw as stupid orders by his Haganah superiors.

One result of the War of Independence was that over 1 million Palestinian Arabs fled their homes and became refugees, mostly in Jordan. Thus was created the festering sore which, above all, has led to the continuing conflict between Israel and the Arab world. From the Arab point of view there could be no possible excuse for what they saw as the deliberate expulsion of those who had lived in Palestine for generations. Refugee camps became havens for an embittered people with but one aim in life – a return to their ancestral homes. It is not surprising that talk of a 'chosen people' and the 'Promised Land' cut no ice at all. The Israelis argued that the Arabs had left voluntarily. In some cases that may be true in the sense that they were not physically driven out by Israeli soldiers. But the truth is that in one incident alone, 254 civilians in the village of Deir Yassin were massacred and that example caused the survivors and many others to leave in fear of their lives. Why else would they leave their homes? Rabin afterwards confessed to feeling uneasy about some of the Jewish actions.[14]

In the last phase of the war Rabin was Chief of Operations on the southern front, where the Egyptians were heavily defeated. He earned the respect of his fellow citizens during the War of Independence but unlike some of his contemporaries, including the dashing Moshe Dayan, he was not loved: his cold, determined personality did not inspire that emotion.

When the war was over Abdullah again entered into negotiations with the Israelis in an attempt to achieve permanent peace and to gain full acceptance of his position as King of Jordan, including the West Bank. However, the Israelis, after their astonishingly complete victories in the War of Independence, were becoming arrogant and the momentum of the negotiations fell away as they appeared to refuse to make any compromises. It looked as if Abdullah was incurring great unpopularity with all his fellow Arabs but without any payoff. He even found himself losing some of his personal authority in Jordan because he had to take account of the very many Arab Palestinian refugees in his country. Indeed, after the 1948 war, the Kingdom of Jordan had a majority of Palestinians in it.[15] His great enemies, the Husseinis (led by the Grand Mufti of Jerusalem, who had been in Germany during the war and had returned), were gaining influence over the Palestinian Arabs.

On 20 July 1951 Abdullah went to pray at the Al-Aksa Mosque in Jerusalem. As he crossed the threshold, a young man stepped from behind the door, pressed a pistol to his ear and fired a shot, killing him instantly. Abdullah's bodyguard immediately slaughtered the assassin. Although there is still argument about the origins of the plot to assassinate him there can be little doubt that it was instigated by Abdullah Al-Tell, a dissident officer of the Arab Legion who had gone to Egypt, together with Dr Musa-Al-Husseini, a relative of the grand mufti who was personally responsible for planning and financing the crime. The actual assassin was a tailor's apprentice from Jerusalem with a criminal record and a member of the grand mufti's radical paramilitary organization. Six of the eight accused were caught, tried and hanged.

There was almost certainly more than one motive behind the assassination, the primary one undoubtedly stemming from a bitter opposition to Abdullah's attitude to Israel and frustration at the apparent inability of the Arab world to prevent the establishment of what seemed to be an ever-increasing Israeli state. However, there may well have been other factors – the Nashashibi/Husseini feud within Arab Palestine; the rivalry between Ibn Saud and Abdullah arising from the Saudi expulsion of Abdullah's father; and even King Farouk of Egypt's desire for Arab domination. Assassinations were almost becoming a way of life in the Arab world.

After the King's murder, a Cairo newspaper published a list of Arab public men who had been assassinated in the five years from 1946 to 1951. It included two Kings – King Abdullah of Jordan and the Imam Yahya of the Yemen; one President of a Republic – Husni az Zaim of Syria; four Prime Ministers – Ahmed Maher Pasha and Nokrashy Pasha of Egypt, Muhsin al Brazi of Syria and Riyadh as Sulh of Lebanon; one Commander-in-Chief – Sami al Hennawi of Syria; the Leader of the Moslem Brotherhood in Egypt – Shaik Hasan al Benna; one cabinet minister – Amin Osman of Egypt; and several police chiefs and judges. Numerous unsuccessful attempts at assassination were made on other Prime Ministers, ministers and public men.[16]

Whatever the causes, the deed had immediate repercussions on British influence in the Middle East. A potential Arab ally of the Israelis disappeared as did a great supporter of Great Britain, whose influence on the area had already begun to wane and was to fade even more in the comparatively near future.

The flamboyant and corrupt reign of King Farouk came to a predictable end in July 1952 with Sadat playing a leading role in Nasser's successful military coup. He did not immediately join the government, however, but started a newspaper, *The Republic*, to present the views of the new regime. There was a great deal of unrest in Egypt, partly because the immediate rewards of the coup were, as is usual with coups, not apparent and partly because of the rise of the fundamentalist Moslem Brotherhood which was banned by the Revolutionary Command Council. There were several plots and assassination attempts including one on Nasser's life in October 1954. Sadat became one of the judges of the 'people's court' set up in order to try 'traitors'. Over a thousand people were tried and six members of the Brotherhood were sentenced to death. In 1959 Sadat became speaker of the Parliament and in 1964 one of the four Vice-Presidents to Nasser. He became Egyptian representative at various international Islamic conferences and in December 1969 Nasser appointed him as his sole Vice-President and, therefore, potential successor.

He had little personal role in either the 1956 Suez War between Britain, France, Israel and Egypt or in the six day war in June 1967 when Israel inflicted a crushing defeat on the Egyptian and Syrian armies. According to his wife, although continuing to support

Nasser, he opposed the draconian measures used against the Moslem Brotherhood and other opposition figures. In his autobiography, Sadat inveighs against the intrigue, cruelty, corruption and hatred which he sees as being characteristic of Nasser's later years in power. 'Although externally uneventful, the period from June 1967 to September 1970 was one of intense suffering, unprecedented, I believe, in the entire stretch of Egyptian history.'[17] On Nasser's death in September 1970 he became acting President, being elected as President the following month (as the only candidate).

After the 1948 War of Independence, Rabin became involved in an internecine dispute between the dissident Irgun Zvai Leumi led by Menachem Begin and the new Israeli Government led by Ben Gurion. Begin had agreed to merge his fighters into the new National Army, but when a ship, the *Altalena*, carrying arms for the Irgun appeared off the coast, Begin refused to hand over its cargo. Ben Gurion feared a putsch from the Nationalist right, which had never accepted partition. The ship arrived off Tel Aviv, and he was determined to take the arms by force if necessary. Rabin was put in charge of the party on the beach. After a firefight, in which fourteen of their men were killed, the Irgun surrendered. The idea fostered by some Zionists, that Jew does not kill Jew, had been shattered once and for all.

Rabin continued his meteoric rise in the Israeli army in spite of a major row with the Prime Minister, Ben Gurion, when he attended a reunion of Palmach veterans protesting against the disbanding of their previously elite body. He attended the British Staff College in Camberley in 1952/3, one of his fellow students being Faez Maher who was eventually to serve as Jordan's chief of staff. He became head of the Northern Command in April 1956, though he did not take part in the Suez War.

On 1 January 1964, at the age of forty-one, Rabin became Chief of Staff. The Israeli army fought brilliantly under his direction in the 1967 war, launched by the Israelis in response to the closure of the

Straits of Tiran. Although suffering from an attack of nerves during which he disappeared for a day, Rabin's reputation was greatly enhanced. Israel captured the whole of the West Bank including east Jerusalem, the Golan Heights, the Gaza Strip and the whole of the Sinai peninsula. The area of land under Israeli control was tripled. Then, for the first time, Rabin entered the political sphere, being appointed by the Prime Minister, Eshkol, as Israeli ambassador to Washington.

When Nasser died and Sadat took over as President, it was at first expected that he would continue the previous policy of internal repression and confrontation with Israel. But he was his own man. He lifted censorship, ordered the release of thousands of political prisoners and announced a new initiative towards the Israelis, offering to reopen the Suez Canal if Israel withdrew its forces from the Sinai – an offer that, sadly, was refused by the Israelis.

After the Suez affair Nasser had become almost entirely dependent on the Soviet Union in many ways, in particular for military equipment and training. Sadat determined to change this and to ally his country more closely with the United States. In July 1972 he ordered all the Russians to leave Egypt within ten days, a radical and, at the time, shattering decision requiring great courage and self-confidence. He hoped that the Israelis, largely protégés of the United States, would make some response – but they did not. Sadat felt that he could not continue with an intolerable situation whereby the Israelis were occupying a large slice (the Sinai) of Egyptian territory. He was also affronted by the ignominious defeats the Egyptian army had suffered in the past, and wished to create a new and better reputation for the Egyptian army and air force. He planned an attack over the Suez Canal on the Israeli occupying force. After a succession of exercises designed to lure the Israelis into a false sense of security, it took place in October 1973. The attack was coordinated with Syria and the aim of both was to recover the land which had been seized from them in the 1967 war.

Unprecedentedly, the Egyptian army was, successful in the early stages. But, after massive supplies of arms were sent to Israel by the United States, the Israeli army began to re-exert its superiority, and the war came to an end when Russia threatened to intervene and the Americans brokered a cease-fire. The initial Egyptian military successes were a great boost to Egyptian morale. However, the opposite was the case in Israel. There was a loss of confidence in Prime Minister Golda Meir and the defence minister Moshe Dayan. Golda Meir had to resign and Rabin, who had become minister of labour on his return from Washington, became Prime Minister. Shimon Peres, who had been for some time a personal enemy of Rabin, became Minister of Defence.

Both sides now wanted peace, and negotiations between Rabin and Sadat were started under the auspices of the shuttling Kissinger. Rabin had secret meetings with Jordan and the King of Morocco, whom he once visited wearing a shaggy dark wig.[18] Both Rabin and Sadat were prepared to make some concessions but they both had difficulties with their own hawks. These meetings came to an end when Rabin had to resign as Prime Minister in 1977 because of a very minor financial scandal in which his wife had been involved when he was ambassador in Washington.

Rabin's successor, Begin, as we have seen, the very aggressive leader of the Irgun during the British mandate, had a tough and uncompromising reputation. However, Sadat was determined to persevere with his search for peace and, in an unprecedented gesture, in November 1977 invited himself to visit Israel and addressed the Knesset, the Israeli Parliament, calling for peace in an impressive speech. This made him extremely unpopular with his fellow Arab leaders and with hard-line elements in Egypt, in particular with the Moslem Brotherhood. This journey was followed by the Camp David meeting in the United States which Sadat and Begin attended under the auspices of President Carter. On 26 March 1979 Sadat, Begin and Carter shook hands on the achievement of a peace agreement. Sadat and Begin both received the Nobel Peace Prize. Sadat plumbed new depths of unpopularity with the other Arab states and Egypt was suspended from the Arab League. Sadat became increasingly isolated both within and without his country and, in order to maintain his position at home, he became more and more authoritarian. He dissolved Parliament two years short of its normal tenure, and rigged the first multi-party election in June 1979. He expelled the last of the Soviet civilian experts and became even more dependent upon the United States for economic survival. Inflation rose and there was much hardship. Sadat banned strikes and demonstrations, becoming increasingly intolerant of any opposition. In September 1981 he ordered some two thousand arrests.

On 16 October 1981 Sadat was celebrating what he saw as Egypt's proudest anniversary – the moment in 1973 when Egyptian soldiers had crossed the Suez Canal. There was a military parade, and as Sadat was watching, an army truck suddenly pulled out of the line of artillery vehicles and stopped in front of the reviewing stands. Three soldiers ran towards the stands with machine guns. A grenade exploded, the machine-guns opened fire and Sadat was shot and killed. The assassins were militant members of the Moslem Brotherhood. The peacemaker was killed by those who could not tolerate peaceful coexistence, indeed any dealings whatever, with the hated state of Israel.

As often seems to be the case civil wars are the bitterest, and internecine warfare within the Israeli political Establishment at least equalled, if it did not exceed, the tension that existed between Arab and Israeli. The right wing in Israel had never accepted partition, and at the birth of the state of Israel Begin bitterly attacked the division of Palestine (and those Jews who willingly accepted it) as 'a crime, a blasphemy, an abortion'.[19] He said, 'Whoever does not recognize our national right to our entire homeland does not recognize our right to any part of it.' However, as do many opposition leaders when faced by the realities of decision-making, on becoming Prime Minister he modified his position. He did sign the Camp David accords but saw them not as the final answer but as one stage on the road.

In 1982, under Begin's leadership, the Israeli army entered the Lebanon in an attempt to liquidate the Palestine Liberation Organization (PLO) presence in south Lebanon, from where attacks were being made into Israel. A massacre of about two thousand people took place in two Palestine Arab refugee camps carried out by a Christian militia aligned with Israel. There was a vast international outcry and much soul searching in Israel. Begin resigned in August 1983, a sick man.

At this stage Israel was a very divided country with much bitterness between the moderates and the extremists, whose political parties were Labour and Likud respectively. After an election in 1984 there was deadlock between the two. A 'National Unity Government' was formed, under which Peres, the Labour leader, and the Likud leader, Shamir, would rotate the Prime Ministership, each serving for two years. Rabin remained Defence Minister for the entire period. Although he had initially supported the incursion into the Lebanon, by January 1985 he was calling the war a mistake.

There now followed a period of widespread unrest and rioting (known as the Intifada) by Palestinian Arabs, within or on the borders of Israel. As Defence Minister, Rabin was responsible for the Israeli response. He tried to suppress the rebellion with force but was only partially successful. Even during this period he was privy to the secret negotiations being carried out by some Labour Party members with the PLO. In November 1988 a further general election was held, which was again inconclusive with Rabin retaining his defence portfolio. This was followed by a period of intense internal intrigue ending with Rabin ousting Peres as leader of the Labour Party, which won a sweeping victory in the election of 27 June 1992, Rabin becoming Prime Minister for the second time. Both Rabin and Peres were above all committed to the peace process. They had been arch-enemies for many years but they made up their quarrels and Peres became Rabin's Foreign Minister. Rabin and Peres continued their negotiations with the PLO, officially in Madrid but effectively at a series of secret meetings in Norway. All this was total anathema to the Israeli right wing, to whom the PLO was an evil terrorist organization set on demolishing the State of Israel.

Eventually, a Declaration of Principles was signed by Arafat for the PLO and Rabin for Israel at the White House in Washington on 13 September, 1993 whereby there would be a five-year interim period of self-rule in the Occupied Territories. The Palestinians would hold elections and Israel would withdraw from Gaza and Jericho. The bitterest pill for Rabin to swallow was formal acceptance by Israel of the PLO as representing the Palestinian Arabs. This led to the necessity of Rabin shaking hands, in full view of the world's press, with Arafat, the man against whom he had fought for many years and who had led the organization which he saw as responsible for many terrorist outrages. In spite of all this, however, Rabin and Arafat developed a grudging respect for each other.

The agreement with Egypt was followed by a peace treaty with Jordan on 26 October 1993. Lastly, the Nobel Peace Prize was awarded jointly to Arafat, Rabin and Peres – the latter two having finally become fully reconciled: indeed, they were to become friends. However, extremists on both sides continued and even increased their terrorist actions. On 25 February 1994 a Jewish Orthodox extremist, a medical doctor named Baruch Goldstein, murdered twenty-nine Arabs at prayer at Hebron. There were massive demonstrations in Jerusalem addressed by Benjamin Netanyahu, the leader of Likud. Rechavan Zeevy, leader of the far right Homeland Party said, 'This is an insane government that has decided to commit national suicide.'[20] Civil war was not far off. Violence by Palestinian extremists escalated. Twenty-two civilians were killed in an explosion in a bus at Tel Aviv and in January 1995 twenty soldiers and a civilian were killed at a bus stop near Netanyah. This was seized on by Netanyahu, who castigated the whole peace process. However, Rabin and Peres were both determined on peace and pressed on with meetings with Arafat. A further agreement was signed with Jordan in September 1995. Tension in Israel was by then at a high level and this agreement was only accepted by the Knesset by sixty-one votes to fifty-nine. Tens of thousands of very angry people demonstrated as Orthodox fury appeared to have no limits. There were pictures of Rabin dressed in SS uniform and shouts of 'Rabin is a homo', 'Rabin is the son of a whore', 'Death to the Arabs', 'Death to Rabin'. Netanyahu addressed the demonstrators: 'This base murderer [Arafat] is now being carried along by the present Government of Israel which, in its blindness, is allowing him to carry out the first stage of his plan – the destruction of the Jewish state.'[21]

Rabin's peace policies were opposed by the entire Israeli right – the most vociferous of which were the Orthodox Zionists. Many of these people believed that the 'End of Days' was nigh and Jewish control of the land of Israel was an essential step towards final redemption. The agreement to give up part of their land to the hated enemy was therefore not only highly dangerous to security but also an act of extreme sacrilege. To further their cause, they had established settlements in areas which were due to be handed over and they refused to move. By June 1992 when Rabin became Prime Minister for the second time an estimated 105,000 Israeli settlers lived in the Occupied Territories.

The extremists believed that there was only one guideline for fixing the borders of the land of Israel: the divine promise made to Abraham, that 'To your descendants I give this land, from the river of Egypt to the great river, the river Euphrates' (Genesis 15:17). Today, this would enclose all the land from Egypt to Iraq. The extremists considered this to be the Lord's will which must be obeyed whatever the cost. Furthermore, Orthodox rabbis had revived two Orthodox precepts, which were by then wholly obsolete – *din rodef* (the duty to kill a Jew who imperils the life or property of another Jew) and *din moser* (the duty to eliminate a Jew who intends to turn another Jew in to non-Jewish authorities). Some rabbis began to insinuate or even to pronounce that, by signing the agreement with Arafat, Rabin fell into those categories. Indeed hundreds of Orthodox rabbis in the United States signed a statement to that effect.[22]

On Sunday 29 October 1995 Rabin had been warmly received at an economic conference in Amman, a conference attended by delegates from all over the Arab world. On the 31st he received a tumultuous welcome when he attended the Israeli Oscar ceremony in Tel Aviv.[23] However, led by Netanyahu, the opposition Likud Party continued to make violent attacks on him and on the peace process. The demonstrations, speeches and newspaper articles condemning Rabin and Peres were receiving great worldwide publicity and it seemed that the mass of the Israeli people were opposed to the peace process. However, Rabin, Peres and their advisors were convinced that a considerable majority of Israeli opinion was behind them. In order to demonstrate this, it was decided to hold a peace rally in the great Kings of Israel Square in Tel Aviv on 4 November 1995. Two hundred and fifty thousand people turned up, five times more than expected. Rabin made a moving speech to rapturous applause. He praised the PLO, 'a partner in peace': 'This rally must send a message to the Israeli public, to the Jews of the world, to the multitudes in the Arab lands, and to the world at large that the nation of Israel wants peace.' As he left the square he was shot and killed. Subsequent official enquiries showed that security had been almost unbelievably lax in view of the obvious danger to Rabin. This led to a belief in some quarters that Rabin's assassination had been condoned by someone in the security services – a belief which was shown to have no foundation.

Yagal Amir, Rabin's assassin, was twenty-five years old, the son of a rabbi, whose education at school and at university had been ultra-Orthodox. He had organized student protests and meetings and was well known as an activist on the extreme right. He was reported as saying, 'Peres and Rabin are snakes. Cut off their heads and the snake will lose its way. . . . They must both be killed.'[24] After the massacre at Hebron, he had been to Dr Goldstein's funeral (the grave later became a shrine). He had seen Goldstein as an agent of God whom he hoped to emulate. He later said, 'It began after Goldstein. That's when I had the idea that it's necessary to take Rabin down.'[25] At his trial he showed no remorse and was clearly elated that he had carried out what to him was a religious duty. Clearly, many Israelis, although publicly showing regret, in fact agreed. There was no evidence of a widespread plot and it was never proved that Amir had direct rabbinical approval for his act although his brother Haggai said he had. Amir himself has always equivocated on this point. It is true that he had indeed talked to some fellow students about a projected assassination of Rabin, and other abortive attempts had been made. A small group – Amir, his brother Haggai, a friend named Dror Adani and, later, Amir's girlfriend, Margalit, who was convicted of complicity in September 1998 – had been planning the assassination, but in the end Amir had acted on his own.

Rabin's death shocked the world. His funeral was attended by many world leaders, including President Clinton, King Hussein of Jordan, President Mubarak of Egypt, the Prince of Wales, Shevardnaze, the new president of Georgia (and ex-foreign minister of Russia) and the Secretary General of the United Nations, Boutros Boutros-Ghali.

Rabin was succeeded as Prime Minister by his party colleague, his erstwhile enemy, then friend, Peres. At the general election of May 1996 Peres was defeated and Netanyahu became Prime Minister. Three years later, he, in his turn, was defeated by the Labour leader, Ehud Barak, a highly decorated soldier and an accomplished classical pianist, who saw himself as the political heir to Rabin. At the time of writing, the so-called peace process, which had languished under Netanyahu as Prime Minister, received a boost – Barak apparently accepting the possibility of the existence of a Palestinian state. But Israel's electoral system leads to a plethora of small political parties, many representing special interests, some of which have to be placated with concessions in order to achieve any kind of consensus. The future remains obscure.

So, where does all that leave us? Did the assassins of King Abdullah of Jordan, Anwar Sadat and Yitzhak Rabin succeed in their political objectives and was the Arab/Israeli situation changed by these events?

The death of Abdullah certainly did not make any appreciable difference to the continuing Arab/Israeli conflict. His son Talal, who was expected to reverse his father's policy of seeking an accommodation with Israel, did not do so. In the event he only reigned for just over a year before being retired on medical grounds. Talal's successor, Hussein, Abdullah's grandson, like Abdullah accepted that the Arabs would have to deal with the Israeli state sooner or later and they had better make the best of it. With supreme skill and great courage he managed to keep his throne and maintain his role as a force for moderation. His grandfather would have been proud of him. He died in February 1999. At the time of writing the future of Jordan, under his son, King Abdullah II, is not yet clear.

Anwar Sadat was succeeded by Hosni Mubarak, the air force commander during the 1973 war and his Vice-President. Like Sadat he was a moderate and a seeker after peace, and he continued with Sadat's policies. Egypt was accepted back into the Arab League in 1993. Mubarak, too, had great difficulties with the Moslem Brotherhood, who had achieved little, if anything, by killing Sadat. Certainly Mubarak played a powerful role in bringing about the accord between the PLO and Israel in 1993.

Only in the case of Yitzhak Rabin could it be argued that the assassin achieved something of his, and his friends', aims. In fact the immediate effect of the assassination was to damp down right-wing protests, but the Likud Party did win the election of May 1996. Whether this would have happened anyway is impossible to say. Peres, Rabin's successor, pursued similar policies to those of Rabin but Rabin was certainly a more charismatic figure than the rather dull Peres. In power, Netanyahu had to negotiate – but he was clearly far more obdurate than Rabin would have been. However, Barak's victory in May 1999 seems to have redressed the balance. In the long run, therefore, Rabin's assassination has changed very little, if anything at all. The truth is that peace cannot come to the Middle

East until both sides are prepared to make real concessions. A change of heart by millions is required and this cannot be achieved by the presence or the absence of one man, however eminent and influential he may be. Passions are too widespread and run too deep to be dissipated by individuals. The 'certainties' created by religious hatred and intolerance do not yield easily to example or persuasion, even if the persuaders themselves, as was the case with all three men studied in this chapter, have impeccable religious credentials.

NOTES

1. In fact, Russia was included in this extraordinary document which was finalized in an exchange of letters between Britain, France and Russia in October 1916. Russia was to acquire Constantinople (Istanbul), a strip on both sides of the Bosphorus and large parts of the four provinces of Turkey bordering Russia. (Incidentally, Britain and France had fought the Crimean War to avert any development of that nature.) The pact, which was intended to be secret, was disclosed by the Bolsheviks in December 1917.
2. Much of the foregoing is taken from the L. Stein, *Balfour Declaration*, Vallentine Mitchell, London, 1961.
3. J. Morris, *Farewell the Trumpets*, Faber and Faber, London, 1978, p. 252.
4. D. Gilmore, *Dispossessed*, Sidgwick and Jackson, London, 1980, p. 49.
5. Ibid., pp. 259, 260.
6. A. Shlaim, *Collusion across the Jordan*, Clarendon Press, Oxford, 1988, p. 20.
7. Gilmore, *Dispossessed*, p. 51.
8. Jehan Sadat, *A Woman of Egypt*, Bloomsbury, London, 1987, pp. 78, 79.
9. Anwar Sadat, *In Search of Identity*, Collins, London, 1978, p. 6.
10. Jehan Sadat, *Woman of Egypt*, p. 72.
11. Anwar Sadat, *Identity*, p. 59.
12. Jehan Sadat, *Woman of Egypt*, p. 108.
13. King Abdullah, *My Memoirs Completed*, Longman, London, 1978, p. 20.
14. D. Horowitz, (ed.), *Yitzhak Rabin: Soldier of Peace*, Halbern, London, 1996, p. 26.
15. Gilmore, *Dispossessed*, p. 167.
16. J.B. Glubb, *A Soldier with the Arabs*, Hodder and Stoughton, London, 1957, p. 281.
17. Anwar Sadat, *Identity*, p. 181.
18. Horowitz, *Soldier*, p. 56.
19. C. Schindler, *Israel, Likud and the Zionist Dream*, Taurus, London, 1995, p. 37.
20. Horowitz, *Soldier*, p. 181.
21. M. Karpin and I. Friedman, *Murder in the Name of God*, Granta, London, 1999, p. 27.
22. Ibid., pp. 9, 106, 108.
23. Horowitz, *Soldier*, p. 4.
24. Ibid., p. 88.
25. Karpin and Friedman, *Murder*, p. 16.

CHAPTER 8

HENDRIK VERWOERD /
MARTIN LUTHER KING /
MALCOLM X

Problems of racial conflict have bedevilled mankind at least since Moses led his people out of Egypt, if not long before. With recent massacres in Bosnia, Rwanda, Sri Lanka, the Sudan, Indonesia and Kosovo, there is no sign of any diminution of race hatred.

In the second half of the twentieth century there were two areas of the world where race problems received great publicity, South Africa and the United States of America. They are of particular interest in the Western world because they touched chords in the Western body politic which have had great resonance. Passions have been aroused which have chimed with other political views, often creating common patterns of antagonism.

Much of the structure of society in these two countries has been dependent on the way the whites, in each case the dominant race, have treated the blacks. This chapter will consider three leading personalities who have been intimately linked with these problems – Hendrik Verwoerd, Martin Luther King and Malcolm X. All three thought they had answers to the common problem and all three were assassinated. In the simplest terms, Verwoerd believed in segregation (or separate development as he called it), as did Malcolm X, certainly until very late in his life, whereas Martin Luther King believed in integration. All three were killed because of their beliefs – King and Malcolm X clearly so. As for Verwoerd, although his assassin was a madman, there was a method to his madness. He had hated Verwoerd for some considerable time because of his racist policies and had gradually got himself into a position from which he could kill him without great difficulty.

It is always tempting to make moral judgements: few of us can resist the temptation of easy condemnation, or indeed approval. However, the fact is that all three of these men held passionate beliefs. We do not know their inner motives: indeed we cannot do so. All we can be certain of is that they tried to implement what they believed in and were assassinated as a result.

Hendrik Verwoerd was born in Holland on 8 September 1901. His father, Wilhelm, emigrated to Cape Town three months after Hendrik was born. The move was probably motivated by an urge to do missionary work in Africa. Wilhelm qualified as a lay missionary at Wellington, near Cape Town, and when Hendrik was nine years old, the family moved to Bulawayo in Rhodesia where Wilhelm helped in the missionary work of his parish of the Dutch Reformed Church.

In 1915 the Verwoerds left Southern Rhodesia for the Orange Free State, where Wilhelm opened a religious bookshop hawking Bibles and other religious tracts all over the province. The atmosphere among Free State Afrikaners was predominantly anti-British: indeed there was a rebellion against South African participation in the First World War led by De Wet and other Boer War leaders. Hendrik determined to become a minister in the Dutch Reformed Church and went to Stellenbosch University near Cape Town to pursue his theological training. Verwoerd was a brilliant scholar, graduating in sociology, psychology and logic (he had quickly abandoned his theological studies) and obtained a doctorate in philosophy in 1924: his thesis ('the Blunting of the Emotions') was the first to be written in Afrikaans, which only replaced Dutch as an official language in Parliament in 1925.

In the immediate aftermath of the First World War there was among Afrikaners a very understandable and deep distrust and dislike of all that was British. The two Boer wars were only twenty years or so in the past and the British concentration camps, where thousands of women and children had died, still lay deep in the Afrikaner consciousness. The British annexation of Natal and the Transvaal, the Jameson Raid in 1895 and the whole saga in the 1830s of the Great Trek and subsequent unsuccessful attempts by the Voortrekkers to avoid British rule were a vital part of Afrikanerdom. The grant of self-government to the Union of South Africa in 1910 had not assuaged the hatred of England; the Nationalist Party, formed by General Hertzog in 1912, came to power in 1924 in alliance with the Labour Party (composed mainly of English-speaking labourers), defeating Smuts's and General Louis Botha's South Africa Party which had accepted the British connection.

Of course, Verwoerd was not born an Afrikaner and therefore did not directly inherit the Afrikaner sense of shame and humiliation, but he quickly absorbed these feelings and beliefs. Shunning the scholarship to Oxford which was offered to him, in 1925 Verwoerd went to Germany where he continued his studies in psychology and sociology at the universities of Hamburg, Leipzig and Berlin. While in Germany he married Betsie Schoonburg, whom he had met at Stellenbosch and who had become a lecturer in Afrikaans in the Stellenbosch Education Department. Verwoerd then obtained the post of Professor of Applied Psychology at Stellenbosch, and the pair settled down in Cape Town – a happily married couple. In 1933 Verwoerd transferred to the Chair of Sociology and Social Work, and it was this which inspired his move into the political field. He took up the cause of the poor white Afrikaners. Many Afrikaner farmers had been ruined by the Boer War and had moved to the towns where, with their poor education and lack of skills, they were unable to find work. In many cases the jobs they would have been able to take were done by blacks, and they were destitute.

In 1934 Verwoerd made a speech to the new Purified Nationalist Party, formed by Dr Malan (this had broken away from Hertzog's Nationalists because of the coalition with Smuts's South African

Party). Verwoerd argued that, 'If someone has to be unemployed, a white or a native, then in our present society, with its existing differences in living standards, it is more economical for the nation that the native should be unemployed.' He went on to say that if this led to mass 'native unemployment' this could be dealt with either by the natives taking the place of imported mine workers or through 'improved economic development of the reserves'. To the present-day Western mind the sophistry of these remarks is staggering but, sixty-five years ago, all those who agreed with him were not necessarily evil by definition. In any event the speech was of historic significance as the germ of the idea which eventually led to the system of separate development. The conference that Verwoerd had addressed went on to demand the cessation of residential mixing of whites and non-whites and suggested many other discriminatory laws which eventually were enacted.

There was a further strand of Verwoerd's thinking which impelled him into political life – the impulse towards a revival of Afrikaner Nationalism and away from any kind of alliance with English-speaking white South Africans. A secret organization, the Afrikaner Broederbond, had been formed by Afrikaner intellectuals in 1919. It was 'born out of a deep conviction that the Afrikaner nation was put into this land by God and is destined to continue in existence as a nation with its own nature and calling'. One of the requirements of joining this organization was that the applicant, his parents and his grandparents had to be born in South Africa. Verwoerd managed to circumvent this requirement, and by 1935 he had become one of its leaders.

As is so often the case with future political leaders, Verwoerd now turned to journalism in order to further his cause. He was offered the position of editor-in-chief of the new Transvaal Nationalist organ, *Die Transvaler*. He accepted it and the family moved to the Transvaal. From that moment on Verwoerd threw himself full time into the political struggle. His newspaper dealt at length with 'the maintenance of white civilization', 'the Asiatic flood in South Africa' and 'the Jewish question'. It preached an extreme

Nationalism. For instance, a document produced by the Broederbond, fully supported by Verwoerd, laid down that 'all Afrikaner children should be educated on the basis that the Christian and Nationalist spirit of the Afrikaner nation must be preserved'. History should be seen as the fulfilment of God's plan for humanity, of the struggle between the Kingdom of God and the Empire of Darkness, while 'native education should be based on the principles of trusteeship, non-equality and segregation and its aim should be to inculcate the white man's view of life, especially that of the Boer nation, as the senior white trustee of the native'.

The Nationalist Party in the Transvaal began to make considerable progress, increasing their seats from one in the elections of 1938 to eleven in 1943. The Second World War had added to the mistrust and hatred which many Afrikaners still felt for the English – in comparison, the Scots, Welsh and Irish were immune from damnation. In fact, the South African declaration of war against Germany was only carried by eighty votes to sixty-seven in the South African Parliament on 4 September 1939.

After the declaration of war there were many twists and turns to the internal political struggles within Afrikanerdom, which it would be tedious to follow here in detail. Hertzog, Malan and Verwoerd found themselves at odds in their approaches to the question of unity, reconciliation with English-speaking South Africans and the creation of a Republic. There were extremists within the Nationalist Party who veered towards National Socialism and other splinter groups. Verwoerd moved through the tangle with supreme political skill, emerging as a leading figure in the Nationalist Party under Malan, which eventually triumphed by winning the General Election of 1948 with seventy seats to the United Party's sixty-five – an overall majority of five, the other minor parties cancelling each other out. Verwoerd actually lost his own seat but was appointed by Malan, the first Nationalist Party Prime Minister, to the Senate to lead the Nationalists in the Upper House.

Verwoerd was made Minister for Native Affairs on 19 October 1950, in the place of Dr Jansen who had become Governor General.

This was a key post and his very considerable intellectual and practical abilities were tested to the full. His formidable task was to translate the general apartheid policies (or separate development of whites and blacks) of the Nationalist Party into law. He was not the originator of apartheid, but it was he who brought coherence to what had been a random collection of regulations and laws enacted in the past on an ad hoc basis. Above all, it was he who enunciated a system which combined remorseless logic (on his own premises) with the ostensible morality which the Afrikaner Volk longed for. As good churchmen, they sought biblical justification for their policies, even if they appeared to have stopped reading beyond the Old Testament. All major white political parties had fully accepted the overall policy of white government for the benefit primarily of the whites, who were almost exclusively entitled to vote: the opposition led by Smuts had also turned down the idea of equality and integration on the basis that inevitably, it would lead sooner or later to black domination. The Africans were to advance under European guidance but there were controls over their movements, places of residence and jobs. The Nationalists under Malan had stated that their two main principles were that there should be no racial equality in the white areas and that the natives should develop along their own lines in their own areas.[1]

As a result of wars during the past two centuries, Africans lived in a number of ethnic homelands or on white farms or as migrant workers in white-owned industry. Verwoerd decided that these ethnic homelands should eventually evolve into independent states linking up with South Africa in a confederation of self-governing units. The theory was that, initially, the existing blacks in the white areas would remain and, indeed, more would have to enter in order to supply the white demand for labour, but that saturation would occur and that in the end most black Africans would return to their homelands as the whites replaced their labour in the white areas. The black homelands were to be helped by the development of their agriculture and the creation of a series of white-owned and -run industries and businesses on the borders of the Bantustans, as the black homelands came to be called by their critics. Verwoerd also tried to re-establish the decaying African tribal system, appointing and training chiefs to carry out his policies.

Like Karl Marx's theory that in a Communist society the all-powerful State would eventually 'wither away', the forecast of the creation of two equal societies, black and white, living happily and peacefully together side by side was pie in the sky – and many Nationalists, perhaps including Verwoerd, must have known that. Apologists for apartheid argued that the Afrikaners had by their hard work, skills and dedication created a South Africa which was founded on Christian principles and economically successful to the extent that many Africans from the north came down to work there. They went on to argue that there were two possible courses for South Africa – the creation of one nation in which the whites would be overwhelmed by the blacks and as a result lose their nationhood, or separate development whereby both races would survive and indeed prosper. Verwoerd made the point in a speech to the House of Assembly on 25 January 1953:

> There are two moral courses. One is the course which leads to the fact . . . that in the final result all the people in the country would be equal and intermingled . . . the other is that eventually everybody can be equal but separate. . . . The policy of integration is an immoral policy viewed from the angle of the rights of the whites to whom this country belongs by virtue of their having settled here and having developed it and not through having conquered it and taken it away from anyone else. . . . The permanent continued existence of the whites is impossible in South Africa along any course other than by implementing apartheid to its logical consequences. This is the only way in which the existence of the whites can be insured practically and effectively.

There is no reason to think that, however mistaken he may have been, Verwoerd did not believe his own words; indeed to his dying day he was completely certain that he was right. Doubt was not a feature of his make-up.

Malan had been succeeded on his death by Johannes Strydom, who died in August 1958. In his turn he was succeeded as Prime Minister by Verwoerd, who was not surprised when the decisive internal party ballot was declared in his favour. Using words which many would now regard as sacrilegious, he said, 'I believe that the will of God was revealed in the ballot'. In his broadcast that night he repeated, 'It must be stated at the outset that we, as believing rulers of a religious country, will seek our strength and guidance in the future, as in the past, from Him who controls the destinies of nations. . . . In accordance with His will, it was determined who should assume the leadership of the government in this new period of the life of the peoples of South Africa.'

Martin Luther King was born on 15 January 1929 in Atlanta, Georgia. He was awarded the Nobel Peace Prize in 1964. In 1983 Congress added his name to the list of major American heroes whose birthdays had become a national holiday, putting him alongside George Washington and Abraham Lincoln, whose birthdays are celebrated together. He was a remarkable man.

The abolition of slavery in the United States under Lincoln's auspices in 1865 had not been the end of racial discrimination; very far from it. The whites in the South had re-established their domination over the blacks using every possible means at their disposal. The blacks were disenfranchised, inter-racial marriage and sex was outlawed, education for the blacks was segregated and public and private facilities of all kinds were segregated by law. The Ku Klux Klan, a white racist organization inclined to terrorism, enjoyed wide popularity throughout the South, and even in parts of the North. In the North, although there was little or no legal discrimination against the blacks, in practice they suffered heavy discrimination in housing and jobs. They were undoubtedly looked down on as inferior by most whites in the United States, and their enforced lack of education and opportunity merely served to reinforce this attitude.

In both North and South, however, there were areas of comparative black affluence where black people had by their own efforts moved into a black middle class. King was born in one of these. His father, Martin Luther King Senior (or Daddy King), had succeeded his father as pastor of the Ebenezer Baptist Church. The Christian Church with its comforting message of life after death and equality before God, had had a profound effect on the black community, particularly in the South, and especially in black middle-class areas where it had become, as well as the answer to religious problems, the centre of social life.

King was highly intelligent. He went to Morehouse College, an excellent, though segregated, educational establishment where the President, Dr Benjamin Mays, had a great influence over him, in particular teaching him to question the obscurantism and naïve, uneducated simplicities of many black preachers. It was at this establishment, too, that King rejected the idea that religion and politics should be kept separate. His father had been involved in the National Association for the Advancement of Coloured People (NAACP), the leading civil rights organization. In this regard, King followed in his footsteps.

King moved to Crozer Theological Seminary in Chester, Pennsylvania, and thence to Boston University where he took a doctorate in theology. His thesis was on the divergent theisms of two celebrated theologians, Paul Tillich and Henry Nelson Wieman, dealing with the complicated and rather esoteric question of whether God was transcendent or immanent. During these years King studied many, if not all, of the major world philosophers and struggled with many of the religious, social and economic problems besetting humankind. He emerged with a deep Christian faith, rejecting Communism and violence in any shape or form but passionate about black inequality and discrimination. He made a profound study of comparative religion. The life and works of Gandhi had a great impression on him. He argued that Gandhi 'was probably the first person in history to lift the love ethic of Jesus above mere interaction between individuals to a powerful effective social form on a large scale'.[2] Nevertheless, King was not a puritan. He lived life to the full. In June 1953 he married a black woman from Alabama, Coretta Scott, who was studying music at the New English Conservatory.

A glittering academic career clearly awaited him if he wished to pursue that path but he had other ideas. He decided to return to the South to serve the people from whom he sprang. He accepted a pastorate at Dexter Avenue Baptist Church in Montgomery, Alabama. This was a fateful step with enormous repercussions both for him personally and for the black people of the United States. In 1955 a black seamstress, Rosa Parks, refused to surrender her bus seat to a white man. She was arrested. In 1896 the Supreme Court had tried to reconcile the southern segregation laws with the Fourteenth Amendment to the Constitution by insisting that segregation laws should be 'separate but equal'. In the buses where the black seats were at the back over the hot engines, segregation was separate but clearly unequal. In fact the symbolism was even more important than the actual lack of equality. The blacks decided to boycott the buses and prevailed upon King to be their leader. The struggle was long, lasting for 381 days. Every form of intimidation and legal wrangle was deployed against the blacks. King's house was bombed, and many arrests were made. These events became famous throughout the United States, particularly because King had insisted throughout that protests must be non-violent. His speeches were outstanding and very moving even when read, but when listened to their power was stunning. King had decided to use the Church as a major weapon in the protest: as a means of communication and fundraising it had no rival. On 5 June 1956 the federal judiciary decided that Alabama's bus segregation was unconstitutional. King had won.

This victory not only vindicated King's stand against violence but it vastly increased black self-confidence. They had won against everything the southern whites had been able to throw at them.

A new organization was formed – the Southern Christian Leadership Conference (SCLC). King was elected President in January 1957. The SCLC was essentially composed of northern black intellectuals and southern preachers. A number of other black civil rights organizations were created over the next few years, all with differing policies, objectives and political orientation. Inevitably, there was tension between them. King remained President of the SCLC until he was assassinated eleven years later. At no stage did he depart from belief in the inherent value of his country despite what he saw as its, he hoped temporary, aberrations. He remained convinced of the need for mass non-violent and patriotic dissent. Unlike some black activists (notably Malcolm X with whom we will deal later) he believed fervently in black/white integration, not separation.

King's prestige had soared. *Time* magazine gave him a laudatory cover story: he was invited to Ghana's Independence Day ceremony, and he met President Eisenhower and Vice-President Nixon. He went to India, meeting Nehru, and was asked to speak all over the United States. He had become a major national and international figure. Clearly there was great scope for further civil rights action. Although the Montgomery bus boycott had gathered great publicity, the resulting public support had to be focussed on a specific objective.

The Presidential election of 1960 (Kennedy versus Nixon) gave King the opportunity of using his fame for the civil rights campaign. However, he refused to endorse either candidate but brought the issue into national prominence by joining a black student sit-in at a segregated restaurant in Atlanta. He was arrested and refused bail. Robert Kennedy intervened and he was released. Jack Kennedy's election led to hopes that the civil rights movement would receive a boost and that the new President would intervene massively on its side. However, in practice, when elected President, Kennedy was chary of pushing his civil rights activities too far for fear of alienating the southern white Democrats whose support had been vital for his narrow election win. In the deep South integration was non-existent: in the eleven southern states only 0.1 per cent of blacks attended mixed schools and very little was being done to bring about school desegregation despite the Supreme Court's ruling in 1954 that segregated schooling was unconstitutional. A Student Non-violent Co-ordinating Committee (SNCC) was formed with King's encouragement. Groups of young blacks and whites ('freedom riders') rode into the deep South on Greyhound and Trailways buses calling for desegregation in schools. They were beaten up and imprisoned.

In December 1961 King was asked to 'come and join the Albany movement', which had been instigated by two young SNCC workers protesting against the flagrant disregard of some federal laws by the Albany City Council in Georgia and local laws supporting segregation. King led a march there and with five hundred or so others was sent to jail. In this case, however, unlike in Montgomery, the authorities and, in particular, the police chief took great care not to alienate national public opinion by overreacting. No violence was used in spite of considerable marching and demonstrations. As a result, the movement never really took off in public relations terms, and it gradually fizzled out.

King now began to realize the vital importance of public relations. In 1963 he determined to lead a campaign in Birmingham, Alabama, the most extreme, racist and violent city in the South. Bull Connor, the ironically named 'commissioner of public safety' in charge of the police and firemen, was an ignorant, bull-necked racist of the most extreme kind. He was ideal for King's purpose, and he duly obliged: his police beat protesting children, and his firemen turned hoses on them as television cameras whirred. King was again sent to jail, from where he wrote his celebrated 'Letter from Birmingham City Jail' in response to a statement published by eight fellow clergymen (including one rabbi) from Alabama attacking him for his 'unwise and untimely' activities. The letter was written on the margins of newspapers and other scraps of paper. He set out at some length his belief in non-violent civil disobedience as the response to the totally unjust situation with which blacks in the United States were confronted. His language was forceful:

It is easy for those who have never felt the stinging darts of segregation to say, 'Wait'. But when you have seen vicious mobs lynch your mothers and fathers at will and drown your sisters and brothers at whim; when you have seen hate-filled policemen curse, kick and even kill your black brothers and sisters; when you see the vast majority of your twenty million Negro brothers smothering in an airtight cage of poverty in the midst of an affluent society, when you suddenly find your tongue twisted and your speech stammering as you seek to explain to your six year old daughter why she can't go to the public amusement park that has just been advertised on television and see tears welling up in her eyes when she is told that Funtown is closed to coloured children and see ominous clouds of inferiority beginning to distort her personality by developing an unconscious bitterness towards white people. . . . When you are forever fighting a degenerating sense of 'nobodiness' – then you will understand why we find it difficult to wait.

The events in Birmingham had an electrifying effect on opinion in the United States and particularly on the blacks. Throughout the South there were massive black protest marches. King capitalized on the momentum of protest and decided to organize a march on Washington. Clearly in response to this threat, Kennedy sent a Civil Rights Bill to Congress embodying new sweeping federal powers against segregation in schools, discrimination in employment and black disenfranchisement. He implored King to call off his march, arguing that violence would certainly ensue and that Congress would react against the Civil Rights Bill as a result. King refused to be deterred. The administration changed its mind, arranged food and drink and encouraged white unions and churches to participate. The march went ahead on 28 August 1963 and it was a massive success, with 250,000 people, one third of them whites, demonstrating in front of the Lincoln Memorial to hear King's world-famous speech, 'I have a dream' – an oration equalled in eloquence and impact perhaps only by Churchill's 'We shall fight on the beaches' and Lincoln's Gettysburg address.

> I have a dream that one day this nation will rise up and live out the true meaning of its creed, 'We hold these truths to be self-evident, that all men are created equal.' I have a dream that one day on the red hills of Georgia, sons of former slaves and sons of former slave holders will be able to sit down together at the table of brotherhood. I have a dream that one day even the state of Mississippi, a state sweltering with the heat of injustice, sweltering with the heat of oppression, will be transformed into an oasis of freedom and justice. I have a dream that my four little children will one day live in a nation where they will not be judged by the colour of their skin, but by the content of their character. I have a dream today. I have a dream that one day down in Alabama . . . . little black boys and black girls will be able to join hands with little white boys and white girls as sisters and brothers. I have a dream today!

President Kennedy's assassination on 22 November 1963 led to a desire for consensus across the whole American political spectrum, and his successor, Lyndon Johnson, was able to pilot the Civil Rights Bill through Congress. It was signed on 2 July 1964. However, the white supremacists in the South, were very far from being defeated. The Ku Klux Klan blew up a Baptist church in Birmingham, killing four young black girls, and continued its campaign with a number of other racist murders. King attacked the FBI for its failure, together with that of the local police, to arrest the bombers and murderers.

The FBI director, J. Edgar Hoover, a very powerful figure, was incensed. He started a campaign of vilifying King as a dangerous Communist and a sexual monster, using all the very considerable means at his disposal. This campaign continued until King's death. King was certainly no Communist: apart from anything else his Christian faith excluded Marxist materialism. However, he was guilty of some sexual peccadilloes, which Hoover used and magnified.

King also found himself in conflict with black extremists advocating violence, in particular with Malcolm X and his mentor, Elijah Mohammed, whose Nation of Islam preached hatred of all whites and a deep distrust of the 'white con-trick' – Christianity. King was therefore under attack from white racists as a dangerous Communist revolutionary and by black extremists as a toadying 'Uncle Tom' pretending to fight racism but in fact condoning the status quo.

By now King was world famous, receiving the Nobel Peace Prize in December 1964. He passed through London on his way to Oslo to receive the prize. In England he was treated as a major foreign figure, speaking to MPs at the Palace of Westminster and preaching to four thousand people in St Paul's Cathedral. He was no hair-shirt orator, staying at the Hilton hotel and enjoying the luxury it afforded. On his return to the United States he led a campaign at Selma, Alabama, to register the black voters there. Although only one per cent of the registered voters was black, there were, in fact, more blacks than whites living in the city. George Wallace, the Governor, and Jim Clarke, the sheriff, were extremist, uncompromising opponents to the civil rights movement with no hesitation in using violence, which they duly did. A demonstration was set upon by state troopers using clubs, whips and tear gas – all shown graphically on national television. In response Johnson sent in federal troops to protect the marchers. Congress passed a Voting Rights Bill: King had won again.

However, he was not so successful in the North. Beside the civil rights issue, there were two other obvious problems: the Vietnam War and northern black poverty. King hesitated before attacking American involvement in Vietnam, which he believed to be profoundly wrong. His hesitation was in part because he did not wish to divert attention from his primary aim – civil rights – and partly because, if he called for withdrawal from Vietnam, he would certainly alienate President Johnson who was totally identified with the Vietnam intervention. He had similar difficulties with urban ghetto poverty, and many of his supporters urged him to leave these two issues alone. However, in 1966 he led a campaign against poverty in Chicago and in 1967 he attacked the war in Vietnam.

Of the three leading figures considered in this chapter, Malcolm X is the most controversial; he came under heavy personal attack at one stage from all sides of the political spectrum. Although the inner Malcolm X may well not have changed, outwardly he twice became a different person. On the first occasion he himself likened his transformation to that of St Paul on the road to Damascus, and the second metamorphosis was no less startling. He was indeed a remarkable man.

Malcolm Little, as he was originally named, was born in Omaha, Nebraska, on 19 May 1925. His father, Earl Little, came from Georgia and his mother Louisa had come to the United States from the island of Grenada in the Caribbean. They were both enthusiastic supporters of the United Negro Improvement Association (UNIA), which had been founded in 1914 by Marcus Garvey, also from the Caribbean. The oppression of blacks in the South had led to a considerable migration of black people to the North where, however, they were far from popular, being seen as invaders, taking white jobs and generally debasing standards of all kinds. Racism was rampant. Garvey's organization was a focus for opposition to white supremacy and was committed to 'racial purity, racial integrity, racial hegemony'. He advocated separation and a black theology within existing religious structures. By the middle of the 1920s, UNIA had 1,100 branches in over forty countries, mainly in the United States, where it was attacked by other black organizations as being a black version of the Ku Klux Klan.

Earl Little was president of the Omaha branch of UNIA, travelling round preaching Garvey's ideas, often from the pulpits of African-American churches, with the active and enthusiastic support of his wife. Malcolm's future life was undoubtedly moulded by the powerful influence of his parents insisting on the pride which blacks should have in their race, allied to a hatred of white racism. They did not see this as in any way contradictory: they believed in segregation not domination by either race.

Earl Little had been married before with three children and Malcolm was the fourth by Louisa. He was no angel: he beat his wife and children and was a compulsive womanizer. Nevertheless, Malcolm admired him and continued to do so throughout his life.

The family left Omaha after attacks on their house by the Ku Klux Klan. They moved to an all-white neighbourhood outside Lansing in Michigan. Having bought their house there, they were told that it was, by law, an all-white neighbourhood and that they would have to move. During the legal battle that ensued, the house was burnt to the ground. Earl insisted that the whites were responsible: others argued, and still do so, that he himself was the arsonist.

The family moved again to another all-white neighbourhood not far away. Shortly after this Earl was killed when he was hit by a streetcar in the dark. Louisa firmly believed that he had been murdered for political reasons, a theory that Malcolm held for the rest of his life. Louisa then tried to bring up her large family as best she could with very little money, and undoubtedly at times the children went hungry. Malcolm was a very difficult boy and was moved from school to school without achieving much, if anything, in the academic line. Eventually he was taken away from his mother and lived with foster parents. Louisa became more and more desperate and unstable until finally ending up in a mental institution. Although there was no racial segregation in schools in the North, Malcolm often suffered indignities because of his colour. (In fact he was not very dark skinned and later was rather ashamed of his 'whiteness'.) He was particularly upset when a teacher told him that his ambition of becoming a lawyer was futile because of his colour: he would do better to study carpentry.

Malcolm's childhood was pervaded by racist indignity and by violence. Of his father's brothers, one committed suicide, one was shot dead by a white policeman, one was killed by another black man and one was shot by a black woman whom he had assaulted. Malcolm believed his own father had been murdered by whites. On top of this, one of his homes was attacked by the Ku Klux Klan and another by racist whites who wanted to push his family out of the area. It was a mixed-up youth who, at the age of sixteen, found his way to Boston to live with a half-sister, Ella, and thence to Harlem, New York.

Autobiographies, inevitably pervaded by self-justification, are notoriously unreliable sources and Malcolm X's is no exception. His autobiography is heavily influenced by a long series of conversations he had with Alex Haley, the black author of *Roots*, and, therefore, there are two angles, Malcolm's and Haley's, on a very complex truth. The temptation for Malcolm was to add to the drama by exaggerating his many problems both at home, at school and in Harlem, where he seems almost to relish the story of his iniquities. It is to the remarkable nature of his two conversions which he wishes to draw our attention. In fact they are remarkable enough without embellishment, as will be seen. In any case, there is no doubt about the main events of his life in Harlem and Boston as he moved between the two.

He became a hustler, descending or, as he would have seen it at the time, ascending the hierarchy from numbers runner to pimp, to drug dealer and eventually to professional burglar. He fancied himself as a dancer, and jumped from bed to bed, appearing to be particularly attracted to white women. He sported a zoot suit, and 'shopped' his friends when it was to his advantage to do so. Inevitably, he was eventually caught and was sent to prison for a period of five to eight years together with two of his associates: he thought that what he saw as the severity of the sentence was due to the fact that two of his other associates were white women and his crime was judged to be particularly heinous because 'blacks had no business to go with white women'.

In prison Malcolm continued with his indifferent and contemptuous attitude towards authority, particularly white authority. He showed a complete irreverence towards the Bible and God, earning the nickname of Satan among his fellow inmates. However, it was not long before his life began to change. A fellow prisoner was John Elton Bembry, clearly a man of very strong character and considerable intellect. Bembry was widely read and well educated, and he was listened to with awe by the other prisoners. He convinced Malcolm that he had some brains and that he should take advantage of the prison correspondence courses and the library. As the years went by Malcolm was moved from Charlestown Prison to Concord Reformatory and thence to Norfolk Prison Colony, which had considerable education facilities. Malcolm took a number of correspondence courses and read very widely.

In his absence his entire family had joined an organization known as the Nation of Islam whose leader was Elijah Mohammed. Malcolm's brother, Philbert, wrote to him in prison and stimulated an interest in this movement. 'The Nation', as it was first called, had been founded by a man of mysterious origin with the name Wallace Farrad, later shortened to Fard. He claimed that he was descended from the prophet Mohammed and that he had been born in Mecca. He taught that blacks were actually a lost Asiatic tribe wandering in the wilderness of North America. He urged the abandonment of Christianity: 'Me and my people who have been lost from home for 379 years have tried this so-called mystery God for bread, clothing and a home. And we receive nothing but hard times, hunger, naked and out of doors. Also was beat and killed by the ones that advocated that kind of god.'[3] He convinced his followers that he had supernatural powers and began to organize a series of temples where worship and instruction would take place. He insisted on a strict lifestyle for his disciples. Pre- and extra-marital sexual relations were prohibited, and alcohol, tobacco and pork were banned. He managed to make an impact on the existing black Christian churches, achieving a number of converts. However, he was harassed by the police and eventually left the country in February 1934.

His place was taken by Robert Poole, a migrant from Georgia, whose name was quickly altered to Elijah Mohammed. He changed the name of his organization to 'the Nation of Islam', deified Fard and taught that he, Elijah, was Fard's messenger on earth bringing infallible truths to black people. On joining the Nation of Islam, converts were expected to drop their surnames, which were the legacy of slavery, and add the letter 'X' to their first name while waiting for Fard to tell them what their original names were. He taught that Satan was not a supernatural being but rather the inherently evil and inferior white race.[4] Allah (Fard) was going to unleash a final, devastating catastrophe upon the white man's world from which only his black followers would escape.

The ridiculous nature of much of the teaching of the Nation of Islam at that time becomes clear in Malcolm X's autobiography:

> The first humans, original man, were a black people. They founded the holy city Mecca. Among this black race were twenty-four wise scientists. One of these scientists . . . created the especially strong black tribe of Shabazz, from which American Negroes descend. About sixty-six hundred years ago, when seventy per cent of the people were satisfied and thirty per cent were dissatisfied, among the dissatisfied was born a 'Mr Yacub'. He was born to create trouble. . . . He began preaching in the streets of Mecca making such hosts of converts that the authorities . . . finally exiled him with 59,999 followers to the island of Patmos. . . . Though he was a black man Mr Yacub decided, as revenge, to create upon the earth a devil race – a bleached out white race of people.[5]

The book then goes on to describe how Mr Yacub created a white race of devils. Mr Yacub died on the island at the age of 152, having left laws and rules for the whites to follow. Yacub's bleached white race ruled the world for six thousand years. It was written that the black original race would give birth to one whose wisdom, knowledge and power would be infinite. This man was Fard and Elijah Mohammed was his messenger.

Although this may appear absurd to most people now, it did not seem so to Malcolm in prison. He changed his lifestyle, refusing to eat pork, spending much of his time in meditation and prayer and becoming a model prisoner except for his refusal to accept inoculation – a further tenet of the Nation of Islam. On his release from prison in July 1952 he went to see Elijah Mohammed and became totally convinced of his authenticity, the rightness of all his teachings and the urgency of conveying them to the black race in the United States. From a licentious atheist he was changed into a puritanical, devoted follower of a man who, he was convinced, had the answers to all the problems of the blacks in the United States and indeed elsewhere. He was determined to devote the rest of his life to the spreading of Elijah Mohammed's teachings throughout black America.

On Malcolm's release from prison, the Nation of Islam, which had been beginning to disintegrate, took on a new and dynamic image. Malcolm was a brilliant orator and an arresting, incisive performer on television, particularly on the chat shows which later came almost to dominate that medium in the United States. Elijah Mohammed quickly realized his potential and Malcolm became a major missionary for the Nation of Islam, travelling far and wide, establishing new temples and consolidating and reviving old ones. He had particular success in Temple Number Seven in New York City, in Harlem. He told his audiences that Jesus Christ was a black man: 'The black Jesus, killed by whites, was still dead and buried in Jerusalem. Jesus could not return and save the black man, only Elijah Mohammed could save them. Heaven was in Mecca, not in the sky. The white man had thoroughly deceived black Christians into thinking they had no claim to this earth, while in reality the earth belonged to black people.'[6] In Philadelphia he affirmed Mohammed's doctrine that whites were the devil and the source of all sin. He claimed that the whites were made from the blacks and they had all the wickedness, and this is why the Bible said they were devils: 'Everything on the earth that is good is dark. . . . Black soil is richest and if God made man from the earth, He too must have been dark like you and I.'[7]

Malcolm said that aeroplanes would first drop pamphlets in Arabic and English warning blacks to join their own kind at once (by this time the Nation would already have been evacuated from North America). Next an ear-piercing trumpet would sound, driving men insane and causing pregnant women to give birth. Finally, Allah (Fard) would return in an aeroplane and light a match, setting an inextinguishable fire that would consume the white man's world. The attack had been delayed for the time being to give Elijah Mohammed a chance to get his followers out of North America.[8]

There seemed to be no boundaries to what Malcolm preached or to the credulity of those who followed him and, through him, Elijah Mohammed. When it came to specifics, however, his message was blurred. It was not clear, and indeed never became clear at any stage, precisely what the Nation of Islam was working towards. The idea had often been floated of promoting the repatriation of black Americans to Africa, where they would prosper and build up that continent to rival and eventually overtake North America, although in fact the Nation of Islam never advocated this policy. Alternatively, the proposal was that blacks would be given, or obtain in some way, areas of the United States in which they would have total control, similar to the Bantustans in South Africa. But that idea soon collapsed as being impractical. What was left was a platitudinous aspiration for freedom mixed with vague promises of independent black power. All this was pervaded by an almost pathological hatred of the whites, a complete repudiation of integration and a great distrust of all those, black and white, who were working towards reconciliation between the races. There were implicit, and sometimes explicit, leanings towards violence as the only possible method of redressing the situation with its injustices and white domination. The *Dictionary of American Biography* quotes Malcolm X as deriding the idea that African Americans could achieve freedom non-violently: 'Revolution is bloody, revolution is hostile, revolution knows no consequences, revolution overturns and destroys everything that gets in its way.'

The demonstrations, marches and speechifying of Martin Luther King and his associates, together with other black proponents of reconciliation, were damned as mere palliatives designed to appear to be fighting for black freedom while in fact perpetuating the evil white man's domination over the blacks. Malcolm claimed that King and other leaders of the march on Washington had taken over the event, with the help of white liberals, in order to subvert its militancy:

> The whites . . . infiltrated [the march] . . . they engulfed it. They became so much a part of it [that] it lost its original flavour. It ceased to be angry. It ceases to be impatient. In fact it ceased to be a march. It became a picnic.[9]

Malcolm X was a very intelligent man. As we have seen, his original education when young was scanty, but he had realized this when in prison and had read widely in prison libraries. However, he had chosen for himself what to read; he had not been confronted by contrary views. As would any intelligent being, he began to have doubts as to the truth of all he was teaching, but his devotion to Elijah Mohammed was such that he forced himself to banish these worries. Mr Elijah Mohammed, as he called him, was a messenger from God. Who was he to question his teaching? He prided himself on his total, unswerving loyalty to his leader.

Malcolm's fame increased and, in spite of his considerable efforts to avoid any such development, the perception began to grow that it was he and not Elijah Mohammed who was the leader of the Nation of Islam. Elijah Mohammed's family and others around him began to be jealous, and this emotion eventually affected the 'messenger' himself.

President Kennedy was assassinated on 22 November 1963, to the horror of much of the United States including many blacks who saw him as their friend and supporter. Elijah Mohammed immediately realized the danger to his movement if any of his supporters used the occasion to attack Kennedy. He ordered that the Nation of Islam should remain silent and not comment. At first Malcolm observed those orders, but then at a meeting, in answer to a question he compared the assassination to those of Lumumba, Diem and Ngo Dinh Nhu, all of whom had died in coups the Kennedy administration had encouraged or condoned. Malcolm said he was 'an old farm boy himself: chickens coming home to roost never did make me sad; they always made me glad.' Elijah Mohammed was furious and ordered Malcolm to remain silent for forty days.

Malcolm had in fact been becoming increasingly unhappy with his situation. He had discovered that Elijah Mohammed, in spite of his puritanical moral teachings, had been having sexual relations with a number of young black women and had several children by them. Malcolm had found it extremely difficult to come to terms with what seemed to him to be a total betrayal of all that he believed in. He tried to find some kind of spurious answer to the inevitable questions he would receive on this matter, but he knew them to be false and shallow. He was worried about the very opulent lifestyle in which Elijah Mohammed and some of his family were living at the expense of the movement. Malcolm himself had always avoided any ostentation. Furthermore he had begun to doubt the teaching that *all* whites were evil. Some orthodox Moslems were telling him that the Nation of Islam's teachings had very little to do with the true beliefs of Islam. Once the bubble of Elijah Mohammed's infallibility had burst, Malcolm saw no reason to continue with what was to him now a false, even evil, doctrine and movement. On 4 March 1964 he publicly repudiated the Nation of Islam.

He announced that he was going to organize his own Moslem mosque. At first he argued that he would not steal the thunder and the membership of the Nation of Islam, but this pretence did not last long. He said that he would preach the gospel of black Nationalism the way Billy Graham spread the gospel of Christianity, encouraging believers to stick to their own churches.[10] He also said that he would cooperate with the civil rights movement, an activity which had been banned by Elijah

Mohammed. However, distancing himself from Martin Luther King, he reiterated his views on violence, saying that the choice was between the ballot and the bullet. If the ballot failed they would have to use the bullet.

Malcolm needed a replacement for the religious certainties provided by Elijah Mohammed which he now perceived to be dubious to say the least, and he made a bold decision: he would make the hajj. He travelled to Mecca via Cairo, and found the whole experience totally electrifying. He faithfully carried out all the rituals demanded of him and underwent his second conversion, fully accepting all the beliefs of orthodox Sunni Islam. Apart from the great solace of the new certainties he found in Islam, he realized that the Nation of Islam's tenet that whites were devils was rubbish, as was all the mumbo-jumbo surrounding that claim. In Islam all believers were brothers and, apart from the fact that many Arabs were near-white, there were other pilgrims with him who had 'fair hair and blue eyes'. For him the hajj was a profound statement of devotion to God, rejection of sin and a celebration of the brotherhood of all Moslems.

After Mecca, Malcolm visited a number of states in the Middle East and Africa – Lebanon, Egypt, Nigeria, Ghana (where he met Kwame Nkrumah), Liberia, Senegal, Morocco and Algeria. On his return to the United States in May 1964 he set up the Organization of Afro-American Unity (OAAU) as a non-religious organization in order to promote the unity of a diverse group of African-Americans without obliging its membership to participate in Moslem affairs. Elijah Mohammed had concentrated entirely on the United States and had discouraged his followers from attempting to internationalize the activities and membership of the Nation of Islam. Malcolm's intentions with the OAAU were the precise opposite. The fundamental goal remained the acquisition of human rights for black Americans but, in order to achieve that, he believed it to be vital to build international black solidarity. He set off on a further tour of Africa: indeed he spent half of the last year of his life in that continent. Among his other activities he met the leadership of nearly every country that he visited, and he attended the second Organization of African Unity Conference in July 1964, with observer status as chairman of the OAAU.

His long absences from the United States were not popular with his followers but probably welcome to his enemies in the Nation of Islam. A hate campaign was started against him. On his return, a plot was hatched to assassinate him but the would-be assassin warned Malcolm about it. Proceedings were started by the Nation of Islam to reclaim the house which it had given to Malcolm and to evict him and his family. Further threats to his life were made, and Malcolm felt that time was fast running out.

To return to the very different scene in South Africa, Verwoerd's emergence in 1958 as Prime Minister was enthusiastically welcomed by Afrikanerdom. During his time in office as Minister of Native Affairs, apartheid laws and regulations had been widened and strengthened in response to rising opposition by Africans under the leadership of the African National Congress and the more militant Pan Africanist Congress. The ultimate step was taken in 1953 with the Public Safety Act under which the government could declare a state of emergency and rule without Parliament. Of course the blacks had no direct influence in Parliament anyway, but this injustice was compounded by the Criminal Law Amendment Act whereby protests against any law could be punished with heavy fines, imprisonment and lashes. Verwoerd went on to deal with African education: 'I will reform it so that natives will be taught from childhood to realise that equality with the Europeans is not for them.'[11]

A high proportion of the Afrikaner community in South Africa had supported Verwoerd in all his doings. On his arrival in Pretoria he was welcomed in the following terms by 'Brother De Klerk', Minister of Labour and father of the future Prime Minister, who was acting as master of ceremonies:

The election of Dr Verwoerd as leader of the Nationalist Party and Prime Minister of South Africa was not a mere accident but part of God's plan for this nation on the southern corner of Africa. . . . The Prime Minister is qualified for his role in many ways. His militancy, his brain power and his physical strength are well known. Under God's guidance he now enters the future.[12]

Verwoerd's emergence as Prime Minister, however, did not lead to general contentment. African opposition increased, to be met by redoubled police action. On 21 March 1960 the police fired on defenceless demonstrators in Sharpeville near Johannesburg, killing 67 people and wounding 186. This led to even stronger action, and 18,000 arrests were made. Violence increased throughout the country, provoking even more stringent action against African 'troublemakers and Communists'. It was a vicious circle.

Many Nationalists, and in particular members of the Broederbond, had for long campaigned for a Republic. With the many other problems faced by the Nationalist Government this matter had not been pursued, but in September 1960 Verwoerd decided to hold a referendum on the matter, himself urging a 'yes' vote. On a high turn-out of white voters, 850,458 voted in favour and 775,878 voted against. The majority was small but Verwoerd decided to go ahead. He flew to the Commonwealth Prime Ministers' Conference hoping that South Africa would be allowed to remain a member of the Commonwealth. There was heavy opposition to this and South Africa became a Republic, in fact leaving the Commonwealth. On his return he was enthusiastically received by the Afrikaner public.

Sharpeville, six months earlier, had led to warnings of disaster for South Africa but the fact is that the five years following departure from the Commonwealth were the most prosperous in South Africa's history. The gross national product rose by a third, gold and foreign exchange reserves reached the highest level ever and trade with Britain increased considerably.

However, economic success had not led to acceptance of the situation by the majority. In 1959 the system whereby Africans had had a limited representation by whites in Parliament was ended and the so-called self-rule for the Bantustans was hardly more than a limited form of local government under white authority. Millions of Africans living in urban areas were not able to vote for the Parliament which ruled them. The theory was that, in return for this, they could vote for an assembly with limited powers in their so-called homeland, which in fact they might well never have visited.

At an election in March 1966 Verwoerd's party won 126 seats out of the 170-man parliament. The United Party opposition was reduced to thirty-eight. Verwoerd had virtually complete power. He had been Prime Minister for over seven years. He dominated his cabinet to an extent that Mrs Thatcher would have envied. He dismissed the growing domestic and international criticism of apartheid as misinformed and inspired by irrational hostility towards the Afrikaners. When Harold Macmillan made his famous speech to the South African Parliament stating that they could not ignore the 'winds of change' which were blowing through Africa, Verwoerd made an accomplished extempore reply to the effect that the rest of the world simply did not understand South Africa. He was a complete autocrat, totally convinced of the correctness of his own judgements about everything. Indeed, when he proposed what was probably the most important of all apartheid laws, the Bantu Self-Government Act, which established ten black homelands, he had not even bothered to seek prior approval from his cabinet. His ministers were dumbfounded, but dared not complain.[13] As far as Verwoerd was concerned they were merely his agents, existing in order to implement the policies which he, alone, formulated. He was a dour, uncompromising man with little, if any, leavening of humour.

On 8 September 1966 he was stabbed to death as he sat in Parliament waiting for the day's session to begin. His assailant, Tsafendas by name, had been born in 1918 in Mozambique of a

Greek father and a Portuguese-African mother. After a very mixed career he had tried to enter the United States but was deported to Greece. He worked there until 1949, when he was deported to Portugal. Held in prison there for three years without trial, he eventually escaped and managed to enter and work in England, the Middle East and elsewhere, before finally moving to South Africa. Being of mixed descent, over the years he had developed an obsessive hatred of apartheid, which he saw as a deliberate affront to his dignity as a human being, and of Verwoerd, whom he regarded as the architect of this evil doctrine. Although in fact extremely unstable (he had been in eight mental institutions), when he arrived in South Africa he managed to present himself as an intelligent and stable person to the extent that he was able to get himself a job as a messenger in the white holy of holies – the South African Parliament. His job was to deliver letters and messages to the Members of Parliament and generally to make himself useful to, among others, the press gallery, many of whose members knew him well. He was not very efficient but always appeared equable and certainly not the type to assassinate anybody. By virtue of his job, he had complete freedom in the parliamentary building and was, therefore, ideally placed to carry out his intention of killing Verwoerd. After the event he said that he had been told to do the deed by a tapeworm which had controlled his life for years. He was tried and committed to detention in jail as insane.

Verwoerd had acquired almost prophetic status among the Afrikaners and his assassination was a terrible shock. He was succeeded by Johannes Vorster, who had been Minister of Justice in his government. During the Second World War Vorster had joined the anti-democratic, extreme right-wing, pro-Nazi National Socialist Ossewa Brandwag, of which he became leader. He was arrested on 27 September 1942 and interned until February 1944. In 1949 he claimed a change of heart and joined the Nationalist Party.

As Minister of Justice, Vorster had quadrupled the police force and used his vast arbitrary powers to the full, arresting hundreds of political opponents and often placing them in solitary confinement. However, he was very different to Verwoerd. For a start his equally dour appearance masked a sense of humour, albeit mordant. A photographer once asked him, 'Prime Minister, could we have a smile?' 'I am smiling,' he replied. Another story recounted about him was that when he was told that the opposition United Party had split, he said, 'A jelly does not split. It merely wobbles.'

Although Verwoerd's assassination was a traumatic event for the bulk of Afrikanerdom, there were those in the higher reaches of the Nationalist Party hierarchy, and especially in the cabinet, who were in fact not sorry to see him go – they felt that he had become, or perhaps always had been, a priggish bore who brooked no dissent. A journalist living near a cabinet minister's house saw, on the night of the assassination, a number of official cars arrive there. He thought that they were probably about to conduct some kind of wake. However, many hours later it was clear from the general noise of merriment that the event was not a wake, but a celebration, and a rather drunken one at that.[14]

Above all, Vorster was a pragmatist. Having promised, initially, not to change Verwoerd's policies, it was not long before he did precisely that. He realized that South Africa could not confront its internal and external enemies within the ideological straitjacket created by Verwoerd. He soon began to experiment with concessions – some multi-racial sport, carefully controlled, and an outward policy in Africa, trying to establish trade and other contacts with African states. Bolstered by Portuguese rule in Angola and Mozambique, he thought that South Africa could use its overwhelming economic strength to persuade black states in the area to mollify their opposition, in private, if not in public. This policy had some modest success; for example President Banda of Malawi came to South Africa on a state visit. As part of his policy of détente with black Africa, also, Vorster gradually withdrew South African support from the white rulers of Rhodesia, a policy which played a major part in the establishment in Rhodesia of 'one man one vote' and a black government under Mugabe. It also earned for

Vorster the bitter hatred of Ian Smith, chronicled in his book, *The Great Betrayal*.[15] None of this would have been conceivable under Verwoerd and indeed it led to the breakaway of a far right group, the Herendigde Nationale Party or HNP (the reunited National Party) under Dr Albert Hertzog MP.

When Vorster resigned in 1979, P.W. Botha took over and, by the time he handed over to de Klerk, he had repealed a hundred apartheid laws. He retained white supremacy without its ideological underpinning and de Klerk surrendered even that supremacy.

The question is, of course, whether apartheid would have collapsed if Verwoerd had not been assassinated and, if it had, whether this would have happened sooner or later with more or less upheaval. With the benefit of hindsight – the historians' unfair tool – the eventual collapse of apartheid was inevitable: for a start there was the fact that there were three and a half blacks, let alone coloureds, to one white in South Africa, as well as the massive economic and moral pressure exerted by virtually the whole of the rest of the world. But Verwoerd's death almost certainly meant that the process was more gradual than it would have been if he had remained in power. His continuance in total authority for many years (and he would not have given up office easily) would probably have led to a far greater conflagration when the system did, eventually, collapse.

To sum up, the eventual outcome in South Africa would have been the same with or without Verwoerd's assassination. Had he lived, the upheaval consequent on the change would probably have been far greater. As for timing, it is impossible to say.

Assassination was not part of the South African tradition and Verwoerd had not expected it, although there had been an attempt several years before when he had been shot and badly wounded by a white farmer. King, on the other hand, and Malcolm X as we shall see, fully expected an early and violent death. All three men generated deep hatred and they lived in violent societies. They were, all three of them, fighting for what they saw as the right, indeed the only, answer to the deeply divisive problem of race. Verwoerd was hated by most of the blacks in South Africa; King was hated by many of the whites in the United States, and Malcolm X was hated by large elements of both races and in particular by the movement of which he had been a leader and which he had disowned.

The FBI had logged fifty conspiracies aiming to assassinate King and he was only too well aware of the danger. But he tried to overcome his fear: 'I cannot worry about my safety; I cannot live in fear. I have to function. If there is any one fear I have conquered, it is the fear of death. If a man has not found something worth giving his life for, he is not fit to live.'[16]

King was becoming depressed about the results of his life's work. The civil rights movement was very divided and his campaign on Vietnam seemed to be getting nowhere. The Black Power movement with its overtones of violence and hatred of the whites was gaining strength. The Student Non-violent Co-ordinating Committee (SNCC) was becoming increasingly militant under the charismatic leadership of Stokely Carmichael. It called for blacks to defend themselves with arms during their demonstrations and to bring about a revolution. However, King retained his firm view that violence could only lead to more violence, thereby distorting the issues and ending in the moral degradation of all those who used it. As regards Black Power, King thought that blacks could not isolate themselves from white society and that any attempt to do so would be certain to lead to hatred and disaster.

King decided on a new approach to the problems besetting the United States. In October 1967 he unveiled plans for a Poor People's Campaign. His idea was that a 'non-violent army' of 3,500 poor people of all races would camp in Washington. They would dramatize the plight of the poor and, unless Congress took notice, he would organize mass civil disobedience disrupting the functioning of the capital of the United States. In March 1968 he addressed a rally in Memphis, Tennessee, to express support for the city's garbage workers who were striking for union recognition and a wage rise. He returned there on 28 March to lead a march to the City Hall. For the first time in his career one of his own marches ended in violence and a sixteen-year-old youth was killed by the police. King was devastated. He nearly cancelled the whole Poor People's Campaign but was persuaded to continue and to return for a further non-violent march. On 31 March, to King's great pleasure, President Johnson announced that he would not run for re-election and would seek negotiations with North Vietnam. On 3 April King addressed a strike rally in Memphis:

> Like anybody I would like to live a long life. Longevity has its place. But I am not concerned about that now. I just want to do God's will. And He's allowed me to go up to the mountaintop. And I've looked over. And I've seen the Promised Land. I may not get there with you. But I want you to know tonight that we as a people will get to the Promised Land. So I am happy tonight. I am not worried about anything. I am not fearing any man. 'Mine eyes have seen the glory of the coming of the Lord.'

The following evening, as he paused on the balcony outside his motel room, a bullet tore into his face and killed him.

The news shocked the world. In the United States riots flared up in 110 cities and thirty-nine people were killed. Some 711 fires blazed in Washington. Stokely Carmichael told the blacks, 'When white America killed Dr King she declared war on us. Get your gun.' President Johnson ordered the Stars and Stripes to be flown at half-mast and proclaimed the following Sunday as a day of national mourning. The Pope told of his 'profound sadness' in a cable to the entire American Catholic hierarchy. In the British House of Commons, both parties introduced resolutions expressing horror. In West Germany both Houses of Parliament stood in silent tribute and the Mayor of Berlin led a march of a thousand Germans and Americans through the city to John F. Kennedy Square. At the funeral in King's Ebenezer Church 800 people were packed inside and 60–100,000 surrounded the church outside.

James Earl Ray, a white escaped convict, was convicted of the assassination. His brother, John Ray, who was also thought to be involved, was active in the American Independent Party in the St Louis area, where two businessmen were said to have offered $20,000 and $50,000 respectively for King's life. There were rumours that the FBI had been involved, but a Congressional Committee set up to investigate it acquitted the FBI and decided that Ray was a lone assassin. This, of course, is not conclusive but the consensus is that the FBI was indeed not involved. There are many other theories and King's own family now believes that Ray, who died in 1999, was innocent. In December 1999 a jury ruled that King was not the victim of a lone assassin but of a conspiracy. But whatever the truth may be, the likelihood is overwhelming that King's assassination was engineered in some way by white opponents of his civil rights movement and his more recent campaigns on Vietnam and poverty, with the aim of removing this extremely powerful and effective campaigner from the scene.

Did the assassination succeed in its aim? Did King's assassination lead to a reversal of what he was fighting for? As far as the Vietnam War was concerned the answer is undoubtedly 'No' – The war was ended. As regards poverty the answer is not clear and, in any case, King was not identified with that campaign long enough to have much of an impact either way. King made by far his greatest impact on the civil rights issue: indeed he is almost exclusively known for this. Certainly his death did not reduce his impact: if anything the opposite was the case. As so often happens, the drama of his assassination added to the effect of his oratory and personality. He became a martyr and an icon and, to a large extent, remains so. Whether this would have been the case had he not been assassinated must remain doubtful. In any event the American record on civil rights has certainly improved over the years and Martin Luther King's life and death has been, at least in part, responsible for this.

On his return from Africa Malcolm X found his organization (the OAAU) in a poor state of morale. He had been away too long. He embarked on a hectic series of meetings and speeches, and began a spate of attacks against Elijah Mohammed, accusing him of religious fakery and immorality. Threats against his life were redoubled. When he went to court in an attempt to avoid eviction from his house by the Nation of Islam, he was guarded by eight OAAU men and twenty uniformed policemen.[17] Malcolm continued with his near frantic tours, visiting Canada, Chicago and Selma, Alabama, among other places. He also made fleeting visits to France and Britain. On 13 February 1965, when he was asleep at home with his family, Molotov cocktails were thrown through his window. Malcolm and his family escaped, but the house was half destroyed. On Sunday 21 February Malcolm was due to speak to a rally in New York. He had just started his speech when four black men, one with a shotgun and three with revolvers, opened fire and killed him. A fifth man threw a smoke bomb, adding to the pandemonium.

One man was arrested on the spot and two later. All three were convicted of murder and sentenced to life imprisonment. Although there was a spate of contradictory rumours about responsibility for the crime including, predictably, the FBI, there is no doubt that it was the Nation of Islam (or the Black Moslems as they were also called) who instigated the assassination. With characteristic generosity Martin Luther King stated that he was 'deeply saddened and appalled' at Malcolm's death: 'This vicious assassination should cause our whole society to see violence and hatred as evil forces that must be cast into unending limbo.'[18]

Elijah Mohammed initially refused to comment. He later denied any responsibility on the part of the Nation of Islam but at a rally in Chicago on the same weekend that Malcolm's funeral took place he recalled earlier happier days: 'In those days Malcolm was safe. . . . After he left the movement he went everywhere. . . . He criticized . . . he criticized . . . he criticized . . . he tried to make war against me. . . . However, I am not going to let crackpots destroy the good things Allah sent to you and me.' Mohammed went on, 'No man will be successful in opposing me.'[19] Whether or not Elijah

Mohammed ordered Malcolm's assassination will probably never be known but Malcolm was undoubtedly killed by those who were appalled by what he was doing to the Nation of Islam and wished to silence him once and for all.

The Nation of Islam is still in existence and remains, some would say, a sinister force in the black community in the United States, holding similar views to those expressed at the time of Elijah Mohammed's leadership. Nevertheless, Malcolm X's assassination did not succeed in its aim of removing him from the public consciousness. He remained a powerful force in African-American affairs. The funeral was a massive event attended by at least a thousand people including a host of civil rights dignitaries. His biographer, Bruce Perry, ended his book with the following words – 'He irrevocably altered America's political landscape. His ability to conquer his fear – and to inspire his followers to conquer theirs – suited him uniquely to this vital historical task.'[20] The *Dictionary of American Biography* adds that Malcolm X's 'contribution was the transformation of the consciousness of a generation of Afro/Americans from racially based self-hatred to that racial pride necessary to the struggle for equality'.

And so these three leaders, one white and two black, were all assassinated in the atmosphere of hate which surrounded them. In none of these cases did the assassins achieve their aims, but did the removal of their targets have any impact on the course of history? In the case of Verwoerd the answer must be that it did not. He had laid down a blueprint for separate development which would have run its course and come to an end whether or not he had been killed. In the case of Malcolm X, it is difficult to be certain: the probability is that his life and death will be seen as a mere blip on the developing story of the struggle for civil rights for blacks in the United States. Martin Luther King may well have a similar status in the future but, like Gandhi, his undoubted selfless heroism may have a far longer and deeper effect on people than many would now imagine.

He did show that non-violence can be successful in affecting the course of events and it is just possible that his example will have a lasting impact. If so, his assassins would have helped, not impeded, that result by conferring martyr status on him.

NOTES

1. A. Hepple, *Verwoerd*, Pelican, London, 1967, p. 113.
2. Oates, *Let the Trumpets Sound*, Harper Perennial, New York, 1994, p. 32.
3. L.A. Decaro, *On the Side of My People*, New York University Press, New York, 1996, p. 23.
4. Ibid., p. 29.
5. *Autobiography of Malcolm X*, ed. by Alex Haley, Ballantine Books, New York, 1964.
6. Decaro, *My People*, p. 104.
7. Ibid., p. 105.
8. Ibid., p. 106.
9. B. Perry, *Malcolm*, Station Hill, New York, 1992, p. 211.
10. Ibid., p. 255.
11. House of Assembly Debate, 17 September 1953, as quoted in Hepple, *Verwoerd*, p. 124.
12. De Transvaler, 13 November 1958, quoted in Hepple, *Verwoerd*, p. 143.
13. F.W. de Klerk, *The Last Trek: A New Beginning*, Macmillan, London, 1998, p. 30.
14. Private information.
15. I.D. Smith, *The Great Betrayal*, Blake, London, 1997 – the other 'Betrayal' was, of course, as Smith saw it, by Great Britain.
16. Oates, *Trumpets*, p. 455.
17. *Autobiography*, p. 421 (Epilogue by Alex Haley).
18. Decaro, *My People*, p. 279.
19. Perry, *Malcolm*, p. 377.
20. Ibid., p. 380.

CONCLUSION

In this book we have examined eighteen assassinations, in very diverse countries and eras. The reasons for assassination (using that word in the case of Jesus Christ for what was, more correctly, judicial murder) vary, but the one constant is a belief that the removal of the intended victim will radically change, and greatly improve, a situation which has become intolerable to the assassin, his associates or, in the case of Trotsky and Becket, his master.

Very often, there is also a personal element of deep hatred involved. Prime examples of this are to be found with Charlotte Corday, a passionate young woman to whom Marat had become a monster, and John Wilkes Booth, whose hatred of Lincoln, whom he believed had destroyed his beloved South, was obsessive to the point of madness. Those who assassinated Abdullah, Anwar Sadat and Yitzhak Rabin were moved by what they conceived to be deep religious faith. It was an outrage to them, an affront to their whole being, that God-ordained and totally necessary wars looked as if they would be averted by the very men who themselves should be leading the fight. Similar emotions, without the religious element, led to the murder of Michael Collins. As far as Jesus Christ is concerned, he must have been a most tiresome and potentially extremely dangerous threat to the chief priests, who would have felt that their personal status as religious leaders was at stake. There seems to have been a venom about their actions that can only be explained by personal hatred.

Even with Julius Caesar, although not as far as Brutus was concerned, there may have been an element of personal hatred on the part of those whom he had forgiven and befriended, a species of hatred recognised by Talleyrand in his reported question: 'Why does that man hate me? What have I ever done for him?' Only in the cases of Trotsky and, perhaps, Becket, does there appear to be no evidence of personal hatred by the assassins, who instead thought they were carrying out the wishes of their masters – indeed with Trotsky the assassin certainly was doing so.

In each case, however, the underlying cause of the assassination was political; personal hatred, where it existed, merely added venom to the deed. But what were the results? The answer is that successful assassinations, in the sense that the political aims are achieved, are extremely rare.

Julius Caesar's assassins thought that his death would lead to a period of peace and tranquillity, together with a return of the power of the Senate and the ending of autocratic rule by one individual. In fact, the assassination was followed by a long period of civil war and the eventual emergence of Augustus as Emperor with great personal powers – the precise opposite of what was intended.

Becket's murder, apparently intended to please Henry II, certainly did not do so. He was shattered, and overcome with remorse. His difficult relations with the Pope were greatly exacerbated and the assassination failed to redress the balance between Church and State in the powers of the courts. Far from getting rid of Becket, it turned him into a martyr and Canterbury Cathedral into a shrine for pilgrimages. Church influence increased, not decreased, as a result of the deed.

Gandhi's assassins hoped that as a result of their actions the reconciliation between Hindus and Moslems, which Gandhi was trying to achieve, would not take place; they hoped that violence would escalate so that the Hindus, who greatly outnumbered the Moslems, would prevent partition by force. Ironically, they appeared to think that Gandhi supported partition, whereas in fact he was personally devastated by the division of India. In the short term, again the result was the exact opposite of what the assassins wanted. Inter-communal riots and murders subsided, albeit temporarily. Their hopes that partition would be averted came to nothing. In the long run, of course, hostility between Hindu and Moslem remained, but Gandhi's assassination had little if anything to do with that. He was an old and frail man and probably would have died soon anyway. Furthermore, his assassination made him a martyr, adding to the impact of his philosophy of non-violence.

As far as Jesus Christ is concerned, the result of his crucifixion is clear. It did not, as the chief priests had hoped, destroy the impact of his teaching. The precise opposite was the case, as the legacy of his life and death changed the world, permanently.

Charlotte Corday's assassination of Marat was followed by the bloodbath of 'The Terror', not by the victory of the moderate Gironde. The vicious circle of hatred, retribution and death was given an additional savage twist by what was seen as the beginning of a counter-revolution.

Lord Frederick Cavendish's murder in Phoenix Park undoubtedly slowed down Ireland's move to independence, which it was designed to expedite. Gladstone had been making considerable progress with Parnell, but Cavendish's murder stopped it in its tracks. Indeed, it is just possible that partition might have been avoided if Home Rule had come to Ireland sooner than it did. In any event, the murder of the inoffensive Englishman was hardly likely to endear the Irish Republican cause to those in England who had the power of decision.

As for Archduke Franz Ferdinand, the result of his murder by Serb Nationalists was the invasion of Serbia by Austria and a world war. It might just be possible to argue that, in the medium term, the Serb Nationalists obtained what they wanted – an independent nation (Yugoslavia) dominated by the Serbs. But this was nothing whatever to do with the assassination itself which failed totally in its immediate objective – the freedom of Bosnia from Austria-Hungary. Indeed, as ever, the Balkan future remains obscure, fraught with those deep and apparently everlasting hatreds, which existed before and after Franz Ferdinand's assassination.

The assassination of Tsar Alexander II had the precise opposite effect to what the assassins intended. Russia, under Alexander's successor, reverted to full-scale authoritarian rule with a rigid clampdown on freedom of all kinds. The successes of the two revolutions and the eventual accession to power of the Communists under Lenin may have ended the rule of the hated Tsars, but eventually they culminated in the much crueller domination of the far more hateful Stalin.

Lincoln's assassination by a fanatical supporter of the southern cause was a disaster for the South. It removed from the scene a man whose whole aim at the time was one of reconciliation and who, with his considerable reputation and standing in the country, undoubtedly could have achieved a great deal in that direction. His successor, Andrew Johnson, who tried rather ineffectually to follow his predecessor's policies, was unable to do so because of powerful figures in the Congress who were determined to punish the South. Indeed, Johnson was nearly impeached in the process. 'They know not what they do' certainly applied to John Wilkes Booth and his associates in their blind ignorance and folly.

The assassinations of Wilson and Collins certainly did not achieve the assassins' aims. Wilson's death made it absolutely certain that the British Government would insist on the treaty being fully implemented in every particular. After the assassination there was no question of any further compromise by Britain. As far as Collins was concerned, those who supported the treaty were strengthened, not weakened, by his violent death. The fact that even Michael Collins, the great revolutionary leader with his charismatic charm and his devotion to the cause of Ireland, had supported the treaty, indeed had negotiated it, had been perhaps the most powerful argument in its favour. His murder did not change that: it merely added to the hatred many Irishmen felt at the time for the IRA and the opponents of the treaty. A legend is not destroyed by murder: if anything it is enhanced. Collins's assassination certainly did not change the view of the mass of the people in the south of Ireland. Indeed, it was not long before the civil war was ended with the total defeat of the anti-treaty forces.

King Abdullah of Jordan, Anwar Sadat of Egypt and Yitzhak Rabin of Israel were all assassinated because they were trying to bring peace to that tragic part of the world, the Middle East, with its tortured and complicated history. At the time of writing, peace has not come, so it could be argued that the assassins succeeded in their aim. However, only in the case of Rabin could the assassinations conceivably be said to have contributed to this sad state of affairs. After the very short rule of his son, Abdullah was succeeded by his grandson, Hussein, who continued the search for some kind of modus vivendi with Israel with even greater integrity, intelligence and persistence than had his grandfather. Sadat, whose brave journey to Jerusalem in November 1977 caught the imagination of the world, was succeeded by Mubarak who, also, has been a powerful moderating influence. In the case of Rabin's assassination, the immediate result was to calm, not stoke, passions. His successor, Peres, was as intent on the peace process as he had been. However, it is true that the next election was won by Netanyahu of the hard-line Likud Party and it can be argued that Rabin's assassination was a factor in this. Rabin, with his war record, was a more appealing personality than was Peres. But, perhaps, the pendulum was due to swing anyway. In the event, Netanyahu, too, had to negotiate, albeit with policies which gave no real chance of success. However, in the election of May 1999 Barak, a man of similar background and mentality to Rabin, was elected, thus, it might be said, restoring the status quo which existed before Rabin's assassination. However, the creation of peace in Israel is a vastly complicated process involving, above all, a readiness on both sides to make real compromises. There has to be a general will to peace. It is the peoples of the area, rather than their leaders, who really matter.

Hendrik Verwoerd's assassination did not bring about an immediate move towards the ending of apartheid. Vorster, his successor, promised faithfully to carry out his predecessor's policies to the letter. However, he was a pragmatic man and, gradually, there was an easing of the rigidities of apartheid as practised by the puritanical and humourless Verwoerd. Although many of the evil practices of the system were continued for a time, there was a gradual relaxation, both externally and internally, culminating in the wholesale abandonment of what was known as petty apartheid by Vorster's successor, P.W. Botha. Eventually, under de Klerk, Mandela was released and the whole system of apartheid was dismantled, followed by black majority rule. However, in retrospect, one can see that the ending of apartheid was inevitable whether or not Verwoerd had lived. It is impossible to know whether, if Verwoerd had not been assassinated, it would have ended sooner, with perhaps a greater explosion in the process, or later.

The assassinations of Martin Luther King and Malcolm X, too, did not really achieve a great deal, if anything. The civil rights movement in the United States was in full flow by the time King was murdered and he had played a leading part in its progress. His assassination turned him into an icon for millions of all races throughout the world. In spite of Hoover's nefarious and illegal attempts to besmirch his reputation, King's is still a name to be conjured with. Whether that would be the case had he not been assassinated must be doubtful.

Malcolm X, though at the time a very powerful figure and, in his earlier days, a focus for the feelings of angry and embittered blacks in the United States, will probably turn out to be no more than a blip on the shifting screen of black advancement. He did give black Americans a sense of their own worth and this was recognized in 1999 by the issuing of a postage stamp bearing his image. He might have achieved more had he lived longer, but that is not at all certain.

Only in the case of Trotsky can the assassination be said, clearly, to have achieved what was intended. Stalin wished to silence his powerful critic and to demonstrate to his people his worldwide powers of life and death. His associates were terrified of him and Trotsky's murder must undoubtedly have added to this terror. In the long run, however, Trotsky's death did not have much impact on the world in general or Russia in particular. As a result of the heroism of the Russian army and the stupidities of Adolf Hitler, the Germans were defeated on their eastern front and Stalin, as leader of a victorious Soviet Union, held supreme power within his country and was able to dominate or influence much of the post-war world. It is difficult to see how Trotsky, if he had lived, would have changed that. In retrospect, too, it is clear that the ideology of Communism, as practised in the Soviet Union, was doomed. Trotsky, alive or dead, would not have altered that situation.

So where does all that leave us? Returning to the theories of Hirschman, put forward in the Introduction, about the results of pressures for change – Perversity, Futility and Jeopardy, and adding a fourth, Success, we can see where those assassinations examined here fit into that hierarchy. Of the eighteen studied, ten are in the Perversity (result opposite to that intended) column: Julius Caesar, Thomas à Becket, Jean Marat, Jesus Christ, Lord Frederick Cavendish, Tsar Alexander II, Abraham Lincoln, Michael Collins, Henry Wilson and, just, Martin Luther King because of his acquired status as a martyr. Then there are six in the Futility (nothing much happens) column: Mahatma Gandhi, Hendrik Verwoerd, Malcolm X, King Abdullah, Anwar Sadat and Yitzhak Rabin. Some of these could be moved, marginally, into the Perversity or even the Jeopardy column. In the Jeopardy (something happens but not what is intended) column, is, very firmly, Archduke Franz Ferdinand. Lastly, in the Success column is Trotsky alone (an assassination with a very limited aim).

In over half of the assassinations studied, therefore, the result was the exact opposite of what was intended; in one-third of the cases nothing much happened; in one case something else, a world war, was the result and in only one instance can it conceivably be said that the assassin's sponsor succeeded in his political aims. There is an argument[1] that assassinations in democratic countries with 'established power hierarchies merely result in the smooth substitution of a lieutenant who continues the same policies'. However, the argument continues, in 'feudal, tribal or dictatorial countries' assassinations have 'far-reaching political consequences (albeit often the opposite of what the assassins intended)'. This study does not bear out that theory. Of the six assassinations in the Futility column which, according to this argument, should have taken place in democratic countries, three (Verwoerd, Abdullah and Sadat) did not. Of the other twelve, which should have occurred in non-democratic countries, five (Cavendish, Lincoln, Collins, Wilson and King) lived in democracies. Even if some of these positions would be open to dispute, there does not appear to be enough evidence to support any kind of rigid demarcation on these grounds.

What, then, are the reasons for this state of affairs? It is of course possible that the assassins and their associates were blinded by personal hatred and, as a result, their judgements were flawed, so that they did not understand or accept the contexts in which they were in fact operating. In other words, the miscalculations were due to simple human error. Indeed, in some of the cases examined, there certainly was a strong element of the politics of desperation, a response to a feeling of powerlessness. However, there may also be a deeper, and perhaps more basic, reason for the plethora of mistaken projections of the future by assassins. All assassins believe that individual leaders are responsible for situations that cannot be tolerated. If that is not the case, why kill them? What if, as suggested in the Introduction, individual leaders are merely the froth on the wave: the result, not the cause, of great collective historical movements? If that is the case, then, come what may, like the Mississippi, history will just keep rolling along. The removal of one individual leader will not affect it. But, if that is so, why does the opposite of what is intended so often happen? Why does the Futility theory not apply in every case?

It is suggested here that this is because assassinations are almost always committed in order to try to reverse a tide which nevertheless continues until it has reached its high or low. The deed highlights, and thus often speeds up, the process. The really important aspects of history are the great movements of ideas, feelings and events that are caused by a multiplicity of factors, beyond detailed analysis here because of their vast numbers and scope. There seems to be an inexorable drive in one direction or another at various points. The individual leader can speed it up, slow it down or even slightly alter its direction but he or she cannot halt it. This is not a Tolstoyan determinist answer. Individuals do indeed have a limited effect and if large numbers of individuals agree at any one point, their impact can be decisive.

As far as Julius Caesar is concerned, the conditions for the arrival on the Roman scene of someone of his ilk were there in the first place. He certainly did grab the opportunities and impel Rome to greatness, but the possibility of doing so existed in full measure. His removal did not change things all that much. His eventual successor was equally powerful. As has been said of Napoleon: 'If he had not existed, France would have invented him.' Similar remarks can be made about all our victims. Marat was only one of those who tried to ride the tiger of revolution in France. He may have slightly increased its savagery, but savage it was always going to be with the situation in France at that time. The tide could not be stopped by the actions of Charlotte Corday, however valiant her purpose.

In spite of his good intentions, Tsar Alexander II could not change Russia, at a stroke, into a modern democratic state. The tide of authoritarianism was too strong and there were too many vested interests involved. His assassins, by removing one important liberalizing element from the scene, merely allowed autocracy to resume its path towards the disaster of full-scale revolution. The same argument applies to virtually all the leading figures examined. Jesus Christ is an exception, because Christianity would not have existed without him. He *did* change the world. But would he have done so if he had not died on the cross?

If this general line is accepted, and there are of course exceptions to it, then the conclusion must be that assassination can affect the course of history, but only marginally so. Given the right circumstances, individual leaders, can speed up or even temporarily impede a movement that already exists, either in fact or in potential. Their removal, therefore, can have an effect but not on a scale which is sometimes imagined, above all by those who plot assassination. And, often, the effect is the opposite of that intended.

Human behaviour is highly complex and, naturally, leaders, in trying to evolve policies, will simplify the issues, particularly so when attempting to gain support from their peoples for their decisions. It is much easier to argue that Adolf Hitler or Slobodan Milosevic were personally responsible for the disasters that they appeared to initiate. Anger against a personality is easier to arouse than it is against a political system. But it was the resentful Germany of the 1930s with its hyperinflation and deep sense of inferiority that allowed Hitler to lead it. The tide of aggressive German Nationalism had to reach its peak before ebbing. Three wars in the last half of the ninteenth and two in the first half of the twentieth century were the result not so much of individual leaders as of the German character as it had developed for historical and geographical reasons over many centuries. The heroic, saintly and heavily anti-Nazi von Moltke, who was executed shortly after the Hitler bomb plot, was right to oppose the assassination of Hitler and to work for a cataclysmic defeat in order to demonstrate to his fellow Germans the tragic error of their ways and not to allow them any alibi, such as the alleged 'stab in the back' of 1918 and the subsequent Treaty of Versailles.[2]

It seems that, very often, the moment throws up the man, not vice versa. Milosevic did not create Serbian Nationalism; he personified it.

Nevertheless, although leaders may only be able to lead when the conditions are right for them to do so, often they do guide their countries into situations which would not exist were it not for them. Thus, Germany was impelled into war in 1939 by Hitler. If he had not existed, or had been assassinated in, say, 1935, a world war might well not have taken place. Similarly, although the conditions of the time were such that Saddam Hussein was able to persuade his fellow Iraqis to agree enthusiastically to the invasion of Kuwait, that probably would not have happened if he had not been the leader at that time.

It is, of course, impossible to prove a negative. All we can say for certain is that Hitler and Hussein were leaders at those periods and did lead their countries into war. We also know that their peoples followed them keenly into conflict. It is not the argument of this book that precisely the same would have happened to Germany and Iraq if Hitler and Hussein had not been leaders at the time. However, something of the kind would inevitably have occurred. The pressures of history were such that, in both cases, there would have been an unpleasant explosion. The same applies to Milosevic. There have been many leaders in the Balkans over the last 150 years. Their removal, or death, has not changed the frantic antagonisms in the area, which have continued to erupt in almost bestial violence.

Too often, villains are created in order to rally public opinion, particularly in these days of mass communication. As well as Milosevic, there have been other examples since the Second World War where highly complex situations have been simplified by the creation of largely imaginary villains, the result of which has been disaster. Nasser of Egypt and Aideed of Somalia are vivid examples of this. The antidote to situations that have become intolerable must be based on a deep understanding of the causes of problems and a consequent careful analysis of the options, not on vastly over-simplified beliefs that particular individuals are solely responsible for the troubles.

It was Winston Churchill who said of his own wartime exploits, 'It was the British people who had the heart of a lion. I merely had the good fortune to be called upon to give the roar.'

It would be folly to argue that leaders never propel events in directions which they themselves wish. Of course they do. However, it is the argument of this book that they can only do so if the right conditions exist for this to happen. The flow can be speeded up or even, sometimes, slowed down. However, assassination is an attempt to stem, and even to turn round, the tide, which, as King Canute discovered, is beyond the power of man.

Disraeli, in a speech to the House of Commons on 1 May 1865, a fortnight after Lincoln's death, said, 'Assassination has never changed the history of the world.' Except in the unique case of the judicial murder of Jesus Christ, he was right.

NOTES

1. Article by Andrew Roberts in *The Sunday Times* of 26 July 1998.

2. H.J. von Moltke, *Letters to Freya – A Witness against Hitler*, Collins, Harvill, London, 1991. (Helmuth James von Moltke was the great-great-nephew of the famous Moltke of Bismark's wars. A leading international lawyer, on the outbreak of war he joined the foreign division of the Abwehr, the German intelligence service, as legal adviser to the High Command of the Armed Services, where he worked under Admiral Canaris who, like Moltke, was executed for opposition to the regime. His final letters to his wife before his execution are most remarkable documents.)

APPENDIX

The word 'assassin' was originally applied to a branch of the Ismaili sect of the Moslem religion. After the death of the Fatimid Caliph in 1094, the Persian Ismailis, under their leader Hasan-i-Sabbah, refused to recognize the new caliph in Cairo and transferred their allegiance to his deposed elder brother, Nizar. However, both he and his son were murdered in prison in Cairo, but, according to assassin tradition, a grandson was smuggled out to Persia and formed a new line of Nizari Imans. This sect developed a new policy of 'assassination' – the murder of the leaders of their enemies as a sacred religious duty. Hasan-i-Sabbah seized the castle of Alamut in an impregnable valley and became known as the 'Old Man of the Mountains'. He and his successors established a network of strongholds all over Persia from where his agents murdered the leaders of those who supported the old caliphate, including some of the caliphs themselves. At the beginning of the twelfth century, the Persian assassins extended their activities to Syria. They seized a group of castles and from there waged a war of terror against the Turks and Crusaders, the number of their enemies having greatly increased by then.[1]

One of the earliest descriptions of the sect occurs in the report of an envoy sent to Egypt and Syria in 1175 by Emperor Frederick Barbarossa. He said that on the confines of Damascus, Antioch and Aleppo there was a certain race of Saracens in the mountains. They had among them a master who struck the greatest fear into all the Saracen princes as well as the neighbouring Christian lords for he had a habit of killing them in an astonishing way. He possessed the most beautiful palaces surrounded by very high walls, so that none could enter except by a small and very well-guarded door. In these palaces he had many of the sons of his peasants brought up from early childhood. These young men were taught by their teachers from their earliest youth that they must obey the lord of the land in all his words and commands and that, if they did so, he who had power over all living gods would give them the joys of Paradise. They were then summoned to the presence of the prince, given a golden dagger and sent out to kill whoever had been selected as victim.[2]

Then, in 1273 Marco Polo passed through Persia and gave a different, though similar, account. According to this, the Old Man of the Mountains turned a certain valley between two mountains into a sort of Garden of Eden full of fruit, beautiful damsels and runnels, flowing with milk, wine, honey and water. No one was allowed to enter save those who he intended to be Ashishini, as they were called. He introduced a number of youths between twelve and twenty years old into the garden by giving them a certain potion which cast them into a deep sleep, so that when they woke up they found themselves there. When he wanted to instigate an assassination he would send for a youth and tell him to carry out a mission and that, when he had successfully performed it, he would immediately return to the Paradise he had just come from. Even if he were killed, the Old Man's angels would take him there.[3]

The Crusaders were much in awe of the assassins because of their reputation as secret and treacherous murderers. However, on at least one occasion, in 1113, the assassins came to their aid by stabbing to death Mawduch of Mosul, a moslem, who had a led a series of jihads (holy wars) against Frankish (Western European) settlers in Syria.[4]

The end of the power of the assassins came under the double assault of the Monguls and their deadliest enemy, the Mameluke Sultan, Bibars. In 1256 Alamut itself fell. After this the sect stagnated as a minor heresy with little or no political importance.

There remains some doubt as to the reason for the use of the word 'assassin' to denote membership of this Ismaili sect. It was suggested in a memoir to the Institute of France in 1809 that it came from the Arabic word 'hashish' which means herbage, more particularly dry herbage or fodder. Later, it was specialized to denote Indian hemp or cannabis, the narcotic effects of which were already known to the Moslems in the Middle Ages. This use would tie up with Marco Polo's description above, and with the idea that the assassins doped themselves before committing their nefarious deeds. However, it seems that this story is almost certainly untrue and that the word was an expression of contempt for the wild beliefs and extravagant behaviour of these people, a derisive comment on their conduct rather than a description of their practices.[5]

NOTES

1. *The Encyclopaedia Britannica.*
2. Bernard Lewis, *The Assassins*, Weidenfeld & Nicolson, London, 1967, p. 234.
3. Ibid., p. 9.
4. Bernard Hamilton, *The Crusades*, Sutton, Stroud, 1998, p. 19.
5. Lewis, *Assassins*, p. 12.

BIBLIOGRAPHY

GENERAL

Encyclopaedia Britannica
Cambridge Biographical Encyclopaedia
Dictionary of National Biography
Dictionary of American Biography
Capouya, E., and Tompkins, E. (eds). *The Essential Kropotkin*, Liveright, New York, 1975
Cutler, R.M. (ed.). *The Basic Bakunin*, Prometheus, New York, 1992
Emsley, C. (ed.). *Conflict and Stability in Europe*, Croom Helm, London, 1979
Gilbert, M. *History of the Twentieth Century*, Collins, London, 1997
Hamilton, B. *The Crusades*, Sutton, Stroud, 1998
Hirschman, A.O. *The Rhetoric of Reaction*, Harvard University Press, 1991
Keegan, J. *The First World War*, Hutchinson, London, 1998
Laucella, L. *Assassination*, Lowell House, Los Angeles, 1998
Lewis, B. *The Assassins*, Weidenfeld & Nicolson, London, 1967
von Moltke, H.J. *Letters to Freya – A Witness against Hitler*, Collins Harville, London, 1991
Woodcock, G. *Anarchism*, Penguin, London, 1963

CHAPTER 1

Buchan. *Julius Caesar*, Daily Express Publication, London, n.d.
Compton, Piers. *The Turbulent Priest*, Staples Press, London, 1957
Firth. *Augustus Caesar*, Putnam, London, 1903
Fry, P.S. *Great Caesar*, Collins, London, 1974
Fuller, J.F.C. *Julius Caesar*, Eyre & Spottiswoode, London, 1965
Gelzer, M. *Caesar*, Blackwell, Oxford, 1968
Ochoa, *The Assassination of Julius Caesar*, Silver Burdett Press, New Jersey, 1991
Pain, Nesta. *The King and Becket*, Eyre & Spottiswoode, London, 1964
Suetonius. *The Twelve Caesars*, The Folio Society, London, 1964
Speaight. *Thomas Becket*, Longman, London, 1958
Ward Fowler. *Julius Caesar*, Putnam, London, 1891

CHAPTER 2

The Earl of Birkenhead, *Halifax*, Hamish Hamilton, London, 1966
Collins, L., and Lapierre, D. *Freedom at Midnight*, HarperCollins, London, 1997
Copley, A. *Gandhi – Against the Tide*, OUP, Oxford, 1987
Fischer, L. *The Life of Mahatma Gandhi*, HarperCollins, 1997
French, P. *Liberty or Death*, Flamingo, London, 1998
M.K. Gandhi, An Autobiography, Penguin, London, 1982

Maloney. *The Living Voice of the Gospel*, Darton, Longman, London, 1987
New Testament
Roberts, A. *The Holy Fox*, Papermac, London, 1991
Watson, F. *The Trial of Mr Gandhi*, Macmillan, London, 1969
Ziegler, P. *Mountbatten*, Collins, London, 1985

CHAPTER 3

Belloc, H. *The French Revolution*, Williams and Northgate, London, 1911
Bullock, A. *Hitler and Stalin*, HarperCollins, London ,1991
Carlyle, T. *The French Revolution*, Lane, London, n.d.
Carr, J.L. *Robespierre*, History Book Club, London, 1972
Cobban, A. *A History of Modern France*, Vol. I, Penguin, London, 1957
Corday. *Charlotte Corday*, translated by Buckley Butterworth, London, 1931
Deutscher, I. *The Prophet Armed*, OUP, Oxford, 1954
Deutscher, I. *The Prophet Unarmed*, OUP, Oxford, 1959
Dugrand, A. *Trotsky in Mexico*, Carcanet, 1972
Gottschalk, L.R. *Jean Paul Marat*, University of Chicago Press, 1967
Mosley, N. *The Assassination of Trotsky*, Joseph, London, 1972
Payne, R. *The Life and Death of Trotsky*, Allen, London, 1978
Segal, R. *The Tragedy of Leon Trotsky*, Hutchinson, London, 1979
Shukman, H. *The Russian Revolution*, Sutton, Stroud, 1998
Trotsky, L. *My Life*, Penguin, Middlesex, 1975
Trotsky's Diary in Exile, Faber and Faber, London, 1959
Wolfe. *Three Who Made a Revolution*, Penguin, Middlesex, 1948

CHAPTER 4

An Approach to British Fair Play, Berlin, 1924
Corfe, T.H. *The Phoenix Park Murders*, Hodder and Stoughton, London, 1968
Crankshaw, E. *The Fall of the House of Hapsburg*, Longman, London, 1963
Foster, R.F. *Modern Ireland, 1600–1972*, Penguin, London, 1988
Foster, R.F. (ed.). *The Oxford History of Ireland*, OUP, Oxford, 1989
Gilbert, M. *The First World War*, Collins, London, 1995
Gilbert, M. *A History of the Twentieth Century (1900–33)*, vol. I, HarperCollins, London, 1997
Grigg, J. *Lloyd George, From Peace to War 1912–16*, Methuen, London, 1985
Kee, R. *Ireland, A History*, Abacus, London, 1980
Jenkins, R. *Gladstone*, Macmillan, London, 1995
Moody, T.W. *The Course of Irish History*, Mercier Press, Cork, 1967
Sampson Low, *The War Guilt*, Wilson, London, 1928
Seton-Watson, *Sarajevo*, Hutchinson, London, 1926
Tuchman, B. *August 1914*, Paperman, Constable, London, 1962

CHAPTER 5

Almedingen, E.M. *The Romanovs*, Bodley Head, London, 1966
Brogan, D.W. *Abraham Lincoln*, Duckworth, London, 1935

Charnwood, *Abraham Lincoln*, Constable, London, 1916

Cowles, V. *The Russian Dagger*, Collins, London, 1969

Donald, D. *Lincoln*, Pimlico, London, 1995

Johnson, P. *A History of the American People*, Phoenix, London, 1997

Ludwig. *Lincoln*, Putnam, London, 1930

Mosse, W.E. *Alexander II and the Modernisation of Russia*, English University Press, London, 1958

Pares, B. *A History of Russia*, Grey, Edinburgh, 1926

Pares, B. *Russia*, Penguin, London, 1940

Parish. *Abraham Lincoln, Speeches and Letters*, Dent, London, 1993

Stern, *The Man Who Killed Lincoln*, Cape, London, 1939

CHAPTER 6

Caldwell. *Sir Henry Wilson*, Cassell, London, 1927

Collier. *Brass Hat*, Secker & Warburg, London, 1961

Duff Cooper. *Haig*, Faber and Faber, London, 1936

Forester, M. *Michael Collins*, Sidgwick and Jackson, London, 1971

Foster, R.F. *Modern Ireland, 1600-1972*, Penguin, London, 1988

Foster, R.F. (ed.). *The Oxford History of Ireland*, OUP, Oxford, 1987

Gwynn. *De Valera*, Jarrolds, London, 1932

Jackson, W.G.F., and Bramall, E.N.W. *The Chiefs*, Brasseys, London, 1992

Kee, R. *Ireland, A History* , Abacus, London, 1980

Mackay, J.A. *Michael Collins*, Mainstream, London, 1996

Moody, T.W. *The Course of Irish History*, Mercier Press, Cork, 1967

Nicolson, H. *King George V*, Constable, London, 1952

O'Connor, F. *The Big Fellow*, Poolbeg, Dublin, 1979

Owen. *Tempestuous Journey*, Hutchinson, London, 1954

Stephens, J. *The Insurrection in Dublin*, Maunsell, Dublin, 1919

CHAPTER 7

King Abdullah. *My Memoirs Completed*, Longman, London, 1978

Bregman, A. *The Fifty Years War*, Penguin, London, 1998

Gilmore, D. *Dispossessed*, Sidgwick and Jackson, London, 1980

Glubb, J.B. *A Soldier with the Arabs*, Hodder and Stoughton, London, 1957

Hiro, D. *Dictionary of the Middle East*, Macmillan, London, 1996

Horowitz, D. (ed.). *Yitzhak Rabin: Soldier of Peace*, Halban, London, 1996

Morris, J. *Farewell the Trumpets*, Faber and Faber, London, 1978

Parkes. *A History of the Jewish People*, Weidenfeld & Nicolson, London, 1962

Sadat, Anwar. *In Search of Identity*, Collins, London, 1978

Sadat, Jehan. *A Woman of Egypt*, Bloomsbury, London, 1987

Schindler, C. *Israel, Likud and the Zionist Dream*, Taurus, London, 1995

Shlaim, A. *Collusion across the Jordan*, Clarendon Press, Oxford, 1988

Stein, L. *The Balfour Declaration*, Vallentine Mitchell, London, 1961

Stevens. *Israel, a Blessing and a Curse*, London, 1960

Weizmann, C. *Trial and Error*, Hamish Hamilton, London, 1949

CHAPTER 8

De Klerk, F.W. *The Last Trek: A New Beginning*, Macmillan, London, 1998

De Villiers, D. *The Case for South Africa*, Stacy, London, 1970

Decaro, L.A. *On the Side of My People*, New York University Press, New York, 1996

Fairclough, A. *Martin Luther King*, Cardinal, London, 1990

Haley, A. (ed.). *Autobiography of Malcolm X*, Ballantyne, New York, 1964

Harmer, H. *Martin Luther King*, Sutton Publishing, Stroud, 1998

Hepple, A. *Verwoerd*, Pelican, London, 1967

Oates. *Let the Trumpets Sound*, Harper Perennial, New York, 1994

Perry, B. *Malcolm*, Station Hill, New York, 1992

Smith, I.D. *The Great Betrayal*, Blake, London, 1997

Shuker, H. *Martin Luther King*, Burke, London, 1988

INDEX